THE WHITE HOUSE AND ITS THIRTY-FIVE FAMILIES

THE WHITE

HOUSE AND ITS THIRTY-FIVE FAMILIES

BY AMY LA FOLLETTE JENSEN

HOWARD C. JENSEN, ART EDITOR

McGraw-Hill Book Company

NEW YORK, ST. LOUIS, SAN FRANCISCO, DUSSELDORF, LONDON,
MEXICO, PANAMA, RIO DE JANEIRO, SINGAPORE, SYDNEY, TORONTO

Permission was granted to use quotations from the following works:

IN THE DAYS OF MY FATHER, GENERAL GRANT, by *Jesse Grant, Harper & Brothers* © 1925.

FORTY-TWO YEARS IN THE WHITE HOUSE, by *Irwin H. Hoover, Houghton Mifflin Company* © 1934.

FROM MCKINLEY TO HARDING, by *Herman H. Kohlsaat, Charles Scribner's Sons* © 1923.

TAFT AND ROOSEVELT, THE INTIMATE LETTERS OF ARCHIE BUTT, by *Archibald W. Butt.* © 1930, *Doubleday & Co., Inc.*

MY MEMOIR, by *Edith Bolling Wilson,* © 1939, *The Bobbs-Merrill Company, Inc.*

THE DEMOCRATIC ROOSEVELT, by *Rexford G. Tugwell,* © 1957, *Doubleday & Co., Inc.*

THE FIRST FORTY YEARS OF WASHINGTON SOCIETY, by *Margaret Bayard Smith, edited by Gaillard Hunt, Charles Scribner's Sons* © 1906.

RECOLLECTION OF FULL YEARS, by *Helen Herron Taft,* © 1914, *Dodd, Mead & Company.*

THE NEW LETTERS OF ABIGAIL ADAMS, *The American Antiquarian Society, Worcester, Massachusetts.*

"MISS GRUNDY LETTERS," by *Austine Snead, The Rutherford B. Hayes Library, Fremont, Ohio.*

MR. PRESIDENT, by *William Hillman, Farrar, Straus and Cudahy, Inc.,* © 1952.

PICTURE CREDITS

American Institute of Architects: 5 (bottom), 29
Benjamin Harrison Home: 142, 143 (top)
Brady-Handy Collection: 52, 55, 56, 62, 68, 71, 73, 74, 77, 78 (top), 82, 84, 85, 88, 92, 96 (top), 102, 104, 120 (bottom), 189
Culver Service: 120 (top), 188, 193, 196 (top), 197
J. T. Dorris: 89
Fogg Art Museum: 41
Franklin D. Roosevelt Library: 76, 241 (bottom), 242, 246 (top), 247 (top)
Frick Art Reference Library: 9, 37, 42, 51, 59, 64, 69, 129
Mrs. William M. Greve: 19 (top)
Japanese Consulate General of New York: 80
Katharine McCook Knox: 4
W. M. Kiplinger Collection: 50, 78 (bottom)
Library of Congress: 3, 11–14, 19 (bottom), 25–28, 32, 33, 35, 38–40, 44, 46–48, 58, 60, 61, 67, 70, 75, 79, 81, 83, 86, 87, 93, 95, 96 (center and bottom), 97, 105, 111, 114, 132, 135–139, 140, 141, 143 (bottom), 144–166, 169–177, 179, 182 (top), 183, 190, 192, 194, 195, 196 (bottom), 198–203, 206–208, 213–228, 229 (bottom), 230, 231 (center and bottom), 232, 233, 244, 245 (bottom)
Maryland Historical Society: 5
Massachusetts Historical Society: 6, 7
McKim, Mead and White: 185 (bottom), 186, 187
Meserve Collection: 108
Museum of the City of New York: 66
National Archives: 2, 30, 204, 209–212, 231 (top)
National Gallery of Art: 10

New York Historical Society: 22, 53, 57
New York Public Library: 5 (center), 8 (bottom), 17, 43, 45, 49, 54, 63, 90, 91, 94, 98–101, 103, 106, 107, 109, 110, 115, 121–127, 130, 131, 133, 134, 180, 184
The New York Times, George Tames, 288–293, 294, 296, 302 (bottom), 304 (top), 305, 314 (top), 320
Pennsylvania Academy of the Fine Arts: 20, 36
National Park Service, Abbie Rowe, 8 (top), 21, 252, 253 (bottom), 254–261, 262 (left)
Rutherford B. Hayes Library: 112, 113, 116–119, 128
St. John's Church, Washington, D. C.: 31
Theodore Roosevelt Association: 182 (bottom), 185 (top), 207
Theodore Roosevelt Collection, Harvard College Library: 181
United Press: 235, 249, 251, 253 (top), 262 (center), 265, 267, 281, 282 (top), 283 (top), 284, 287
U. S. News and World Report: 271–277
Fred Ward, Black Star: 304 (bottom)
The White House: 264, 266, 267 (top), 268 (top), 269, 270; Robert L. Knudsen, 292, 299; O. Winston Link, 286, 295; Abbie Rowe, 285; Cecil W. Stoughton, 283 (bottom), 306–307, 309–311, 312–313, 314 (bottom)–319, 321
Wide World: 191, 205, 229 (top), 234, 236–240, 241 (top), 243, 245 (top), 245 (bottom), 247 (bottom), 248, 250, 262 (right), 267 (bottom), 268, 278–280, 282 (bottom), 297, 298, 300, 301, 302 (top), 303

ACKNOWLEDGMENTS

Throughout the long preparation of this book, the author has drawn heavily on the knowledge, experience, and encouragement of a great number of individuals. Without help of this kind such a book could not be produced. The author here lists some of the persons, with the societies, museums, and agencies which they represent, and expresses her deep gratitude for the patient aid consistently offered.

Library of Congress: Virginia Daiker, Carl Stange, and Milton Kaplan of the Prints and Photographs Division; Hirst Milhollen, Reference Librarian, also of the Prints and Photographs Division

National Archives and Records Service: Josephine Cobb

National Capital Parks: T. Sutton Jett, Abbie Rowe, and Carol Johnson

The Rutherford B. Hayes Library: Watt P. Marchman, Director

The Lincoln Museum: Stanley McClure, Director

New-York Historical Society, Map and Print Room: A. B. Carlson

The Franklin D. Roosevelt Memorial Library: Herman Kahn, Director, and Margaret Suckley

Embassy of Japan: Toshikazu Maeda, First Secretary, Press and Cultural Affairs

Consulate General of Japan in New York: Isamu Masuda, Consul

Frick Art Reference Library

Eastman House: Beaumont Newhall, Curator

Corcoran Gallery: Victor Amato, Photographer

American Institute of Architects: George Pettingill, Librarian

McKim, Mead and White, Architects

Benjamin Harrison Home, Indianapolis, Indiana

New York Public Library: American History Room, Print Room, Rare Book Room

Culver Picture Service

Museum of the City of New York

National Gallery of Art, Washington, D. C.

Ladies' Hermitage Association, Nashville, Tennessee

Theodore Roosevelt Collection, Harvard College Library: Robert Haynes, Curator

Theodore Roosevelt Association: Mae V. Manning, Curator

St. John's Church of Washington, D.C.: David W. Mayberry, Rector

(Continued)

Also contributing greatly were the persons who made available sources of fresh and unpublished text and picture material:

Herbert Hoover, J. T. Dorris, Charles A. Kraft, Mr. and Mrs. Edgar Cox of the Brady-Handy Studios, Harry J. Sievers, S. J.; Mrs. Mary Jane McCaffree, secretary to Mrs. Eisenhower; Mrs. Katharine McCook Knox, Mrs. Gladys Montgomery, Helen Decker, John K. Murphy, Frank Rowsome, Jr., Phillip H. Miller, Marty Monroe, Nelson Demarest, Milton J. Kennedy, Edward August, Brian Brown, George Bryant, Mrs. Arthur Adams, Miss Margaret W. Hodges, Mrs. Gouverneur Hoes, George Gray Zabriskie, Robert Chapin

The White House: Pamela Turnure, Press Secretary to Mrs. John F. Kennedy; Mrs. Elizabeth Carpenter; Miss Simone Poulain; Mr. James Ketchum, Curator of the White House; Mrs. Constance Stuart; Oliver Atkin.

CONTENTS

THE WHITE HOUSE AND ITS THIRTY-FIVE FAMILIES

Deeds of Lands in the Territory of Columbia, by the Governor & Council of Maryland.

Rec'd a Letter from Maj' Elliott about the engraving for a plan of the City —

At a meeting of the Commissioners at George Town on the fourteenth day of March 1792.

Present David Stuart and Daniel Carroll Esquires

The following Advertizements were ordered to be published in the principal Towns in the United States to wit

Washington in the Territory of Columbia

A premium

of 500 dollars or a medal of that value at the option of the party will be given by the Commissioners of the public federal buildings to the person who before the fifteenth day of July next shall produce to them the most approved plan, if adopted by them for a pre-=sidents house to be erected in this City — The Site of the building, if the artist will attend to it, will of course influence the aspect and outline of his plan and its destination will point out to him the number, size and distribution of the apartments — It will be a recom mendation of any plan if the Central part of it may be detached and erected for the present with the appearance of a compleat whole and be capable of admitting the additional parts in future, if they shall be wanting — Drawings will be expected of the Ground plats, elevations of each front and sections through the building in such directions as may be

(necessary)

---

necessary to explain the internal structure, and an estimate of the cubic feet of brickwork composing the whole mass of the walls

March 14th 1792.   The Commissioners

Washington in the Territory of Columbia

A Premium

A house built to order

THE PRESIDENT'S HOUSE, austere and naked-looking in its treeless setting, was far from inviting in November, 1800, when it admitted its first tenants. Indeed, it was forbidding as it stood in isolated splendor in the dismal little village of Washington. President John Adams and his wife, Abigail, taking up their residence in the unfinished mansion, could not understand how eight years had gone into its building.

The great house of white sandstone stood in the midst of rough fields which on the south sloped to the Potomac River. Strewn about the grounds were old brickkilns, pits for storing supplies, and stacks of rubbish. Shacks put up to house the workmen still stood on the grounds. Indoors, only a half-dozen rooms had been made habitable. The main stairway was not up; there was no plumbing, and the open log fires, the only source of heat, strove vainly to dry the damp walls.

The President and Mrs. Adams, reluctantly moving in in time to round out the last few months of Adams's term of office, were highly appreciative of the fact that as first occupants of the home built specifically for the President, they were performing an act unique in history. Nevertheless, they both thoroughly detested the involved move of the government from Philadelphia to this, its permanent home. In the so-called city of Washington that was now to house Congress and the President, only two government buildings were finished. A dirt road newly cut through the brush, called Pennsylvania Avenue, led off to the Capitol building, a mile and a half away. Clustered around its bleak unfinished frame were a few lodgings and buildings erected quickly to house tradesmen. Four or five hundred residences were scattered at random over the swampy landscape.

It had been ten years since President George Washington had put his signature to the bill which began the building of a federal city. In 1790, after Congress had approved the location of the city on the Potomac River, an act had been passed "to provide suitable buildings for the accom-

The village of Washington in 1800, when it became the home of the President and Congress.

3

President George Washington, holding the plan for the city which bears his name, but which he always modestly called the Federal City. This mezzotint, published by E. Savage in 1793, was from the original portrait painted at the request of Harvard University, Cambridge, Massachusetts.

modation of Congress and of the President, and for public offices of the Government in time for their occupancy in 1800."

At the time, a decade had seemed ample for the creation of a capital city. But ten years had not been enough for the planning and imagining, selecting and surveying, financing and refinancing necessary to establishing a permanent seat of government. Nor could President Washington foresee the maddening delays which would balk the carrying out of his plans.

A year had already slipped by when the Board of Federal Commissioners appointed by Congress took an important step. On March 9, 1791, there appeared in the Georgetown *Weekly Ledger* an announcement that "Major Longfont, a French gentleman, employed by the President of the United States," had arrived in the vicinity to look over the area upon which he was to plan a city. "Major Longfont" proved to be the distinguished

4

French-born engineer, Major Pierre Charles L'Enfant; and the city he planned, drawn on a plan already sketched by Washington's Secretary of State Thomas Jefferson, included broad diagonal avenues, parks, and circles reminiscent of the streets of L'Enfant's native Versailles.

It was not until a year later, at their meeting on March 14, 1792, that the Commissioners set about securing plans for a President's House. An advertisement written by Thomas Jefferson and published in the country's leading newspapers offered a prize of $500 or a gold medal of the same value for plans accepted by the Commissioners.

Jefferson, who wanted passionately to see the city modeled on the antique, could not miss this chance of indulging his favorite hobby. Putting his architectural talents to work, he drew up his own plans for the proposed mansion and sent them in to the Commissioners, signing them with the initials "A. Z." His entry was immediately attributed to an Alexandria, Virginia, builder named Abraham Faws.

A second distinguished contestant was the versatile Dr. William Thornton, a doctor of medicine, inventor, city planner, painter, race-horse enthusiast, and amateur architect, who was himself a member of the Commission.

In the open competition for plans both Jefferson and Thornton lost to a little-known architect from Charleston, South Carolina. He was James Hoban, born in Kilkenny, Ireland, and trained in Dublin, where he had taken prizes for his designs for "brackets and cornices."

The American Revolution had scarcely come to an end when Hoban emigrated to the United States and set up for business in Philadelphia, advertising in a newspaper that he was qualified and eager to design "houses for gentlemen." He was working in Charleston when he learned of the competition for plans for the President's House. With his preliminary drawings finished, Hoban traveled to Washington to look over the building site selected by President Washington and L'Enfant. The trip was well worth the effort. In July, 1792, he was notified that he had won the prize offered by the Commissioners and also a long-term job as superintendent of the building.

Jefferson's design for the President's House, and below, Palladio's Villa Rotonda, from which he borrowed.

The seldom-seen plan submitted by the architect of the first Capitol, Dr. William Thornton.

Hoban's drawing after he omitted a third story at Washington's suggestion.

Hoban's original plan showed a Georgian house of three stories above a ground floor, topped by a steep roof. His design, in a manner considered extremely practical by the judges, allowed for wings to be added at a later date. The cost of erecting the house was estimated at about $400,000.

In the heat of the summer President Washington came up from Mount Vernon to fix the exact location of the President's House on the site selected, keeping in mind its relationship to the Capitol site and the location of all future streets. And on October 13, 1792, as Free Masons from Georgetown, the Commissioners, and "gentlemen of the town and neighborhood" looked on, there was laid the cornerstone of the future home of all the Presidents. Afterward, the party returned to the Fountain Inn in Georgetown for dinner, drinking a total of sixteen toasts to, among others, the fifteen states, the President, the city, the Marquis de Lafayette, the fair daughters of America and, finally, peace, liberty, and order.

From the first, Hoban was handicapped by a shortage of money for salaries and supplies. With the burden of erecting a Capitol soon added to that of the President's home, a parsimonious Congress pulled the purse strings even tighter. Schemes for dropping one project or the other were proposed. One Congressman thought rented quarters for the President would do for a while. Another wanted to provide a double-duty building to house both the President and Congress.

6

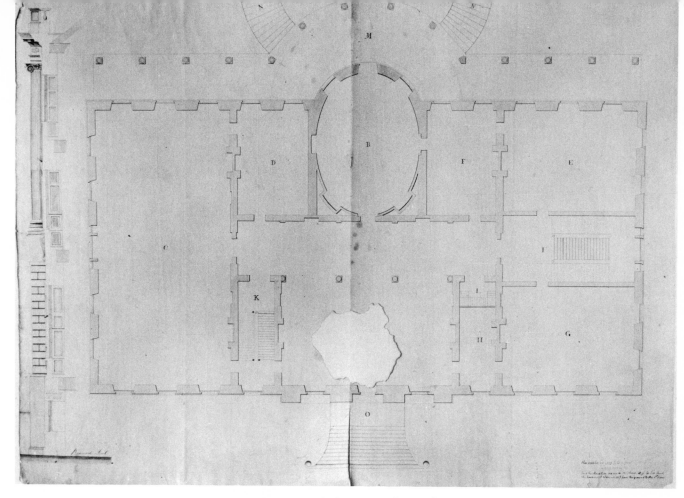

Hoban's drawing of the main-floor plan.

Washington and Jefferson, fearful that Congress might halt the work completely, reasserted their enthusiasm for it. Early in 1793 Washington wrote: "The doubts and opinion of others . . . have occasioned no change in my sentiments on the subject. They have always been, that the plan ought to be prosecuted with all the despatch the nature of the case will admit, and that the public buildings in size, form and elegance, should look beyond the present day."

Before long the original grant of $200,000 given by the states of Maryland and Virginia had been exhausted and a second scheme for raising money was hatched. City lots were to be auctioned off, and Washington, greatly concerned over the impasse, came to the auction in the hope of spurring sales. His presence had little effect. There were few purchasers for the undeveloped, boggy land in a city which was still only a dream in the minds of a few men.

At Washington's suggestion, Hoban had eliminated one story from his first plans. It now became clear that in spite of this economy, construction of the President's House would have to be extended over a long period. Often work came to a complete standstill while workmen loafed around the grounds, drinking and talking as they waited for the river boats to arrive with lumber, stone, and brick.

By spring of 1799 the exterior walls had finally gone up and the roof

7

Above, Leinster House in Dublin, Ireland, with which James Hoban's
design for the President's House was often compared. Below, the
"Design for a Gentleman's House," which most architects agree was
actually the basis for Hoban's plan. The drawing appeared in
A Book of Architecture by James Gibbs, a disciple of Christopher
Wren. Still other observers saw in Hoban's plan a great
similarity to the Condé Palace in Paris.

John Adams, the first
President to occupy the
White House, drawn by
C.B.J.F. de St. Memin.
A detail of the original.

had been put on. The Commissioners still looked around for more funds,
the workmen still dawdled, and the time left for completing the house
for the President and his family had dwindled precariously.

Washington, who with Thomas Jefferson had stood up to so much
opposition in his wish to establish a Capital, was not to see the President's House in anything approaching its completed state. In December,
1799, nearly a year before it was occupied, George Washington died at
Mount Vernon.

Work on the public buildings meanwhile continued at a leisurely pace
despite the rapid approach of the removal of the government from Philadelphia. In June, 1800, at the close of the last session of Congress in
Philadelphia, President Adams came briefly to Washington to take a look
at his future residence. He found it far from completion; the Commissioners had been correct in their report to Congress that "the plaster and
paint must have time to dry." The President stayed at Tunicliffe's Hotel
on Capitol Hill while he saw to the storing of the official furniture in the
Presidential mansion.

The transfer of government in the early summer of 1800 was marked
by complete calm. In May Adams advised his department heads to "make
the most prudent and economical arrangements for the removal of the
public offices, clerks and papers . . . in such manner that the public offices
may be opened in the city of Washington by the 15th of June." The Sec-

9

Gilbert Stuart painted the sturdy, political-minded Abigail Adams, first mistress of the White House.

retary of State had a notice posted on his door to the effect that he was moving away, and changes of address for the departments were published in Philadelphia newspapers. All 136 Federal employees prepared to move.

In the fall, somewhat in advance of his wife, John Adams came down to Washington from Quincy, Massachusetts; and on November 22, House and Senate members met in the Senate chambers of the unfinished Capitol to hear the President deliver his message to Congress. Afterward they traveled the muddy road to the White House, where John Adams, formally dressed in black velvet, held court alone in the upstairs drawing room.

Abigail Adams, arriving later by coach, with full retinue of servants, was characteristically penetrating and outspoken in her description of her new abode. She pictured it in letters to her sister and daughter: "As I expected to find it a new country, with houses scattered over a space of ten miles, and trees and stumps in plenty with a castle of a house—so I found it." She was "distressed" by the shocking state of Washington and pained by the oversized, chilly house in which she must at once take on the twin role of housekeeper and hostess.

"This House is twice as large as our meeting House," wrote Abigail. "I believe the great Hall is as big . . . but this House is built for ages to come. Not one room or chamber is finished of the whole. . . . To assist us in this great castle, and render less attendance necessary, bells are wholly wanting—promises are all you can obtain."

The looking glasses which hung in the few livable rooms of the house were, according to Abigail, "dwarfs"; there were not "a twentieth part enough lamps to light it"; and she had been forced to have the servants hang the wash to dry in the great unfinished audience room because there was no drying yard. In spite of the forests nearby, wood was not to be had. The vessel bringing her clothes had not arrived, her tea china was "more than half missing," and the ladies were clamoring for a "drawing-room." She dismissed the lively town of Georgetown as the "very dirtiest hole I ever saw for a place of any trade or respectability of inhabitants."

There were a few compensations for living in a wilderness. The view of the river from the south windows was beautiful, with vessels passing, and the spot itself was beautiful—"capable of every improvement," wrote Abigail hopefully. She was near the woman she admired most in the world, Martha Washington, who had sent her a haunch of venison from Mount Vernon with an invitation to visit her whenever time permitted.

Abigail and John Adams had only a brief stay in the White House, but during those few months they worked hard to set the social tone they thought appropriate for the home of the President. For years, while her husband had been Vice President, Abigail had observed Martha Washington at close range in New York and Philadelphia before becoming First Lady herself. It was this stiff, ceremonious style, strictly in the Federalist tradition, which she sought to bring to the White House. Upstairs in the Oval Room, filled with mahogany chairs and sofas upholstered in crimson damask, the Adamses each week held court in a manner which would, with modifications, govern the social life of all administrations to come. Adams, dressed in velvet, with silver buckles at the knees, his hair powdered, would bow from the waist as he greeted his guests, while his wife remained seated at his side. The Adamses, it is true, did not have as showy an equipage as George Washington's cream-colored coach in the style of Louis Seize, decorated with cupids and flowers and drawn by six horses. That had not gone down well with the citizens of the Republic. Adams was making a minor concession to the march of democracy.

Their leaving of the White House was not without its touch of tragedy. Adams was deeply aggrieved by his defeat at the hands of the anti-Federalist Thomas Jefferson, their years of friendship long since engulfed by the political ill will of Adams's term. As late as nine o'clock on the eve of Jefferson's inauguration, Adams was still sending nominations of devoted Federalists to a special session of Congress. Abigail, despite the perils of her lengthy winter journey, had set off for Quincy as soon as the news of Jefferson's election became known.

On March 4, 1801, while Thomas Jefferson walked from his boarding-house to the Capitol for the inauguration, John Adams was already in a coach headed for Baltimore, determined not to join the demonstration put on by the crowd for the man who had defeated him. It was not dignified or wise, he thought, for the President to join the *hoi pólloi* in the streets and make his way to the Capitol like a common citizen.

In thus letting his disapproval be known, Adams was indicating his true feelings, that Jefferson's election was a catastrophe. Adams set his standards for the Presidency high. In a letter to Abigail on November 2, 1800, he had written: "I pray heaven to bestow the best of blessings on this house, and on all that shall hereafter inhabit it. May none but honest and wise men ever rule under this roof."

Adams need not have worried. Jefferson and those who followed him were to be men of surprising ability. In the words of Rexford Guy Tugwell, writing in his *The Democratic Roosevelt*, "It is a remarkable comment on the presidency that the processes of party politics, so often corrupt, boss-managed, and infiltrated with venial arts, have never deposited a man in the White House who was wholly unworthy. There have been those who were ignorant, weak, unwise, or overkind to friends; there have been many who were slow to understand their essential duties; but there never has been one who did not grow better, wiser, more dedicated to the public interest."

Only the north wing of the Capitol had been finished when Congress met there for the first time in November, 1800.

The architect Benjamin Henry Latrobe made these water colors of the White House to show the porticoes and terraces which he planned along with Thomas Jefferson. Above, the south front, and below, the east front of the White House, as they were to look when the porticoes were added many years later. The terraces were built in Jefferson's administration.

The artful gentry

THE PRESIDENT was out horseback riding when the delegation of fashionably dressed women was ushered into the President's House. The ladies, waiting in the Oval Drawing Room, had time to reflect indignantly upon the way the new President had cheated them out of their favorite social function, the large weekly levee or reception. Organized into a formidable body, they had come to meet President Thomas Jefferson face to face and shame him into reestablishing this activity so important in the Washington and Adams regimes. When the tall, rangy Jefferson appeared in the doorway, booted and spurred and disheveled from his ride, they were ready for him.

President Jefferson behaved as if he had been expecting them. Pleasure beamed from his freckled face; he was delighted to see them all. Taking no notice of their anger, he explained to the women his view of the routine levee; it was a pointless waste of time and far too suggestive of the court of an old-world king. Patiently he led the subdued ladies to the door.

There was one young woman in Washington who could have warned the ladies that they would never be able to stand up to the logic and charm of Thomas Jefferson. She was Mrs. Samuel Bayard Smith, whose husband had recently been brought from Philadelphia by Jefferson to publish the *National Intelligencer*. Margaret Bayard Smith, unlike her husband, was a Federalist and had not known Jefferson in Philadelphia. When he was characterized by his Federalist enemies as "coarse and vulgar in his manner, awkward and rude in his appearance" she had believed every word.

Mrs. Smith's conversion to the Jefferson camp, as she described it later in her lively journal, *The First Forty Years of Washington Society*, was sudden and dramatic. A stranger appeared at the Smith home one morning to make arrangements about having some printing done. "He turned to me a countenance," Mrs. Smith wrote, "beaming with an expression of benevolence and with a manner and voice almost femininely soft and gentle. I know not how it was, but there was something in his manner,

The fashionable, worldly Jefferson when he was minister to France. A bust by sculptor Jean Antoine Houdon.

13

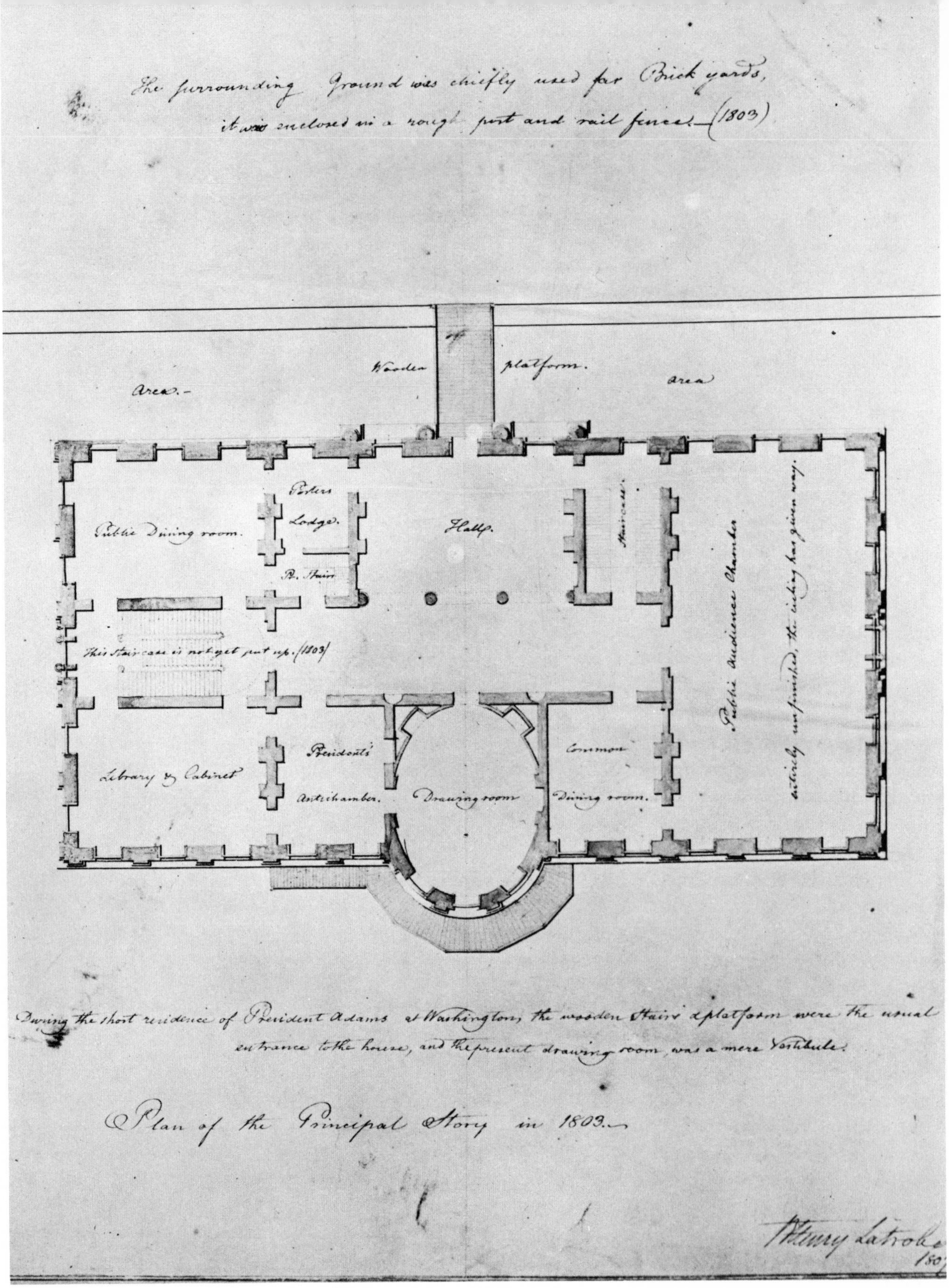

The surrounding Ground was chiefly used for Brick yards,
it was enclosed in a rough post and rail fence (1803)

Wooden platform.

Area.—   area

Public Dining room.   Porters
                               Lodge.   Hall.   Staircase

                               B. Stair

This Staircase is not yet put up. (1803)

Library & Cabinet   President's   Drawing room   Common   Public Audience Chamber
                               Antichamber.   Dining room.   entirely unfinished, the ceiling has given way.

During the short residence of President Adams at Washington, the wooden Stairs & platform were the usual
entrance to the house, and the present drawing room was a mere Vestibule.

Plan of the Principal Story in 1803.

B Henry Latrobe
1803

The main floor of the White House in 1803, drawn by Latrobe.

his countenance and voice that at once unlocked my heart. . . ." When the stranger was introduced as Mr. Jefferson, Mrs. Smith was already captured. "I felt my cheeks burn and my heart throb," she admitted.

The picture of Jefferson in the White House had additional interest for women; the President, except for the servants, lived there entirely alone. Nearly twenty years before, Jefferson's wife had died and the legend endured that the grieving husband had vowed never to remarry.

From the first it was apparent that Jefferson intended to enforce a republican simplicity in the White House. In addition to the levee, the small formal drawing room and the punctilious state dinner were done away with. No more formality, no more precedence was the rule. At dinner parties rank was discarded and the ladies preceded the gentlemen en masse as they entered and left the dining room. The receptions—two only, to be given on July 4 and New Year's Day—were open to all who chose to come.

The elimination of snobbery was, however, the President's only concession to simplicity. Elsewhere, with great savoir-faire, Jefferson plunged into the task of creating an oasis of fine living in the wilderness of Washington. The grounds around the White House might still be littered with workmen's sheds and piles of trash, and carriages winding up the makeshift roadway might still have to cross an open sewer, but indoors the parlors were filled with chairs and sofas in the styles of Hepplewhite, Sheraton, and Louis Seize. From Monticello, Jefferson had brought the bric-a-brac, the pictures, and the furniture he had purchased while Minister to France. Because he was fond of the copperplate prints on cotton then in vogue in Europe, cotton took the place of the stiff silks and damasks favored by Abigail Adams.

A remarkable household staff, rigidly supervised by the French steward Etienne Lemaire, contributed to Jefferson's role of epicure, as did the French chef and the dozen well-trained servants brought from the President's estate. Wines from Spain and France, Italy and Portugal came into the storage rooms by the barrel. In 1804, an election year, Jefferson's bill for Madeira, claret, sauterne, and champagne ran to nearly $3,000.

There was far more to Jefferson's design than the desire to show off his talents as gourmet and man of the world. The President meant to create in the White House, and especially at his dining-table, a favorable setting for carrying on his official business. Dinners were kept small in order to facilitate the free exchange of ideas. Foreign ministers, Congressmen, and all the assortment of citizens invited were soon going away from Jefferson's parties in a state of elation. At Jefferson's table—a circular one which made all seats equal in importance—delicacies imported from abroad delighted the bored residents of Washington. Waffles from Holland, macaroni from Italy, almonds and anchovies from France were all to be found, and ice cream, the recipe for which Jefferson had brought from France, was served in little balls encased in shells of warm pastry.

There were other surprises for the President's guests. A great believer in the wisdom of secrecy, Jefferson had turned his well-known inventive talents toward making some silent helpers for his dining room. Circular shelves set in the wall turned at the touch of a spring, bringing into view filled dishes, ready for serving. Another touch and the shelves swung out of sight. At no time was the President's company interrupted by a servant.

At times when only two or three persons were being entertained, a small dumb-waiter, filled with every necessary item for the meal, would be placed beside each guest, who then proceeded to help himself. This invention seemed wonderful indeed to diplomats from countries in which a servant might be a spy in disguise.

Conversation at the President's House was also surprising to visitors from abroad. Jefferson would discuss astronomy, geology, agriculture, mathematics, or music by the hour, then abruptly switch to amusing his guests with what the young senator John Quincy Adams called Jefferson's "prodigies." These "prodigies," which were simply tall stories, did not amuse the humorless Adams, who nevertheless recorded some of them in his diary. "He said that before he went from Virginia to France," wrote Adams after attending a dinner for ten Federalist Congressmen, "he had some ripe pears sewed up in tow bags and that when he returned six years afterwards, he found them in a perfect state of preservation—self candied."

Adams was on hand when the Tunisian ambassador, the black-bearded Meley Meley, came to dine with Jefferson, bringing along his two secretaries and a Greek interpreter. It was a Mohammedan fast day, and Meley Meley, who had to observe the fast until sunset, was half an hour late for the party. He did not hesitate to hold up the dinner even further while he had a smoke from his exotic pipe, at the same time dipping into his snuff, which, according to the Senator, was "deeply scented with otto of roses." Finally seated at the table, Meley Meley threw caution aside and joined in the repast with ardor, not even asking the ingredients of any dish. Adams also noted that the minister's secretaries indulged themselves in a glass of wine once their employer had left the table.

Jefferson had been President for nearly two years before his two married daughters came to the White House for a visit. Martha—Mrs. Randolph—and Maria—Mrs. Eppes—had been too busy with their own families to assume any responsibilities in Washington and had gladly relinquished the duties of official hostess to the popular Dolley Madison, wife of Secretary of State James Madison. Now, in December, 1802, they decided to come, and Jefferson, who was a devoted and sentimental father, looked forward with pleasure to the moment when the President's House would be overrun with his grandchildren and his daughters would be introduced to Washington. Dinners and parties were planned well in advance.

A social season in the Capital was not taken lightly by the two young women. In spite of their Paris schooling, their country life had left them unsure of themselves in the realm of fashion, and Martha Randolph asked her father for aid in making herself and her sister presentable. In October Martha wrote asking Jefferson to order wigs made for them both—"the color of the hair enclosed and of the most fashionable shapes"—so that they would not be out-of-date among the belles of Washington.

16

A picture of the White House published in a popular book in 1807.

Jefferson immediately turned the whole problem over to Dolley Madison, who went at the job with her usual energy. Several trips to Philadelphia were necessary before she had found the correct gowns and turbans, the pelisses and shawls, which would keep the Jefferson girls from looking countrified.

Mrs. Madison evidently did a good job, for Margaret Bayard Smith was very favorably impressed. "A lovely woman," wrote Mrs. Smith of the practical-minded Martha. For Maria Eppes she reserved the word "beautiful." All Washington looked on with interest as the President's coach, drawn by four showy bays, carried the women on a constant round of amusements. On New Year's Day, 1803, they stood in line with their father and greeted a cross section of the citizenry at the general reception held in the White House.

Mrs. Smith, always ready to take the kindliest view of any move of Jefferson's, claimed that the round table he had had installed in his dining room was put there because the seating arrangement made general conversation easier. Diplomats, however, said that the table was just another facet of Jefferson's design to embarrass foreign ministers by doing away with precedence. The Danish minister and the Spanish minister were sure that this was true and pointed out the President's behavior at his receptions, where he would "show his preference of the Indian deputies on New Year's Day by giving us only a bow, while with them he entered into a long conversation." It remained for the British minister, Anthony Merry, and Mrs. Merry to reach new heights of indignation when they encountered Jefferson's principle of equality for all.

Minister Merry and his wife had become reluctant residents of Washington in November, 1803, upon which occasion Merry remarked, "Why, this is a thousand times worse than the worst parts of Spain," a comment delightedly and frequently quoted by his wife. In due time the new envoy, accompanied by Secretary Madison, went to the White House to present his credentials to President Jefferson. Merry, in "full official uniform," trimmed in gold lace and wearing a dress sword, was annoyed upon entering the President's House to find the audience chamber unoccupied. He was further outraged at being introduced to the President in a narrow vestibule, "from which to make room, I was obliged to back out." The real scandal, however, was the President's personal appearance. President Jefferson was, Merry wrote to a friend, "not merely in undress, but actually standing in slippers down at the heels, and both pantaloons, coat and under-clothes, indicative of utter slovenliness and indifference to appearances, and in a state of negligence actually studied. . . ." Merry took the entire scene as a deliberate insult to His Majesty, George III.

When the time came for the Merrys to go to dinner at the President's, the serio-comic Jefferson-Merry affair immediately involved Mrs. Merry. At a dinner given by the President for foreign ministers and members of Congress, Merry, the ranking diplomat present, took for granted that he and Mrs. Merry would be seated before the other guests. When the time arrived for entering the dining room, he was horrified to see Jefferson offer his arm to Mrs. Madison instead of Mrs. Merry. The others were left to seat themselves as they pleased.

Since there was no female member of Jefferson's family living in the President's home, Mrs. Merry picked Dolley Madison for her attacks. Dinner at the James Madisons was "more like a harvest home supper than the entertainment of a Secretary of State," said Mrs. Merry, and she said it frequently and to persons she was sure would repeat it to Mrs. Madison. Dolley Madison, hardly ruffled by the remark, made a shrewd and composed answer. "The profusion of my table . . . arises from the happy circumstance of abundance and prosperity in our country." Thomas Jefferson, who had already labeled the large, overpowering Mrs. Merry a virago, was more annoyed than Mrs. Madison. He said that if the minister's wife continued her destructive ways she "must eat her soup at home."

It was the Merrys who finally severed all connection with the President's House. Someone suggested that they could just as well live in Philadelphia as in the wilds of Washington, and away went the Merrys out of range of the upsetting Thomas Jefferson.

In the year 1803, Jefferson had the greatest triumph of his years in the White House when Napoleon sold to the United States the great Louisiana Territory for the sum of $15,000,000. Jefferson could not conceal his joy. When the news reached the Capitol, Congressmen held an all-night jamboree at Steel's Hotel and only the most hard-bitten of Jefferson's Federalist enemies complained about the price.

President Jefferson's capacious intellect embraced a world of unusual interests, and among the profusion of books, maps, and pictures brought from Monticello were some singularly fascinating symbols of his interests. One large, high-ceilinged room was given over to piles of enormous bones, prehistoric and otherwise, shipped from the West by the Lewis and Clark expedition and awaiting examination by a scholar friend. Downstairs in his basement office, while his pet mockingbird sat on his shoulder or flitted through the room, Jefferson would sit at his desk (the drawers filled with gardening and carpentry tools, as well as documents) and write letters with a new invention, the polygraph. A Mr. Hawkins of Philadelphia had sent

Jefferson his "machine," a device for "copying with one pen while you write with the other," and Jefferson, using two, three, or even four pens, was able to abandon his cumbersome copying press.

In the closet of his bedchamber Jefferson had installed one of his own useful inventions—a turnstile contrivance for hanging up his clothes. At a touch it revolved, bringing into view the wanted jackets and breeches, vests, and cravats. Dolley Madison sometimes let friends take a peek at this odd invention when she showed them through the White House rooms.

Jefferson had taken great pleasure from the happily married state of his daughters and looked with approval upon their lives away from Washington. This happiness was blasted, however, when, in the spring of 1804, Maria died at Monticello. Of his six children, only one now remained alive, the stable, capable Martha, already the mother of six. The lonely President longed to have his only daughter and her children near him in Washington.

It was not until the fall of 1805, after Jefferson had begun his second term, that Martha Randolph could manage to leave her home in Virginia and come to the White House for the winter. Jefferson was elated. Every moment that could be stolen from work was spent playing with the children. That season a seventh Randolph baby, James Madison Randolph, was born in the White House, the first child to be born there.

Margaret Bayard Smith, calling on Mrs. Randolph one evening, was charmed to find the President alone with his daughter and her family. "While I sat looking at him," Mrs. Smith wrote, "playing with these infants, one standing on the sofa with its arms around his neck, the other two youngest on his knees, playing with him, I could scarcely realize he was one of the most celebrated men now living, both as a Politician and Philosopher."

When Jefferson got down to the constructive business of enlarging and improving the President's House, he by-passed James Hoban, architect of the mansion, and instead engaged Benjamin Henry Latrobe to develop the ideas he himself had already outlined. Latrobe, the architect of the naval dry docks in Washington, was given the appointment of surveyor of public buildings early in Jefferson's tenure. The association was a long one, productive of great changes to the exterior of the Executive Mansion.

Jefferson had already drawn plans for long, colonnaded wings, to stretch east and west from the central building, and it was with these plans as a basis that Latrobe set to work. Although he privately expressed the opinion that Jefferson's taste in architecture was "old-fashioned," Latrobe cooperated to the full with Jefferson on the important extension of the building. Space was provided, with the addition of the terraces, for a variety of necessary adjuncts—offices, stables, a meathouse, an icehouse, and storage rooms for wines, coal, and wood.

Hoban's plan had specified an oval entrance pavilion on the south side and a simple entry on the north. Latrobe, with Jefferson's sketch in front of him, developed the oval porch into a semicircular portico and drew plans for an impressive portico on the north. Their completion would have to

Rembrandt Peale's portrait of Jefferson, painted in 1805.

Martha Randolph, Jefferson's daughter, as portrayed by Thomas Sully.

*Dolley Madison,
Jefferson's hostess,
disliked her Gilbert
Stuart portrait.*

wait a good many years, but while Jefferson was President the foundation work and steps of the North Portico were completed.

Squeezing money from Congress in inadequate yearly amounts, Jefferson and Latrobe made a number of improvements between the years 1803 and 1808. A slate roof replaced the leaky old one, and slowly, as they waited for an appropriation, a stone wall was built around the private grounds. Detesting Hoban's floor plan—"the entrance hall was all stomach"—the architect drew up new ones which were never used.

When Latrobe wrote his 1809 report on the condition of the White House, he listed the changes made and deplored the unfinished interior. He ended, pessimistically, "It is a duty which I owe to myself and to the public, not to conceal that the timbers of the President's House are in a state of very considerable decay." The East Room was still unfinished and the interior walls had hardly been touched since John and Abigail Adams's sojourn, and yet the roof, Latrobe considered, was likely to fall in at any time.

The second term of Jefferson's administration had been more rigorous than the first. Day after day Jefferson's Cabinet Room was tense with discussion of the conspiracies of his former Vice President, Aaron Burr. Personal abuse and the hampering moves of the New England Federalists had contributed to Jefferson's eagerness to retire to Monticello. "Never did a prisoner, released from his chains, feel such relief as I shall on shaking off the shackles of power," he wrote to his old friend, Du Pont de Nemours, two days before his term ended. Though Jefferson's popularity had lessened he was still powerful enough to insure the election of his friend James Madison to the Presidency in 1808. Thousands of people poured into Washington to see Madison inaugurated and to see the great Jefferson hand over the reins of office to his protégé. Madison invited Jefferson to sit in his coach on the way to his inauguration but Jefferson declined and instead joined the parade of horseback riders that trailed behind. He had once again become one of the plain people.

Jefferson also attended the reception given at the Madison home after the inaugural ceremonies and that evening appeared at the inaugural ball— the first ever to take place in Washington—given at Long's Hotel in Georgetown. The ball, scheduled to start at seven o'clock, began when the band struck up *Jefferson's March* and Mr. Jefferson entered the hall. The Madisons had not yet arrived. "Am I too early?" Jefferson inquired of a friend. "You must tell me how to behave, for it is more than forty years since I have been to a ball."

As the new President's party entered the hall, *Madison's March* got a rousing performance and all eyes were turned, not to the little President dressed in black, but to the stunning Mrs. Madison, queenly and full-blown, dressed in buff velvet with a long train, and wearing on her head a buff velvet turban from Paris, trimmed with plumes and white satin. Just as Dolley Madison drew the public gaze on this occasion, so would she for the next eight years be the center of attention in the White House.

20

Although nearly a century was to go by before the name White House became official, it was during the Madison administration that the President's House was first referred to in print as the "white house"—in the Baltimore Whig in November, 1810. It had been called that familiarly almost from the beginning because its white sandstone stood out from the brick and frame of Washington houses.

W HEN MRS. JAMES MADISON received guests in her yellow-damask-draped Oval Drawing Room, standing in front of the yellow "sunburst" fire screen fashioned of fluted damask, she could hardly have been more impressive. Her flamboyance seemed to diminish even further the small, preoccupied President. No one could have suspected that Dolley Madison had grown up wearing the quiet gray of the Philadelphia Quaker; now she dressed in velvet or satin when she appeared at White House functions. Her bespangled and befeathered headdresses, called turbans for lack of a better word, were the talk of the Capital.

" 'Tis not her form, 'tis not her face, it is the woman altogether whom I should wish you to see," effused Mrs. William Seaton, wife of an editor of the *National Intelligencer*, trying hard to put into words the elusive charm of Dolley Madison. Artists tried, with little success, to catch it on canvas. President James Madison, overworked and insomniac, wasted none of his precious time analyzing his wife's great attraction for all ages, sexes, and stations of human beings. He accepted gladly the great boon of her exuberant personality and happily turned over to Mrs. Madison the management of White House affairs.

A pillar of Mrs. Madison's household was the French steward Jean Pierre Sioussat, who had been a doorman for Thomas Jefferson and before that a servant in the residence of Minister and Mrs. Merry. He was called French John or John Suse in the kitchens and the laundry. For Mrs. Madi-

21

The serious and the sunny in the James Madison family. Although both the Madisons were well liked, Dolley Madison was extravagantly admired and praised. Oddly enough, it was a man who made one of the rare criticisms of Mrs. Madison—that she was "fat, forty, but not fair." The President's portrait was painted by Asher Brown Durand, Mrs. Madison's by Ezra Ames.

son he became an indispensable part of her busy life. It was Sioussat who outlined and who regulated Dolley Madison's social and domestic schedule.

The schedule was staggering. With a gusto that belied her approaching middle age, Dolley Madison kept to a timetable that no other First Lady could follow. Under the Madisons the weekly levee that had been dropped by Thomas Jefferson was reinstated and the Executive Mansion became the setting for a constant round of dinner parties, lawn parties, luncheons, teas, and dances.

Mrs. Madison's fabulous Wednesday night "drawing rooms" brought out the cream of society. Washington Irving, who had heard much of the gaiety at the White House on Wednesday nights was determined that he would go at least once to see for himself. Arriving in Washington after an exhausting coach trip from New York City, the famous writer dressed himself in "pease blossom and silk stockings" and hurried to the White House to see the show. He found it worth the effort. So gracefully was the evening carried off by the superlative hostess that within a few minutes Irving felt he was among old friends.

Irving noted the beautiful young ladies and the ugly old ones and set down for future readers such an incisive estimate of the Madisons that, accurate or not, they would never be able to escape its conclusions. "Mrs. Madison is a fine, portly, buxom dame who has a smile and a pleasant word for everybody," wrote Irving. But he thought little could be said for the President's appearance: ". . . as to Jeemy Madison—ah, poor Jeemy!—he is but a withered little apple-John."

The Quaker lady, who rather tardily had been metamorphosed into a social leader of quite extravagant tastes, brought to the role of First Lady some extremely useful abilities. One was her talent for injecting into the most ceremonious occasion the informal gaiety of a country dance or a tea party among old friends.

Mrs. Madison, marvelously adept at small talk and the apt remark, was also not above employing a few superficial props to help break the conversational ice with timid guests. She liked to carry a popular book—she preferred romances—open to a page from which to quote a lively passage. And many a shy young man was put at his ease when Dolley invited him to help himself from her lava snuff box, a trinket she was never without. "You are aware that she snuffs; but in her hands the snuff-box seems only a gracious implement with which to charm," wrote a female admirer.

The President, on the rare occasions when he could clear his mind of the cares of office, could also make sparkling talk and even display a flair for jest and epigram. More often, however, he was lost in his own thoughts and the direction of conversation at White House dinner parties fell to his wife. Dolley habitually sat at the head of the table so that the President could escape some of the responsibilities of taking charge of his guests.

There were lively evenings in the White House when the Madisons gave a small party. The almonds, raisins, apples, and pears, which were served as a sort of second dessert as in the days of Thomas Jefferson, would signal the end of dinner and the Madisons would lead the company into one of the parlors for a little fun. "Mrs. Madison insisted on my playing her elegant grand piano, a waltz for Miss Smith and Miss Magruder to dance, the figure of which she instructed them in," reported Mrs. Seaton after one such evening. For the benefit of cabinet ladies, neglected while their husbands were in cabinet session, Dolley often gave "dove" parties.

The White House drawing rooms saw more of James Monroe and his imposing wife after Madison appointed Monroe to the post of Secretary of State. Mrs. Seaton, after observing Mrs. Monroe at an evening party, could not resist comparing her with her idol, Mrs. Madison. "Mrs. Monroe paints very much," she wrote, "and has, besides, an appearance of youth which would induce a stranger to suppose her age to be thirty: in lieu of which, she introduces them to her grandchildren, eighteen or nineteen years old, and to her own daughter, Mrs. Hay, of Richmond."

"Mrs. Madison is said to rouge," continued Mrs. Seaton, "but it is not evident to my eyes, and I do not think it true."

On a shopping trip to Philadelphia, Benjamin Henry Latrobe, who had remained with the Madisons to do the purchasing for the redecorated mansion, selected at the President's request a state coach, a handsome turnout in reddish brown, with touches of yellow lace inside. Daily the coach whirled along the muddy roads of Washington, taking Dolley on her self-imposed mission of paying and returning calls.

In her own way Dolley used the social scene to further the interests of the President. As the impressment of American seamen and the seizure of American ships by the British on the high seas brought the War of 1812 ever nearer, a succession of military, diplomatic, and government figures was cultivated at White House parties. No opportunity was overlooked for lionizing the currently important individual. The flashy Henry Clay, whose War Hawks would make a second term for Madison a certainty, was frequently seen chatting with Mrs. Madison. British diplomats accepted their rightful share of attention without, however, slowing down in the slightest the drive toward war.

In spite of the threat of war and the British blockade of the French coast, Dolley had to find some way of getting the latest fashions out of France if she were to continue in her role of fashion leader. Fortunately for Dolley, Mrs. Joel Barlow, the wife of the United States Ambassador to France, took upon herself the task of finding Parisian wearing apparel to please the President's wife. The winter of 1811 found Dolley sending a typical request for finery. Mrs. Barlow was asked to purchase and "send by a safe vessel, large headdresses, a few flowers, feathers, gloves and stockings, black and white, with anything else pretty and suitable for an economist."

Letters to Mrs. Barlow also spoke of the impending war and listed the officers selected for its conduct. On June 18, 1812, the President signed papers declaring a state of war between England and the United States of America.

For over two years, through 1812, 1813, and into 1814, the war proceeded in discouraging fits and starts, brightened by occasional naval victories on the Great Lakes. But still it hardly touched the Capital or its people, who believed that Washington was not important enough to become involved in the plans of the British.

New Year's Day of 1814 accordingly found the customary large, public reception in progress at the President's House. Mrs. Seaton recorded that Dolley was wearing a gown of pink satin, trimmed with ermine. Her turban that day was an especially showy one, fashioned of white satin and velvet and nodding ostrich plumes. Mrs. Seaton scrutinized the President's face for signs of anxiety and found them in his pallor, his great reserve, and air of abstraction.

The French minister, too, was displaying some magnificence at the White House that day—one of the last opportunities he would have in Washington for many a year; Mrs. Seaton breathlessly described it in her journal. Having eaten her ice cream and drunk a glass of Madeira at the reception, she was on the point of departing when she espied through a front window what she at first thought to be "a rolling ball of burnished gold carried with swiftness through the air by two gilt wings. Our anxiety increased the nearer it approached, until it actually stopped before the door; and from it alighted, weighted with gold lace, the French minister, M. Serurier, and suite. We now perceived that what we thought were wings were nothing more than gorgeous footmen with *chapeaux bras*, gilt-braided skirts and splendid swords. Nothing ever was witnessed in Washington so brilliant and dazzling. You may well imagine how the natives stared and rubbed their eyes to be convinced 'twas no fairy dream."

The "natives" were no doubt just as slow to believe when in July of that same year they learned that defense plans for the supposedly safe city of Washington were hastily being prepared. They were equally incredulous over news of the rout of American troops by the British in Maryland. By Monday, August 22, the British troops were within sixteen miles of the Capital and citizens were leaving the city en masse, taking their belongings with them.

On that day, too, the President, after admonishing his wife to take care of herself and of the cabinet papers, galloped away to join the militia under General Winder. By Tuesday the guard of one hundred men that had been placed around the White House had also disappeared—some to join the military forces, others to look for more healthful surroundings. A few terrified servants and the reliable steward Sioussat were all that remained.

After she had finished packing documents into trunks and had gathered the silver plate, the velvet curtains, and valuable small pieces for removal to a safe place, Dolley, waiting for word from her husband and determined not to leave until his return, found time heavy on her hands. Overcoming her usual reticence about putting her thoughts on record, she sat down to describe the happenings around her in a letter to her sister Lucy.

"Dear Sister," she wrote on Tuesday, August 23, "My husband left me yesterday morning to join General Winder. He enquired anxiously whether I had courage, or firmness to remain in the President's house until his return, on the morrow, or succeeding day . . . I have since received two dispatches from him written with a pencil; . . . he desires I should be ready at a moment's warning to enter my carriage and leave the city . . . I am determined not to go myself until I see Mr. Madison safe, and he can accompany me. . . ."

The following day British troops and Washington militia met in a brief engagement at Bladensburg, Maryland. The Americans, untrained and raw, scattered in confusion. From the roof of the White House, Dolley saw through her spyglass the hopeless rout of the unprepared soldiers. Her letter to Lucy continued: "Since sunrise I have been turning my spy glass in every direction and watching with unwearied anxiety, hoping to discover the approach of my dear husband and his friends; but, alas, I can descry only groups of military wandering in all directions, as if there was a lack of arms, or of spirit to fight for their own firesides."

By that afternoon Dolley must have realized that Madison would not be bringing a group of gay and victorious officers back to dine at the White House as they had planned. She added to her letter: "We have had a bat-

Sir George Cockburn was at the head of the British fleet when it brought war to Washington in 1814. Here he towers heroically above the flaming ruins.

25

The British swaggered a bit in this well-groomed
version of the burning of Washington. The illustration
appeared in a History of England, *written by*
Paul de Rapin-Thoyas.

tle, or skirmish near Bladensburg, and I am still here within sound of the
cannon. . . . Two messengers, covered with dust, come to bid me fly; but I
wait for him. . . ."

In the most perilous moment of all, just before fleeing the Executive
Mansion for good, Dolley actually did save the Stuart-Winstanley portrait
of George Washington, as history books have recorded ever since. She
finished her letter with an account of just how it was saved.

"Our kind friend, Mr. Carrol, has come to hasten my departure," she
wrote, "and is in a very bad humor with me because I insist on waiting
until the large picture of General Washington is secured, and it requires
to be unscrewed from the wall. This process was found too tedious for these
perilous moments; I have ordered the frame to be broken and the canvas

This cartoon commemorating the English victory over the
Americans shows "Maddy" in full flight, his face distorted
by fear, while British tars and Madison's own countrymen give
voice to a variety of belittling remarks.

taken out; it is done,—and the precious portrait placed in the hands of two
gentlemen of New York for safe keeping.

"And now, dear sister, I must leave this house, or the retreating army will
make me a prisoner in it, by filling up the road I am directed to take. When
I shall again write to you, or where I shall be tomorrow, I cannot tell!"

While Mrs. Madison's coach rocked toward the countryside and the
Virginia shore, British redcoats methodically set fire to the public buildings of Washington. The Capitol, the Departments, the Navy Yard buildings were ticked off one by one as the victors carried torches through the
streets. The light thrown off by the monstrous bonfires was said to be equal
to that of a sunny day.

At eleven o'clock that night, M. Serurier, the French minister, peering

27

*The burnt-out shell of the White House in late
1814 and as it was to remain for many months.*

from a window of his residence at Octagon House a few blocks away, saw a
detachment of soldiers approaching the White House. Hurriedly he sent a
messenger to the President's House to beg protection for the French Embassy. The messenger found the British soldiers busily collecting souvenirs
while some of them piled up tables and chairs in the drawing room in
preparation for lighting a bonfire. The messenger from the Embassy was
assured that no such disaster would befall Octagon House—that "the King's
House," a private home, would be protected.

All night long the flames leapt from the heart of the capital city. On
Thursday a hurricane that had been brewing in the stifling August heat
wreaked its full fury on the town. Violent winds tore roofs from houses and
large trees were uprooted. Riders were blown from the backs of their horses
and foot soldiers ran for cover. Rain, falling in streams, put out the fires
that had burned all night. The White House walls steamed but remained
standing.

On Sunday the Madisons were once again in Washington—a Washing-

*In 1814 open countryside lay between the White House and
Octagon House, seen at the right. A water color by S. Lewis.*

ton largely destroyed, chaotic, and dismal. "Such destruction, such confusion," wrote the horrified Mrs. Madison. "The citizens expecting another
visit and at night the rockets were seen flying near us." Of the President's
House, only the roofless, hollow walls still stood like ancient ruins, stained
and blackened. It was necessary to start all over again and find a new point
from which to carry on.

Octagon House, conceded to be the best house in the area, was soon
left vacant by the removal of the French minister to Philadelphia and it was
in this charming home that the Madisons set up their second Executive
Mansion in the fall of 1814. In spite of the hopes expressed by the anti-
administration press that there would now be a cessation of the endless
drawing rooms and receptions—"the resort of the idle, and the encouragers
of spies and traitors"—Dolley was immediately caught up in her usual
tempo of party giving. Perhaps it was her awareness of the views of many
strait-laced individuals as well as those of her husband's political enemies
that spurred her to keep up her gaiety no matter what the circumstances.

29

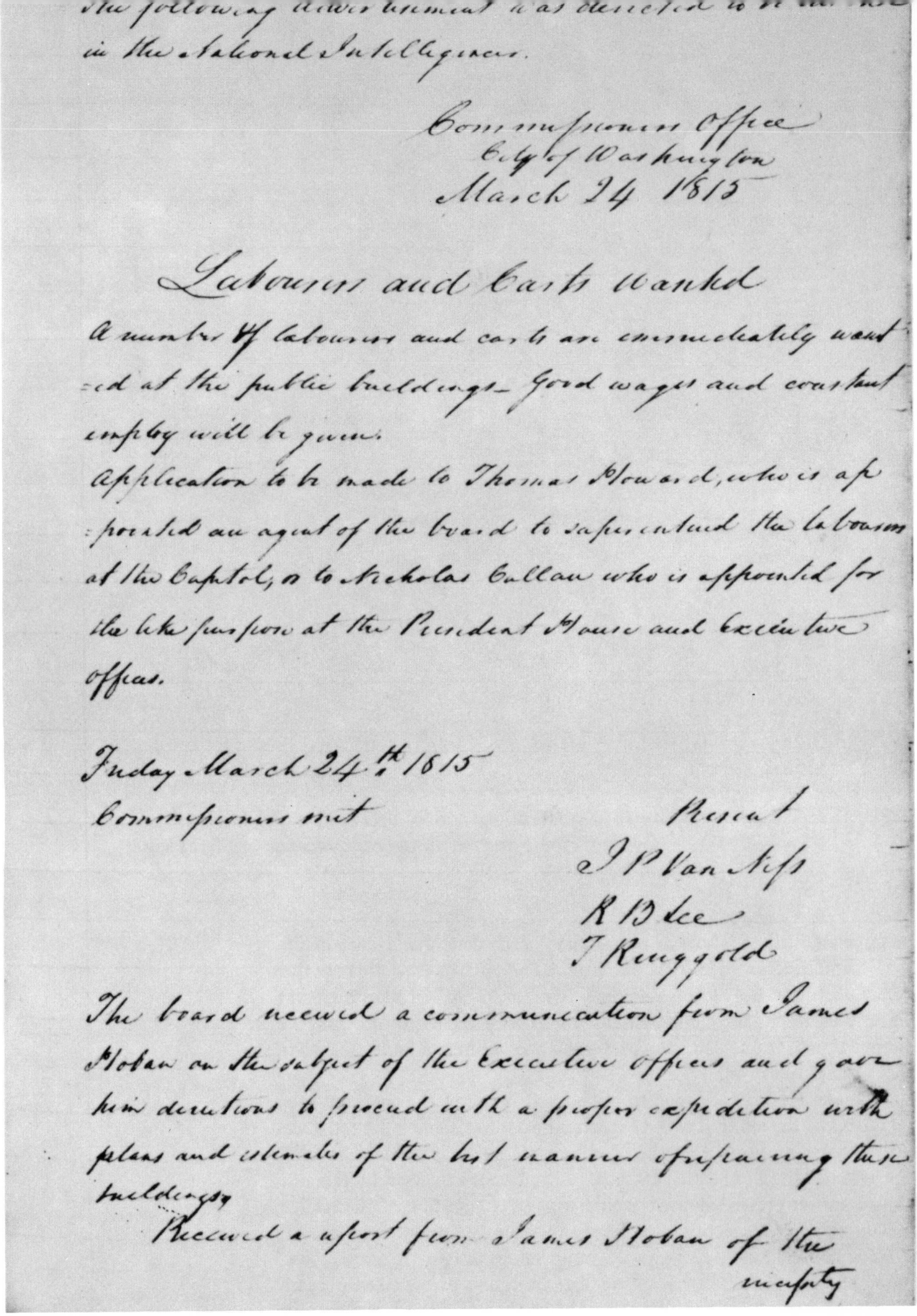

the following advertisement was directed to be inserted
in the National Intelligencer.

Commissioners Office
City of Washington
March 24 1815

Labourers and Carts Wanted

A number of labourers and carts are immediately want
ed at the public buildings—Good wages and constant
employ will be given.
Application to be made to Thomas Howard, who is ap
pointed an agent of the board to superintend the labourers
at the Capitol; or to Nicholas Callan who is appointed for
the like purpose at the President House and Executive
offices.

Friday March 24th 1815
Commissioners met

Present
J P Van Ness
R B Lee
T Ringgold

The board received a communication from James
Hoban on the subject of the Executive Offices and gave
him directions to proceed with a proper expedition with
plans and estimates of the best manner of repairing these
buildings.
Received a report from James Hoban of the
necessity

By the spring of 1815 the City Commissioners were once again
involved in providing a home for the President.

Latrobe's version of the fire-blackened White House with his own St. John's Church in the foreground.

A year later a third Executive Mansion was added to the list—this time a small private house presenting a blank face to the street at the corner of Pennsylvania Avenue and Nineteenth Street. Fifty years later aging men and women would tell how as schoolchildren they passed by the house, pausing to watch Dolley Madison feed her parrot in the window.

Work had proceeded meanwhile on the reconstruction of the President's House. The embers of the ruins had hardly cooled, in the fall of 1814, before a committee from Congress began considering the future of the public buildings destroyed by the British and recommended the modest amount of $500,000 as adequate for reconstructing them. With staggering understatement it reported of the White House that "some parts of the walls, arches and columns are in a state requiring a small expense to preserve them."

With architect James Hoban again in charge, the broader aspects of rebuilding were begun immediately. For a short period the Madisons may have flirted with the notion that they would once more occupy the big rooms of their rightful residence. This dream was of short duration. The work of rebuilding proceeded at a snail's pace. In spite of the signs of activity around the workmen's huts that dotted the grounds—the hurrying to and fro, the stacks of lumber, the masses of brick and stone—little progress was noticeable as the months went by. It was soon clear that the occupancy of the new President's House would fall to Madison's successor.

In December of 1816 the house was still far from the completed state necessary if the incoming President, James Monroe, were to occupy it the following March. Workmen, prodded to greater exertion by Hoban, still were laboriously framing and paneling, painting and varnishing. It had begun to appear even to the casual onlooker as though the President's House would never be ready for occupancy.

31

Something of the shimmering elegance of the Monroe era is caught in
this photograph of three French pieces bought for the 1817 refurnishing
of the White House. They are the famous Minerva clock and two candelabra.

3 | James Monroe 1817-1825
John Quincy Adams 1825-1829

A new house and a new style

On New Year's Day, 1818, the citizens of Washington put on their finery and stood longer than usual before their looking glasses. Everyone was preparing to go to the President's House to meet the new President and Mrs. James Monroe, and see the interior of the rebuilt mansion, said to be extravagantly furnished in the latest French mode.

The announcement that the Executive Mansion was finally to be opened for a general reception had put the public in an expectant frame of mind, and they were not disappointed. Eagerly they thronged to the President's House, gleaming under its coat of fresh, white paint, inspected the shining new rooms, and took a close look at the grave-faced, dignified President Monroe. If he seemed a little out of place in the grand surroundings, at least Mrs. Monroe's regal and worldly appearance fitted into the picture perfectly. The affair was an unqualified success.

The *National Intelligencer* expressed its satisfaction in cautious terms: "The charming weather of yesterday contributed to enliven the reciprocal salutations of kindness and good wishes which are customary at every return of New Year's Day. The President's House, for the first time since its reaerification, was thrown open for the general reception of visitors. It was thronged from 12 to 3 o'clock.... It was gratifying once more to be able to salute the President of the United States with the compliments of the season in his appropriate residence."

Although the reception was in many ways as unpretentious and democratic as any under Jefferson and Madison, the President had been greatly concerned with one phase of the preparations. In the knowledge that diplomats would resent elbowing their way through the crowd, Monroe received them a half-hour in advance of the general public. It was the first indication of Monroe's interest in formal White House etiquette.

To the Monroes had fallen both the pleasures and the woes of furnishing the White House, which had been bare of household goods when pronounced ready for occupancy in the fall of 1817. In order to speed up this

President Monroe's desk, on which he signed the Monroe Doctrine.

33

process, Monroe sold his own furnishings to the government for the sum of $9,071.22½. While minister to France, he had bought many fine pieces of the Louis Seize period, and these were now used along with domestic pieces to furnish two bedrooms and the State Dining Room, with a good start left over for the drawing rooms.

Colonel Samuel Lane, Commissioner of Public Buildings, was placed in charge of expenditures, with $50,000 at his disposal during 1817-1818, for outfitting the mansion. Lane, aided by experts in each field, set a value on the furniture, china, and silver plate bought from the Monroes, appraising the silver down to the quarter-cent. Two dishes, for example, were accordingly priced at $455.31¼; one coffee pot cost $57.37½; one mustard pot, $9.56¼; a fish knife, $10.46½.

President and Mrs. Monroe had learned while abroad to love French furnishings and so decided to order the more important pieces for the ceremonial rooms from France. All purchasing was placed in the hands of the Havre firm, Russell and La Farge, who were before long advising the President that it was no easy matter to obtain furnishings appropriate for the "palace of the President at Washington." All the furniture must be custom-made, and the circular rug for the Oval Room, the *tapis d'Aubusson velouté* being manufactured by Roger and Sollandrouze of Paris, would, they said, take longer than they had expected. The mahogany furniture the President desired for the same room could not be had at all. "We should also add," wrote Russell and La Farge, "that mahogany is not generally admitted in the furniture of a Saloon, even at private gentlemen's houses." The firm took it upon itself to substitute gilded wood instead.

As the Havre firm got deeper into its dealings with the artisans of Paris, it became apparent that prices on mirrors, bric-a-brac, chandeliers, porcelain, clocks, and lamps had gone up as soon as the President's "palace" in Washington was mentioned. Stutterings from Havre to the President became more and more apologetic. "The furniture for the large Oval Room, is much higher than the prices limited," read the President in consternation. "It must be ascribed to the gilt-wood and crimson silk trimmings, fringes, etc., which is 50 per cent dearer than other colors. . . . The christal and gilt bronze lustre is of superior workmanship . . . and if it was to be made again would cost 5,000 francs."

A note of encouragement occurred in one paragraph: "The plate has been manufactured by Fauconnier, an excellent artist, and honest man. The tureens will, we hope, be found of the highest finish."

However members of Congress may have gasped when they saw the bills from abroad, the State rooms of the White House, with the exception of the somewhat bare East Room, were undeniably charming and impressive in their new trappings. The Oval Drawing Room—the Blue Room in later administrations—was a dream of formal elegance. On the green velvet rug with the arms of the United States of America in its center rested a profusion of carved and gilded furniture. The sofas, nine feet long, the *bergeres*, the armchairs and the footstools to match, were upholstered in light crimson satin. Crimson taffeta draperies hung from gilt arches with

34

Hannibal stands motionless and triumphant on a French clock in the Red Room.

an eagle clinging to each; in one claw the eagle held an olive branch, in the other a bunch of arrows. Over the chandelier was draped a fringed, red silk scarf. Ornaments in the latest mode—a Minerva clock, bronze candelabra, porcelain vases—stood on the mantelpiece and on the carved tables. The room glowed with color—crimson and green and gold.

The State Dining Room received a gilded porcelain table service and a dessert service, the latter of which featured the United States arms. Each piece was also decorated with vignettes representing art, science, agriculture, commerce, and strength. A set of gold-plated spoons, destined to become famous in a later administration, added an extra note of luxury.

35

James Monroe, the fifth President of the United States of America, painted by Gilbert Stuart.

The room was lighted by carved and gilded lamps and sconces. Most spectacular of all was the thirteen-foot-long, gilded, carved-bronze center-piece for the State dining table. It consisted of seven main parts, featured representations of Bacchus and bacchantes, and had numerous detachable small figures, pedestals, garlands, vases and candle-holders. This elaborate *surtout-de-table* would be treasured in the White House for generations to come.

In creating such an imposing background for his official entertaining, President Monroe set his pattern for dealing with European ministers. Gone were the days of Jefferson and Madison when diplomats could find the President at home almost any time. They now must wait for invitations to the White House or ask for private audiences which were apt to be stiff and, even worse, brief. Monroe determined to receive the ministers as he, an American minister to France, had been received—with pomp and solemn formality.

From the President's stand on protocol, Mrs. Monroe took her cue, and set up new rules for visits. Unlike Dolley Madison, who had cheerfully worn herself out calling on all who called on her, Mrs. Monroe announced that she would neither make nor return calls. In her place she sent her elder daughter, Eliza Hay, who with her husband, George Hay, lived in the White House. Mrs. Monroe was advised by Mrs. John Quincy Adams to give as an explanation for this arrangement the delicate state of her health. But even given this excuse, the ladies of Washington were furious.

Eliza Hay had her own very strong opinions on precedence and on White House etiquette. Eliza, who had gone to school in Paris with the daughters of royal houses, was not impressed by the gold braid and lace of foreign ministers and thought she knew best how to deal with their wives. She would make no calls on wives of diplomats unless they called on her first. When they did not agree to this arrangement Eliza set about influencing her father toward an even more aloof treatment of foreign ministers.

Before long the busy Secretary of State John Quincy Adams was forced to concern himself with the precedence controversy stirred up by the behavior of Mrs. Monroe and her daughter. The "obstinate little firebrand," as Adams labeled Eliza, was constantly interrupting him with "this senseless war of etiquette visiting." Even Cabinet members and Congressmen took up the issue and began to declare their own war on the White House.

The Monroe dealings with foreign ministers came to a head in December, 1818. The French minister, Hyde de Neuville, was planning a ball in celebration of the evacuation of France by the troops of Germany, England, Austria, and Russia, and had invited President and Mrs. Monroe. The President hesitated, then asked advice of Major Jackson, who had been private secretary to George Washington. On learning that Washington had never under any circumstances visited a foreign minister Monroe declined and asked Eliza Hay to go instead.

It fell to John Quincy Adams to relay Monroe's decision to the French minister, together with Eliza's list of reservations—her statement that she would attend the ball but only as a rankless person, that her presence there would leave her relations with diplomatic wives unchanged, and that her name should appear in no newspaper afterward. Adams noted in his diary that the French minister, on receiving her message, seemed "mortified," but "suppressed his feelings within bounds of decency."

Although the Monroes continued to give dinners and receptions, by the fall of 1819 these had become mostly masculine affairs, with the ladies of Washington boycotting the snobbish Mrs. Monroe. In December Mrs. Seaton gleefully wrote: "The drawing-room of the President was opened last night to a beggarly row of empty chairs. Only five females attended, three of whom were foreigners." Mrs. Monroe's Tuesday night receptions also were being ignored; the only women sure to come were Mrs. Monroe's sisters. The situation had become so serious that it was shortly taken up at a Cabinet meeting.

There was one member of the Monroe family who had not been very active in the world of society up to the year 1820. She was Maria Hester, who was twelve years old when her father was elected to the Presidency. Even Maria had some claim to distinction in the world of fashion, for it was she who back in 1807 had first worn in Washington the pantalettes which were all the rage in France. In 1820 she was sixteen and engaged to be married to her cousin, Samuel L. Gouverneur, who was one of Monroe's secretaries. Her wedding would be the first of a President's daughter in the White House, and one of the most exclusive events of the season.

In the hands of Mrs. Hay the occasion reaffirmed all the earlier snobbery of the Monroe social regime. Even Cabinet members were excluded from the wedding, described as being in "the New York style" with only relatives and close friends invited. When the Russian minister, Poletica, magnanimously inquired what was expected from the diplomatic corps in relation to the marriage, Mrs. Hay sent back word that the diplomats were to ignore it and, furthermore, send no gifts. She had finally managed to embroil her young sister in her feud. For Maria's wedding, the East Room was opened even though the gathering was small. Maria, charming in stiff, blue silk, was united in matrimony with the handsome, dashing Samuel Gouverneur before a select group of friends and relatives.

Monroe dinners served in the "French style" were considered rather frigid affairs. James Fenimore Cooper noted the grave behavior of the guests, the commonplaceness of the conversation, and thought the evening had "rather a cold than a formal air." However this judgment might have displeased the Monroes, they must have noticed, as had Cooper, that although the dishes were passed around by liveried waiters, some of the guests helped themselves to any dish within reach.

At the public receptions, with their medley of visitors, there was necessarily an informal atmosphere. A newspaper article pictured an open house graphically: "The secretaries, senators, foreign ministers, consuls, auditors, accountants, officers of the army and navy of every grade, farmers, merchants, parsons, priests, lawyers, judges, auctioneers and noth-

The regal Mrs. Monroe as painted by Benjamin West.

The "obstinate little firebrand," Eliza Hay, Monroe's elder daughter.

The north façade of the White House in 1820, drawn by George Catlin. It is still without its portico.

ingarians—all with their wives and some with their gawky offspring, crowd to the President's house every Wednesday evening; some in shoes, most in boots and many in spurs; some snuffing, others chewing, and many longing for their cigars and whiskey-punch left at home; some with powdered heads, others frizzled and oiled, whose heads a comb has never touched, and which are half-hid by dirty collars (reaching far above their ears) as stiff as pasteboard." Such, then, was the social life in the White House under the Monroes during the President's first term.

When President Monroe's second term began, Eliza Hay was still snubbing the wives of the diplomatic corps and alienating friends and acquaintances. The criticism of Mrs. Monroe's alleged snobbery, however, had subsided. Fashionables no longer boycotted her weekly drawing rooms but joined the less distinguished citizenry to swell the crowd that flocked to the White House on Tuesday nights. In fact, the receptions had become so popular that extra attendants were needed to handle the crowd. In the parlors, warmed by great hickory-wood fires, Negro servants dressed in livery served wine from silver trays. Late in the evening tea and coffee and little cakes were handed around while visitors indulged in political small talk or merely stood on the sidelines and enjoyed the show.

Many were the tributes paid to the beauty and charm of Mrs. Monroe in this period. Baron Axel Klinkowström, envoy from Sweden, wrote on one occasion: "Mrs. Monroe was very elegantly dressed. . . . Her costume consisted of a white gown of India mull, embroidered with gold, set with pearls, and ornaments of pearls adorned her throat, arms and ears."

During this period, also, unprecedented national unity and a series of brilliant diplomatic moves by Secretary of State Adams had led Monroe to his stand on the independence of the Spanish-American countries. His message to Congress on December 2, 1823, contained in its pages the Monroe Doctrine, asserting boldly that the American continents "are henceforth not to be considered as subjects for future colonization by any European powers."

White House visitors were colorful and varied in the later years of

This dainty and fanciful drawing of the White House and environs
was made by Madame Hyde de Neuville, wife of the French Minister.

Monroe's administration, including, on one occasion, a party of Indian
chiefs, painted with red and yellow and adorned with beads. "They were
of six tribes," recorded John Quincy Adams, "among the most savage of
the desert, part of them all but naked. They were Saukeys or Sturgeons,
Musqukeys or Foxes, Piankeshaws or Miamies, Pah-a-geser Ioways, the
people seen in a fog, Monomone, or Wild Oats, Chippeways and Nacatas
or Sioux, the amiable people." Since there were five Indian languages
represented, and two additional languages, French and English, spoken
by the receiving party, the conference turned into a flurry of translation.
Three squaws and a tiny Indian girl also looked on as the President made
a short speech and was answered by each chief in his own tongue. The
puritanical Adams may have had a part in the changed appearance of
the chiefs when they made a return visit to the White House a few days
later, for on that occasion they were all modestly dressed in store clothing.
The President hung medals from the men's necks and gave small gifts
to the squaws and the child.

But President Monroe was embarrassed toward the end of his second
term by the efforts of members of Congress, led by Tennessee Congressman John Cocke, to find out what had become of $20,000 of the appro-
priation for the furnishing of the reconstructed White House. Samuel
Lane had died without accounting for that amount, and Cocke recklessly
sent President Monroe a message asking him to appear before a Congressional Committee to be questioned concerning it. Monroe's sole
answer was "to tell Cocke that he was a scoundrel." The President then
came forward with his own money to buy back at the original price of
$9,071.22½, his own furnishings which he had sold to the government
eight years before. Adams in his diary deplored the "details of a very humili-
ating character" which came to light in this transaction.

Monroe's last months in the White House were given interest by the
arrival of the Marquis de Lafayette. Lafayette, after a thirty-day voyage
from France and a triumphal tour of the East, came to visit the Executive Mansion, and on New Year's Day, 1825, a White House reception
honoring the aging hero was followed by a dinner for two hundred guests,

After the South Portico
was completed in 1824,
the White House looked
very much like this.

39

A social high spot of the Monroe administration was the ball given by John Quincy Adams for Senator Andrew Jackson, even though Monroe did not attend.

given by Congress in the front rooms of Williamson's Hotel. The President was there to share in the honors. Sixteen toasts were drunk to Lafayette and Monroe.

The gala air of the Lafayette festivities had temporarily diverted attention from the furor over the Presidential election. Although the popular vote had gone to Andrew Jackson of Tennessee, the indecisive vote that followed in the electoral college threw the election into the House of Representatives, where Henry Clay, originally a candidate himself, ruined Jackson's chances of winning by handing his votes to John Quincy Adams.

On the evening of the crucial day an enormous crowd assembled at the White House for the usual Wednesday reception, the last to be held under Monroe. Adams was there, trying unsuccessfully to hide his excitement. Clay, smiling and serene, strolled about with a lady on his arm. There was an abundance of noted men to stare at: John Calhoun, the new Vice President, Daniel Webster, whose rumbling voice carried over the din of the packed rooms, and General Winfield Scott, who had his pocket picked in the crush. None of these, however, was the center of attention, not even John Quincy Adams, the victor in the fight for the Presidency.

The favorite of the evening was, oddly enough, the defeated candidate, gaunt-faced Andrew Jackson, Indian fighter and military hero. Jackson, parading with a "large, handsome woman," knew well that he was being observed and was prepared when, inevitably, he and the President-elect met face to face. Their exchange was cordial. "How do you do, Mr.

40

Adams?" said Jackson affably. "I give you my left hand, for my right as you see is devoted to the fair; I hope you are very well, Sir." Adams echoed concern with the other's health, and the meeting was over.

A spectator, noting the affability of the two, might have gathered that Jackson had taken his defeat lightly. His supporters, however, were plainly furious; at the reception Adams was already being sneered at as "Mr. Clay's President."

Five days later, when Clay was offered the post of Secretary of State by Adams, Jackson followers were ready with their charges of a "corrupt bargain" between Adams and Clay. The charges would not die for four years, and would hound John Quincy Adams through all his days in the White House.

J OHN QUINCY ADAMS entered the White House a bitterly disappointed man. The son of a President, he had felt his entire career as foreign minister, senator, and Secretary of State to be preliminary to his own Presidency. But now he had received neither the popular nor the electoral vote. He recorded in his diary that his election had not been in "a manner satisfactory to pride or to just desire; not by the unequivocal suffrages of a majority of the people."

The violent opposition of the Jackson party in Congress soon added to Adams's woes. Because of its machinations his constructive domestic program, which included the establishment of a national university and the development of projects in science and the arts, came to nothing.

Adams's mood of frustration might easily have forced him into seclusion had it not been for the constant demands of the Presidency. Daily, from shortly after breakfast until five in the afternoon, a parade of visitors filed in and out of his upstairs study—Congressmen, solicitors, heads of departments, all bringing him their problems, large or trivial.

The President conferred with the architect Charles Bulfinch and the Italian sculptor Luigi Persico, and advised them to throw out the figures of "Peace" and "Plenty" they had planned for the Capitol façade and to substitute "Hope" for the heathen "Hercules." He listened to the woes of the Cherokee Indians and to requests for cash from penniless citizens. "I can scarcely conceive a more harassing, wearying, teasing condition of existence," he confided to his diary.

Of all the visitors who consumed Adams's day and stole the hours he needed for reading or writing, the petitioners for office fared the worst. They could reach the President merely by entering the front door and climbing the stairs to the offices, but they generally left as jobless as they had come. However it might inflame the party leaders, it was not Adams's policy to turn out entrenched office holders in order to make room for his own supporters.

Nor were the President's evenings free from interruption. Social duties and visitors took up the precious time he had saved for working on official

The sharp-eyed
John Quincy Adams
sat for Gilbert Stuart
with a smiling face.
Thomas Sully later
added the body and
the background.

41

*The fragile
Mrs. Adams,
also by Stuart.*

papers, for writing long letters of advice to his erratic son, George Washington Adams, or for practicing briefly at the billiard table.

Adams nevertheless managed to adhere to a rigid routine. "The life that I lead is more regular than it has perhaps been at any other period," he wrote at the end of 1825. Daily he rose between five and six o'clock and took a walk of four or five miles, returning home in time to see the sunrise. In warm weather he swam in the broad Potomac, but still complained that he didn't get enough exercise. After making a fire he would read two or three chapters from the Scriptures before breakfast.

On reception nights, visitors could find the President and Mrs. Adams in the Oval Room. The President would invariably be modestly dressed in black, but the appealingly feminine Mrs. Adams would be attired in the latest fashion, with a fanciful and elaborate hairdress to offset her costume. Perhaps it was the chill of the Adams personality that put restraints on the natural spirits of the crowds at these affairs, for there was seldom any rudeness. Outside in the courtyard, however, the waiting coachmen and servants of the more prominent visitors sometimes engaged in a little roughhousing, until Adams was forced to place a constable in charge to maintain order.

Since the Adamses had for many years moved in the worldly circles of Europe and America, guests at the White House were surprised that their dinner parties were so dull. Guests seated near the President had, in the words of one visitor, "a hard time of it," with Adams from time to time managing a constrained smile but incapable of calling up any small talk. Only if he were with persons with whom he had much in common intellectually would Adams forget his restraint. When interested he could discuss a wide range of subjects—art, science, literature, or history.

Most of the excitement came from visiting diplomats, and throughout July and August of 1825, visitors had the thrill of meeting General Lafayette. The General, who was making the White House his headquarters that summer, had left his live alligator in the East Room until he could find a suitable home for it, and was also using the room as a storehouse for the gifts that had been bestowed on him. They were piled haphazardly in the corners and on sofas and chairs.

By early fall plans were being made to send Lafayette safely back to France on the battleship *U.S.S. Brandywine.* While they were breakfasting together one morning, Adams exacted a promise from Lafayette that once home he would remain aloof from French revolutionary projects. The General, perhaps feeling his age, vowed that he would leave such activities to younger men, and Adams was satisfied.

Already sixty-eight years old, Lafayette thought it unlikely that he would ever return to America, and his melancholia over this possibility grew more pronounced daily. Saying good-by to an old friend was a wrenching emotional experience for him and he had still to face his official farewells, planned for the day before his departure for France.

When the day arrived, the White House parlors were packed with civil, military, and naval officers and large numbers of Washington residents. In a florid speed, Adams extolled Lafayette's friendship for America and pledged the undying affection of the nation.

Lafayette, his voice breaking, responded in the same style, with "God bless the American people, each of their States, and the Federal Government" as the substance of his speech. When he had finished, Lafayette and Adams embraced while the tears rolled down their cheeks. As he left Adams's side, the General's feelings overcame him completely and he turned, again threw his arms around the President, and sobbed a last "God bless you!" Onlookers were deeply moved.

In spite of Adams's general unpopularity and the growing strength of the Jackson forces, the public receptions under Adams were well attended. On New Year's Day the populace could regard at close range the personages who ran the government—the Vice President, Supreme Court justices, and Cabinet members, and men on down through the ranks to the pettiest clerk in a minor office.

The crowd on January 1, 1826, was so huge that it was necessary to open the East Room, and some Congressmen present were embarrassed to see that it was almost devoid of furniture. Shamed into action, Congress set up a Committee to consider the question of outfitting the White House. An inventory of the sparse furnishings listed some pieces Monroe had bought in France and some useless secondhand furniture which had served for the Madisons at Octagon House. This had again been put to use after Monroe bought back his own fine furnishings.

John Quincy Adams, always one to do things thoroughly, included a list of his own purchases for the White House in the inventory. In doing so he gratuitously handed his enemies in Congress the raw material for another attack on his administration. A set of chessmen and a billiard table with cues and balls, bought for $84.50, attracted the attention of a Georgia Congressman, who accused Adams of squandering the public's money on "gaming tables and gambling furniture." The President's protests that he had paid for the articles himself went unheard; privately he determined to do little additional purchasing during his tenure of office.

There was a rustic, haphazard look to the exterior of the White House during Adams's occupancy. A dozen sheds leaned against the enclosing walls and clerks who worked for the nearby Treasury and State Departments tied up their horses there when they came to work in the morning. The wings of the mansion had never been finished—they still needed a coat of hard stucco—and architect Charles Bulfinch said that the entire picture was "such as no gentleman of moderate property would permit as his own residence."

Architect James Hoban was clamoring for the addition of the North Portico, which, he thought, would rid the mansion of its bald, ill-proportioned appearance. The White House did not, however, get its North Portico. Nearly all the improvements to the property during Adams's tenure were made on the grounds, which were graded and filled.

Adams's plans for the development of agricultural procedures in America, however, were to some extent put into practice on the White House

An American looks at a distinguished Frenchman. The Marquis de Lafayette, painted by Samuel F. B. Morse.

Strollers on Pennsylvania Avenue in 1826 saw a still-uncompleted White House.

grounds. He took great delight in the rows of trees and shrubs, the array of vegetable gardens, herbs, and even the weeds. Under the care of gardener Ouseley, the apple and pear trees, the apricots, plums, and cherries flourished and gave fruit. In the seedling beds the President constantly measured the tiny sprouts that would one day be mighty oaks, beeches, locusts, and walnut trees.

By the time of his third summer in the White House gardens Adams recorded in his diary that their beauties had made his more distant walks so "tedious and irksome" that he had stayed home for three days to ruminate among the growing things. In early June of 1827, the President gazed fondly on "the casual poppies . . . all in flower, the mustard and anthemis in full bloom, the altheas still coming up and the wild cherries apparently stationary . . . the catalpa trees in full and beautiful blossom. . . ." Twenty rows of shellbarks, pignuts, black walnuts, and cork oak acorns had been planted in the nursery. In the single month of June, he noticed that ninety-seven Spanish cork oaks had made their appearance.

In addition to two of the President's three sons, the Adams household included during his tenancy three orphaned young people, the children of Mrs. Adams's sister, Nancy Johnson Hellen. The White House became the scene of a progressive romance as Mary Hellen, the eldest of the trio, flirted with George Washington Adams on his frequent visits to Washington and then abruptly switched to John Adams, Jr., then serving as his father's secretary. Although at first the President frowned on the match, he eventually gave in and John, Jr., and Mary were married in the Oval Room in early 1828. Adams's first grandchild, a girl, was born on December 2, 1828. It was the second child to be born in the Executive Mansion.

Other affairs were not so propitious. By the autumn of 1828 Andrew Jackson's triumph over Adams was a certainty. Adams had another burden added to his worry over Mrs. Adams's melancholia and the ever-increasing failures of his son, George. As he had always done, he sought comfort in

44

religion and squeezed time from his labors for reading Cicero, Milton, and Plutarch. He exercised more than ever but still worried about his sedentary life. His old physical and nervous symptoms were closely reviewed for the benefit of his memoirs.

Summoning her energy for a last bow to public duty, however, Mrs. Adams opened the White House for a brilliant party in mid-December, 1828. It followed closely on the heels of her husband's failure to achieve a second term, but the show of gaiety that evening, with dancing in the East Room to the music of the Marine Band, and Paris frocks in abundance, was long talked about.

Behind the scences John Quincy Adams's mood was nonetheless one of bitterness and despondency over the triumph of the Jackson forces and what he considered to be the end of his career. Sitting in his upstairs writing chamber, he recorded on the morning of New Year's Day, 1829: "The year begins in gloom. My wife had a sleepless and painful night. The dawn was overcast, and, as I began to write, my shaded lamp went out, self-extinguished. It was only for lack of oil; and the notice of so trivial an incident may serve but to mark the present temper of my mind . . . I began the year with prayer, and then, turning to my Bible, read the first Psalm."

As his father before him, Adams did not take part in the inaugural ceremonies for his successor. Although he would have been glad to make a gesture of civility toward the incoming President, Jackson by his behavior had made it impossible for Adams to attend gracefully. Even Adams's Cabinet, with a lone exception, opposed his going.

Nearly three weeks had gone by since Andrew Jackson had arrived in Washington and taken his old lodgings at Gadsby's Hotel, and he had not yet paid a courtesy call on the President. Since Jackson had not communicated with him, Adams sent word that he would be willing to move out of the White House in time for Jackson to receive his visitors there on Inauguration Day. Jackson at first declined, urging the Adamses to stay as long as they wished, then reconsidered and asked to have the White House for his inaugural reception.

On the evening of March 3, John Quincy Adams drove out to the rented house on Meridien Hill to which his family had already moved. On the same day a notice appeared in the *National Intelligencer:* "The citizens of Columbia and others, friends of Mr. Adams, who might be disposed, conformable to the usage heretofore, to pay him a friendly visit, after the Inauguration of the President elect, on Wednesday the 4th inst., are requested by Mr. Adams to dispense with that formality which the distance of his residence from the Capitol would render inconvenient to them. He thanks them for all the kindness which they have constantly extended to him, and prays them to accept the assurance of his best wishes for their health and happiness."

Even in his defeat Adams had phrased his request with gentle dignity. A few days later he confided to his diary a characteristic prayer: "From indolence and despondency and indiscretion may I be specially preserved."

The latest-model velocipede got plenty of attention on Pennsylvania Avenue in 1827.

A quarter of a century after Andrew Jackson entered
the White House in 1829 this equestrian statue showing
him as a military figure was placed in Lafayette Park.

4	Andrew Jackson	1829 - 1837
	Martin Van Buren	1837 - 1841
	William H. Harrison	1841 - 1841
	John Tyler	1841 - 1845

A crowd in the house

Andrew Jackson pictured as master of the Hermitage.

Down Pennsylvania Avenue came the shouting, exuberant crowd, with gray-haired Andrew Jackson on a horse in their midst. The throng that had followed the President from the inaugural exercises at the Capitol surged through the White House gates, pushed its way through the portals of the Executive Mansion, and spread throughout the public rooms. Everyone was putting up a fight to get a look at the old warrior who had been chosen by the people to occupy the President's House. This was People's Day and the People had come to show their love for the living symbol of Democracy.

The crush in the East Room was suffocating. The ice cream and cakes, the punch and ices piled on long tables soon disappeared, and were replaced only to disappear again. China was dropped and broken, and there were jostlings and fistfights as the muddy-booted climbed on tables and chairs to get a better view. Not a policeman was in sight. ". . . a rabble, a mob, of boys, negroes, women, children, scrabbling, fighting, romping, what a pity, what a pity!" wrote Margaret Bayard Smith after going through it all. Some had to leave through a window. Rumor had it that 20,000 people milled in and around the White House that day.

President Jackson, constantly backing up in an effort to get away from the mob, appeared to be in a state of exhaustion. Retreating to a wall, he stood leaning against it while friends linked arms and formed a barrier between him and the crowd. When people had been lured away by the promise of lemonade and ice cream on the lawn, the President made his escape through the south exit, was taken to lodgings at Gadsby's Hotel, and put to bed.

For days Washington had been jammed with the idolizing throngs. They poured in by horse and by mule, in wagons or on foot, sleeping on floors, three to a bed, or on billiard tables—anywhere in order to be on hand for the excitement. Horsemen galloped up and down Pennsylvania Avenue, showing off hickory bridles and hickory stirrups; women adorned them-

George Cruikshank, the British caricaturist, included an obstreperous horse in his drawing of the mob at Jackson's first reception.

selves with necklaces made from hickory nuts. The city was so crowded that there was shortly a threat of a whisky famine. The hero of the Indian wars and the Battle of New Orleans was receiving a show of idolatry never before seen in his country.

Surprisingly, the man responsible for the excitement was in the depths of gloom. At that moment Andrew Jackson would gladly have returned to his estate, the Hermitage, in Tennessee, to die in peace. The campaign, with its bitter warfare, followed by the death of his wife, Rachel, had left him melancholy and feeble. An old scandal concerning the legality of Rachel's divorce from Lewis Robards and her subsequent marriage to Jackson nearly forty years before had been resurrected and mercilessly dwelt upon during the campaign. The gentle Rachel, stamped an adulteress by Jackson's political enemies, had been heartbroken by the attacks, and her health had steadily declined.

On a shopping trip to Nashville soon after the election, Rachel Jackson was resting in the parlor of the Nashville Inn when she overheard some women talking of her commonness, her pipe smoking, and the questionable circumstances of her marriage. When her friends called for her, Rachel was in hysterics. She wept continuously on the trip back to the Hermitage. As a result her illness was aggravated and she died three days before Christmas. Jackson was inconsolable. He blamed John Quincy Adams and, even more, his Secretary of State, Henry Clay, for her death. Grief and rage left him shattered and ill. His friends thought he might not live until spring.

Jackson, however, was tough and stubborn. He made the long trip to Washington by boat and stage in good time for the Inauguration, and, lacking Rachel, took with him into the Executive Mansion as much of Tennessee and the Hermitage as he could. Into the White House came Rachel's nephew, Andrew Jackson Donelson, to be Jackson's private secretary; his wife, Emily, also born a Donelson, to act as official hostess; and Emily's young cousin, Mary Eastin, who soon wrote home that she had a room "fit for a Princess." To oversee the White House accounts there was Maj. William B. Lewis, a long-time Tennessee friend and political supporter. Jackson's favorite slaves were sent from the Hermitage to run the household.

The White House stables where the President kept his running horses were an important part of the White House during Jackson's occupancy, and were as busy and well managed as the East Room and the formal parlors. Frequently Jackson made trips to the National Jockey Club or other tracks to watch his Negro jockeys ride his fillies, Emily, Lady Nashville, and Bolivia.

More important was the improvement of the White House itself. Construction was begun at once on the North Portico, and Jackson quickly began to transform the austere, threadbare interior that John Quincy Adams had left behind into something both beautiful and awe-inspiring. The new East Room decorations cost nearly $10,000. Two thousand dollars went for "three very splendid gilt chandeliers, each for eighteen candles, the style of which is entirely new." Bronzed and gilded tables "with Italian black and gold slab" stood beneath the chandeliers and under the huge mirrors. Drapes of blue and yellow moreen set off the lemon yellow walls, and a rich Brussels carpet of fawn, blue, and yellow, with a red border, contrasted effectively with the blue damask satin upholstery used throughout. The upstairs rooms were made warm and livable for the procession of "company" from Tennessee.

The china, cutlery, and glassware of this period were equally lavish. A dinner and dessert set of sterling silver plate costing $4,308.82 came from France, as did a blue and gold dessert service decorated with the American eagle, made to order for President Jackson. Bills for drinking equipment listed every known type of wine and champagne glass, plus decanters by the dozen.

Altogether, in his two terms, Jackson spent over $50,000 refurbishing the Executive Mansion in such a way as to remove every trace of the hated John Quincy Adams. A newspaper reporter, sent down to Washington from New York to look over the newly decorated mansion, wrote back that it was plain that Jackson was doing it all for the People. John

Although as President Jackson had great dignity, he was often the center of combative scenes. Below, friends balk an attack on him during a trip by river boat.

Magnolia trees, in memory of the dead Rachel, were planted on the south grounds during Jackson's first term.

Quincy Adams had not actually wanted anyone to sit in his presence and had therefore carefully avoided providing enough chairs. Now any plain citizen visiting the President would have a comfortable place to sit. "They won't be kept standing upon their legs as they do before kings and emperors, and as practiced by Mr. Clay's President, till they are so tired as scarcely to know whether they have legs to stand upon." No longer would the mansion be full of "cobwebs, a few old chairs, lumbering benches and broken glass," as in Adams's day. The White House was now quite fit for any king.

Before long Jackson's enemies were saying that the whole business was meant for just that—a king. "King Andrew" was a new title bringing to mind Jackson's arrogance, his ruthless method of turning out his enemies and rewarding his friends, his highhanded ways with his Cabinet and his luxurious living in which so many of Rachel's relatives shared. But when he drove out on a fine day in his beautiful phaeton made from oak salvaged from the frigate *Constitution*, with a picture of the frigate painted on its side, the crowds still shouted their affection.

Part of the devotion lavished on Jackson came from the warm welcome visitors received at the White House. It was first come, first served, at the White House receptions, with the aging President shaking hands until he would have to retire from exhaustion.

It was at the suppers and receptions for invited guests—sometimes as many as a thousand—that the splendor of the Jackson style was particularly on view. Although Jackson praised frugality, he lived sumptuously. Even at ordinary dinners the best of wines flowed freely. The table would be laden with turkey, fish, canvasback duck, and partridges before the Negro waiters took them aside to a buffet for carving. The chicken, cold and "interlaid with slices of tongue and garnished with salled," im-

50

Emily Donelson, Jackson's niece and hostess, who objected strongly to the presence of the trouble-making Peggy Eaton in the White House.

pressed one guest so deeply that he wrote home about it at great length. Coffee and brandies were always served in the parlors. For the official State functions that were held at the White House, Jackson's chef paraded his skill.

Jessie Benton, daughter of the Senator from Missouri and later the wife of the explorer, John Charles Frémont, visited the White House many times in her childhood and joyfully remembered it in a state of readiness for the guests to arrive. "The great wood-fires in every room, the immense number of wax lights softly burning, the stands of camellias. . . . After going all through this silent waiting fairyland, we were taken to the State Dining-Room, where was the gorgeous supper table shaped like a horseshoe, and covered with every good and glittering thing French skill could devise, and at either end was a monster salmon in waves of meat jelly."

There was one notable flaw in the felicity of the Jackson household. Emily and Jack Donelson, however much they adored their uncle, would not countenance the wife of his dear friend and Secretary of War, John Henry Eaton. Eaton had on New Year's Day before Jackson's inauguration married Margaret O'Neale Timberlake, the fascinating and notorious wid-

51

Peggy Eaton, who stirred up a storm within the Jackson inner circle.

ow of ship's purser John Timberlake. It was generally believed Eaton had thus ruined his chances of becoming a member of Jackson's Cabinet, but Jackson, five days after his inauguration, made Eaton his Secretary of War.

Peggy O'Neale Eaton was therefore important enough to receive her first official snubbing on the day of Jackson's inauguration. On that day the Cabinet wives ignored her presence and Emily Donelson and Mary Eastin did not once look in her direction. Mrs. Calhoun, wife of the Vice President, pointedly avoided Peggy. It was the start of social warfare which raged throughout much of Jackson's first term.

Peggy Eaton had grown up in the public rooms of her father's inn, Franklin House, a boardinghouse in which Congressmen frequently took lodgings during the months that Congress was in session. Andrew Jackson, living there in the days when he was Senator, had written to Rachel that Peggy played the piano and sang beautifully, giving little recitals of hymns on Sundays. Another guest at the inn, John Eaton, a widower and Jackson's fellow Senator from Tennessee, had also noticed Peggy's charms, and Peggy, lonely during her husband's long absences at sea, fell into the habit of relying on him for companionship, as her father was relying on him for financial aid.

When Timberlake died of tuberculosis while at sea, Peggy's detractors spread the story that he had committed suicide over jealousy of Eaton. Eaton and Peggy were in a painfully embarrassing position. "Marry her at once," ordered Jackson from Tennessee, thus rushing Eaton into a marriage that he had considered only a remote possibility. "The General's friends are much disturbed," wrote Margaret Bayard Smith; "his enemies laugh and divert themselves."

Jackson's enemies could well be amused, since they had received ready-made a situation perfect for breeding trouble within the President's official and personal families. Cabinet wives carried on an organized cold-shouldering of the beautiful Peggy; Mrs. Calhoun spent her time at home in South Carolina rather than mix with Peggy and her friends; and Peggy was reduced to social life with bachelors and the wives of foreign diplomats, who were likely to look upon the whole thing as a piece of provincial nonsense.

For a while Emily Donelson was exiled by Jackson to Tennessee because of her attitude toward Peggy. During her absence Peggy sat on Jackson's right at a White House dinner and the slanderers spread it around that Jackson was her lover. "She is one of the most . . . silly women you ever heard of," said Mrs. Smith, at the height of the Peggy affair. "The smartest little woman in America," said Jackson, who had been in on Peggy's mimicry of her enemies and had heard her annihilate them with a jest.

One man who realized that Jackson would never give up on the Eaton battle was Martin Van Buren, Jackson's Secretary of State. Van Buren, a widower, would use his championship of Peggy Eaton to oust Calhoun, become Jackson's second-term Vice President, and finally come into the

A lithograph published during Jackson's second term pictures an
imaginary scene in which the President and his Cabinet, plus Peggy
Eaton's father, Jimmy O'Neale, interview Celine Celeste, the
sensational ballerina and actress then appearing in New York.
The cartoon maliciously implies that Celeste is to take over
Peggy's former role.

White House on his own under Jackson's sponsorship. The "Little Magician" paid Peggy marked attentions at White House dinners, made her
the center of his own parties, and repeated her flattering remarks to the
President.

Van Buren saw clearly that Jackson's hot-headed, sentimental defense
of Peggy was actually a defense of his beloved Rachel, whose memory
had never left Jackson. Around his neck he wore a miniature of Rachel,
propping it at night on a table beside his bed. Next to his heart, Van
Buren also knew, lay a bullet fired by Charles Dickinson, whom Jackson
had killed in a duel over Rachel's good name.

When two clergymen charged that Peggy had undergone a miscar-
riage in a pregnancy attributed to Eaton, Jackson was ready to come to
her defense. He invited the ministers to meet with his Cabinet and himself in order to clear up their misconception of Peggy's character.

This was surely the strangest Cabinet meeting the White House had
ever witnessed. Testimonials to Peggy's spotless character—gathered for
days by Jackson's henchmen—were laid in detail before the two infuriated
clergymen. When one of them tried to speak, Jackson cut him short with

53

The people dig into Jackson's monstrous, smelly cheese.
Its odor lingered in the White House for months afterward.

the reminder that he had been invited to give testimony, not to discuss it. The minister, retorting that he could prove his attacks in "any court of law," left in a huff. Jackson delivered his personal verdict and the case of Peggy Eaton was closed. "She is as chaste as any virgin," pronounced the President.

On a freezing day in March, 1833, when Jackson was inaugurated for the second time in the simplest of ceremonies in the Chamber of the House of Representatives, Van Buren was his Vice President. The White House was not opened to the public, and Jackson, fatigued and ill, retired to his bedchamber at an early hour. While the new Vice President and Jackson's young folk danced at two inaugural balls, Jackson lay in bed, resting and reading the Bible that had once been Rachel's.

Soon more than ever the White House was filled with youthful relatives and family sentimentality. Emily's son, named Andrew Jackson Donelson, was six years old at the beginning of Jackson's second term, her daughter, Mary Rachel, a child of three. In the winter Andrew Jackson, Jr., Jackson's adopted son, brought his tiny brunette wife Sarah Yorke Jackson and their four-month-old infant, the President's first grandchild, to the White House for a long stay. The baby had been named for Jackson's wife and at once became the apple of her grandfather's eye. "My baby, my pet," crooned the old man as he walked the floor with her at night when she was wakeful. "My dear little Rachel," the old man habitually called her and swore she was the solace of his old age. Jackson fretted as much over the welfare of all the children as though they had been his own. Their measles, their mumps, and teething were problems of paramount interest to him.

A friend of Emily Donelson's left a description of the peaceful domestic scene in the evening at the White House: "There was light from the chandelier, and a blazing fire in the grate; four or five ladies sewing around it; Mrs. Donelson, Mrs. Andrew Jackson, Mrs. Edward Livingston, etc. Five or six children were playing about regardless of documents or workbaskets. At the farther end of the room sat the President in his arm-chair, wearing a long loose coat and smoking a long reed pipe, with a bowl of red clay; combining the dignity of the patriarch, monarch and Indian chief. Just behind was Edward Livingston, the Secretary of State, reading him a dispatch from the French Minister for Foreign Affairs. The ladies glance admiringly now and then at the President, who listens, waving his pipe towards the children when they become too boisterous."

The White House vibrated with youthful gaiety. Relatives and connections of relatives of the Donelson clan came to the White House for long visits and went away with their future lives permanently enhanced. Young girls who came to stay with Emily Donelson or Mary Eastin found they were automatically belles, with a young naval officer or an embryo diplomat ready to squire them at a moment's notice. Mary Ann Lewis, daughter of Major Lewis, was courted by Alphonse Pageot of the French Legation and was given a big White House wedding by Jackson.

In Jackson's last winter in the White House Emily Donelson found her health failing and returned to Tennessee for a rest. While her husband was still in Washington, Emily died of consumption, leaving Jackson a sorrowing man on departing the White House, just as he had been on entering.

Ever the People's President, Jackson added a common touch to his last reception, given on Washington's Birthday, 1837. For this final monstrous gathering a huge cheese, weighing 1,400 pounds and measuring 4 feet in diameter and 2 feet through, was put on display in the center of the vestibule. It was sent by the same New York State dairyman who had kept Jackson supplied with cheese for eight years.

The White House had not been open two hours when the public, invited to help itself, had demolished the cheese, either bolting it on the spot or carrying away small hunks of it wrapped in newspaper. The scent of cheese permeated the entire house; it was impossible to get away from it. The press throughout the public rooms was so great that men were forced to leave their hats on their heads as they munched the smelly stuff. "The company reminded one of Noah's Ark—all sorts of animals, clean and unclean," wrote an observer. Many members of the crowd had traveled long distances. Whole families had come by train from Baltimore or from Alexandria by boat in order to be in on this last of the big shows staged by the "Yankee King."

A tired former President sits for a Brady daguerreotype at the Hermitage, shortly before his death in 1845.

55

The "Little Magician," Martin Van Buren, eighth President of the United States.

Martin Van Buren's victory in the Presidential sweepstakes was a triumph for Jackson himself. When Jackson rode out of the White House grounds for the last time on the morning of March 6, 1837, with a doctor sitting beside him in his *Constitution* carriage, the cheering crowds that had gathered to bid him farewell were just as dense and just as admiring as they had been on the occasions of his two inaugurations. On his trip back to the Hermitage by coach, train, and steamer, Jackson could reflect, if he wished, on his own prodigious popularity.

Suave little Martin Van Buren had inherited Andrew Jackson's crown but not his incredible good luck. Van Buren was not even settled in the White House when he was faced with a nation-wide financial panic. Banks, factories, railroads, speculative schemes collapsed overnight, and the population sank into poverty. In the larger towns crowds rioted for bread. The Panic of 1837 was on.

It was scarcely the time for the President to carry on his role of epicure and bon vivant, and he astutely postponed any worldly show until the financial storm should subside. Behind the scenes, however, Van Buren transformed the White House into something more appealing to his refined tastes.

The President, widowed and without any official hostess, took personal charge of the renovation. His first move was to get rid of some of the gaudy, worn-out furniture left over from Jackson's administration, auctioning it off for nearly $6,000. Another $27,000, obtained from Congress, paid for housecleaning, china, glassware, rugs, and upholstering. Van Buren installed the first of the screens between the entrance hall and the long corridor, to cut off the chilling drafts which circled the downstairs rooms.

Small, intimate dinner parties were the extent of Van Buren's entertaining during 1837. From England, where he had served briefly as Minister, he had brought a chef noted for his Continental style, and excellent dinners were served to friends and political enemies alike. Calhoun and Clay and other enemies of Jackson frequented the White House and dined at Van Buren's expense.

On New Year's Day of 1838, Van Buren opened the White House to the public for the first time, and in March held his first drawing room. Washington, which had expected something dazzling, was sorely disappointed, not only at the infrequency of the entertainments but also at their simplicity. "We have seen the private dwellings of many merchants in Boston, New York, Philadelphia and Baltimore," one visitor remarked of the White House interior, "the fitting up of which must have cost a much larger sum." Congressmen were piqued because they were invited so seldom—only twice a year, to a stiff, formal affair. If they joined in the public gatherings there was no refreshment, not even a cake or a glass of punch.

Though an English visitor noted the extreme decorum of the "humbler classes" at the open houses, it was observed at the same time that

56

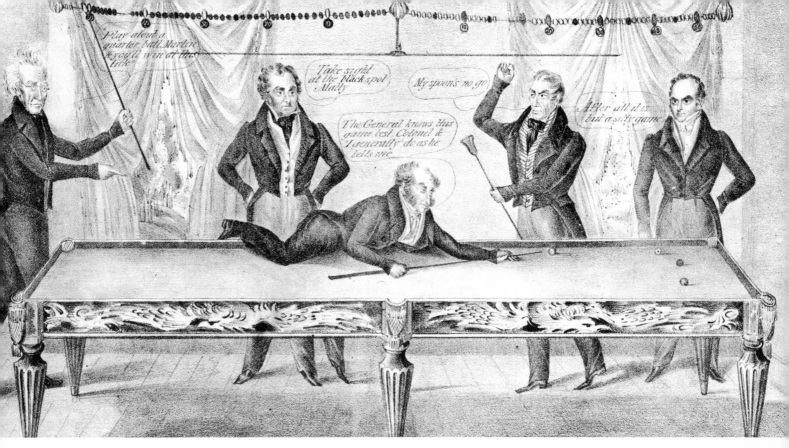

Van Buren was the central figure in a host of cartoons which slyly ridiculed his personal habits and his political dependence upon Andrew Jackson. Here, in a game of billiards, Van Buren gets general advice on his next play but takes that of Jackson. He is saying, "The General knows this game best, Colonel, and I usually do as he tells me."

police had been posted at the White House entrance to screen the citizens who made their way inside. The "mobocracy" could no longer march in, as in Jackson's time, muddy, dirty, or drunken, ready to pick a fight or to insult some who had come with more respect for the surroundings. In short order the public was sharply divided on the rightness or wrongness of Van Buren's move.

Thus brought into the limelight, Van Buren's personality received a thorough scrutinizing. His cultivated tastes and exquisite manners were felt to be precious, even effeminate. He was far too polished. His tone was too elegant. He was certainly no democrat.

Van Buren's four young sons, who lived with him in the White House, shared the President's "elegant tone" and shone at many a dinner party. Abraham, the eldest, who served as secretary for his father; John, who visited England and was made so much of by Queen Victoria that he was forever after called "Prince John" by Van Buren's Whig opponents; Martin, Jr.; and Smith Van Buren were all liked and admired. In spite of their presence, however, the White House still seemed a barren spot, a house painfully in need of a hostess. Dolley Madison, who lived on Lafayette Square, a short walk away, knew exactly what the cold old pile needed.

In South Carolina lived a young relative of Dolley's named Angelica

57

The way to the Capitol in 1840 as seen from the South Portico.

Singleton who would fit the role of White House hostess to perfection. Angelica was just out of a fashionable ladies' seminary in Philadelphia and was still so young that the corkscrew curls in style that year actually became her. She was, of course, far too young for the President, but would do beautifully for Abraham.

It took almost a year to bring off the marriage successfully, but Dolley managed it, and Angelica was on hand to receive with the President in the Oval Room, or "Blue Elliptical Saloon," at the New Year's reception of 1839. Her grace and charm were considered beyond criticism.

On the day after Christmas, 1839, former President John Quincy Adams went to the White House to pay a call on President Van Buren. Adams had already confided to his diary his sour remarks on Van Buren's affectations and the duplicity of his character. On this occasion he limited his observations to one only: "Mr. Van Buren is growing inordinately fat."

What Adams was probably most surprised to note was Van Buren's lack of outward concern over the approaching political campaign in which he faced certain defeat. The Whigs had already selected what they believed to be an unbeatable candidate for 1840, a tough old warrior almost as colorful and homespun as Andrew Jackson himself.

The nominee, William Henry Harrison, a Virginia aristocrat, hero of Tippecanoe and long-term Governor of Indiana Territory, had as his running mate John Tyler, also of Virginia. With great cunning Harrison was put forward as a simple Western farmer, and the log cabin and cider barrel became the symbols of a campaign increasingly dedicated to turning little Van, "a used-up man," out of the White House.

On a fine spring day in 1840, Charles Ogle, Representative from the state of Pennsylvania, stood up in the chamber of the House and began his three-day tirade, the famous "Gold Spoon Speech," against Van Buren and his luxurious way of living. Brandishing a sheaf of bills, vouchers, and assorted papers, many of them dating back as far as Monroe, Ogle addressed the absent Van Buren: "Your house glitters with all imaginable luxuries and gaudy ornaments . . . I put it to the free citizens of this country . . . will they longer feel inclined to support their chief servant in a Palace as splendid as that of the Caesars, and as richly adorned as the proudest Asiatic mansion?"

58

Angelica Singleton Van Buren, who came up from South Carolina to marry the President's son, Abraham.

As his Whig fellows listened enthralled, Ogle figuratively tore the dining room to shreds, dwelling on the exquisite china, the gold spoons and silver plate, and the cut-glass decanters and goblets. "Harrison would scorn to charge the people of the United States with foreign cut wine coolers, liquor stands, and golden chains to hang golden labels around the necks of barrel-shaped flute decanters with cone stoppers," Ogle assured his audience.

The food at the White House, Ogle continued, was hardly fit to eat; he himself preferred "fried meat and gravy, or hog and hominy." As for Van Buren's personal habits, Congressman Ogle claimed that the President spent his time lolling about in a tepid bath spraying his whiskers with French *Triple Distillé Savon Daveline Mons Sens.*

The quality of Ogle's "Gold Spoon Speech" was strictly in keeping with the preposterous style of the Harrison "Log Cabin" campaign. Van Buren, poker-faced to the end, received the news of his defeat as he left church on a Sunday morning. Not for one moment did he betray any disappointment. From that day on, relations between Harrison and Van Buren took on a friendliness unheard of between opponents.

59

A souvenir silhouette of the popular William Henry Harrison, who died exactly one month after becoming President.

O<small>N THE TENTH OF FEBRUARY</small>, 1841, Gen. William Henry Harrison, just turned sixty-eight, called on President Van Buren at the White House. The following day Van Buren, with characteristic courtesy, gathered all his Cabinet members and took them along when he went to see Harrison at Gadsby's Hotel. The President-elect was already being beleaguered by office seekers, and Van Buren, realizing Harrison's fatigue, offered to vacate the White House ahead of schedule so that the aging General could get some badly needed rest.

Harrison chose instead to visit his daughter in Virginia. Although the press constantly stressed his vigor and sprightly step, he was already showing the strain of the campaign months. Before his return to Washington a notice appeared in the papers saying that there would be no handshaking during or after the inaugural ceremonies, since the President-elect had shaken so many hands during the campaign that he now had a sore hand and a sore arm.

There had been a steady stream of log-cabin-float parades during the campaign, and the evening of Harrison's swearing-in, the same sort of crowd followed him into the White House, passed through the north entrance, and paused briefly in front of the President before exiting at the south door. They would always be loyal to the hero of Tippecanoe.

Mrs. Harrison, frail and retiring, who was highly displeased over her husband's rise to the position of President, was not in Washington for the inauguration and therefore missed the two-hour speech, heavy with classical allusions, which her husband delivered while standing in a freezing northeast wind. She had remained in North Bend, Ohio, and in her place had sent her widowed daughter-in-law, Jane Findlay Harrison, to be hostess for the President. Other relatives accompanying Jane Harrison into the Executive Mansion were an aunt, a cousin, and her own three children.

One of Harrison's first wishes was the desire, for diversion, to do his own marketing for the White House table. But in a few days it was plain he was to have no diversion of any kind. The White House was crawling with office hunters. The General met them in the vestibule, in the halls, on the stairways. Once he was forced to fill his pockets and his hat full of their carefully prepared petitions before he was permitted to make his way through their ranks to his own quarters. Members of his Cabinet were incensed because the President did not give in to their demands to turn out the old office holders to make way for the party men. Harrison answered them by continuing to make his own appointments.

Late in March, Harrison, worn out by the harassments of the patronage system, developed a severe cold. When a physician was called in on the evening of March 27, symptoms of pneumonia had already set in. A week later, exactly one month from the day of his taking office, Harrison died. In the delirium of his last hours his mind wandered back to the insurmountable problems of his office. "I cannot bear this," a friend heard him mutter, "don't trouble me."

60

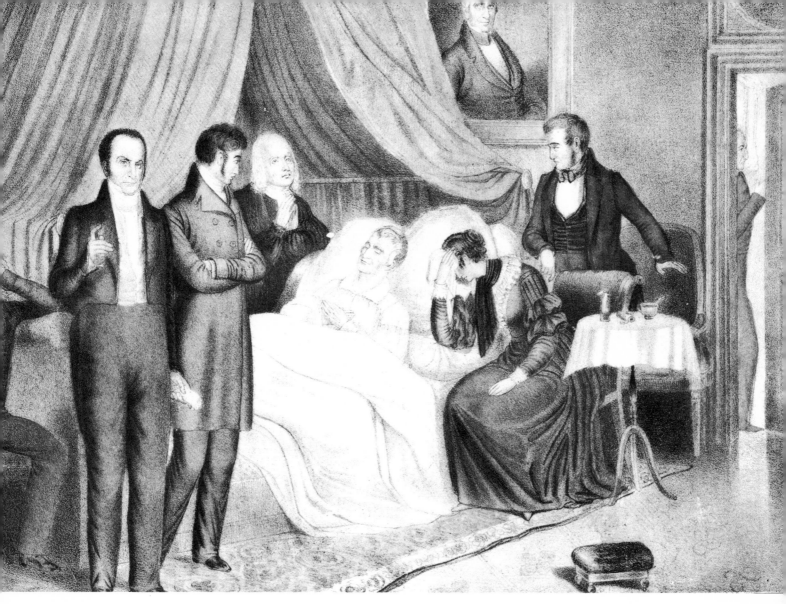

A highly stylized Currier lithograph deploring the death of Harrison.

For the first time, a President lay in state in the East Room. The windows, the doors, the very walls of the great room were swathed in black. At the funeral services, President John Tyler—hurriedly called from his home in Virginia—former President John Quincy Adams, Cabinet members, foreign ministers, and the late President's aides-de-camp from his fighting days were ranged about the coffin. In an era that made much of funerals, this particular funeral was said to be outstanding in its pomp and magnificence. As for the procession that followed, the newspapers agreed that it was "better arranged than that of the Inauguration."

The funeral car was drawn by eight white horses with Negro grooms dressed in white, the car covered with black velvet embroidered with gold. The Harrison relatives followed in somber carriages, and after them the carriage of President Tyler and Daniel Webster, Harrison's Secretary of State. Mounted police waved white batons ornamented with black tassels to keep order in the two-mile-long parade which wound its way to the Congregational burying ground. More than ten thousand people followed the dead President to his last resting place.

61

John Tyler, whose White House years were so full of surprises.

Jоhn Tyler, after his election to the Vice-presidency, had gone back to his Williamsburg home with the idea of four years of quiet, broken only by leisurely trips to the Capitol to preside over the legislative body. He had not received much attention during the wild, mad Harrison campaign, and some believed that if "Tyler too" had not rhymed so handily with "Tippecanoe" he might have been lost sight of altogether. Immediately upon his arrival at the White House, however, Tyler made it plain that he was not "Acting President" as many statesmen, including John Quincy Adams, believed he should be, but rather that he was President in the full sense of the word, with all the rights, privileges, and duties the office normally conferred.

Early in his tenure, Tyler, a stickler for convention, gathered his three daughters and his daughter-in-law, Mrs. Robert Tyler, around him and gave them this advice: "My daughters, you are now occupying a position of deep importance. I desire you to bear in mind three things; show no favoritism, accept no gifts, receive no seekers after office."

Tyler's wife, Letitia Christian Tyler, went into the White House as an invalid—as the result of a stroke she had suffered a few years earlier —and consequently never had an opportunity to display her genuine charm

62

and breeding. When the girls wanted to see their mother, they went to her room in the family quarters which she rarely left. There, seated in a great armchair, with her Bible on a stand at her side, Mrs. Tyler knitted and remained cheerful in spite of the paralysis which would shortly end her life. Only once in the year and a half of life which remained to her did Mrs. Tyler appear downstairs. It was at her daughter Elizabeth's wedding to William Waller of Williamsburg, held in the East Room in January, 1842.

Whatever advice on social procedures the Tyler girls received came from that social paragon of all time, Dolley Madison, who, well past seventy, was still the most popular woman in Washington. Priscilla Cooper Tyler, the young wife of the President's son, Robert, served as hostess during Mrs. Tyler's illness and turned frequently to Dolley for counsel. When she asked Mrs. Madison whether she would have to return all visits or could merely send out cards, Mrs. Madison, remembering her own busy and successful career, said she must make the calls. "So," wrote Priscilla to her sister, "three days in the week I am to spend three hours a day driving from one street to another in this city of magnificent distances."

John Tyler's administration in the early years was remarkably lacking in pomp and formality. Tyler continued to live exactly as he had in Virginia, cared for by the same slaves who had taken care of his family in Williamsburg. It was said he rode in a second-hand carriage, and at State affairs colored waiters wore livery admittedly bought second-hand. Tyler himself was fond of inviting his guests into the dining room to help themselves from a sideboard well supplied with mint julep.

The chief opponents to a more presentable White House seemed to be Tyler's enemies within his own Whig party. They consistently voted against the appropriations needed to refurbish the ceremonial rooms, so that the public rooms each month became dirtier and gloomier than before. Eventually the press was to refer to the White House as the "Public Shabby House." Tyler was forced to pay his own light and fuel bills. In addition, he was attacked so constantly by the Whig press that the American public came to regard him with contempt; when the country had an epidemic of influenza it was referred to as "Tyler Grippe."

In the early part of Tyler's tenancy, Charles Dickens paid a visit to the White House and wrote down his impressions of the man and the mansion. Dickens, in charge of "an official gentleman," made his way to the White House on the morning after his arrival in Washington. They entered a hall, walked through the rooms on the ground floor, noting particularly the "Eastern Drawing Room," and climbed the stairs to an antechamber of the President's office where other visitors had already gathered. "At sight of my conductor," Dickens wrote, "a black in plain clothes and yellow slippers who was gliding noiselessly about and whispering messages in the ears of the more impatient, made a sign of recognition, and glided off to announce him."

In the short waiting period Dickens catalogued what he considered a few American types: "a tall, wiry, muscular old man, from the West

A picture of a fancy-dress party for the President's small granddaughter, Mary Tyler, shows her dressed as a fairy and Dolley Madison's grandniece, Ada Cutts, as a flower girl.

63

Julia Gardiner Tyler,
painted in her prime
by the artist Anelli.

. . . a Kentucky farmer, six-feet-six in height . . . an oval-faced, bilious looking man . . . who sucked the head of a thick stick, and from time to time took it out of his mouth, to see how it was getting on." Dickens noted the constant spitting—"Indeed all these gentlemen were so very persevering and energetic in this latter particular, and bestowed their favours so abundantly upon the carpet, that I take it for granted the Presidential housemaids have high wages. . . ."

When they were finally ushered into Tyler's presence, Dickens was surprised to see that while the President looked tired, "the expression of his face was mild and pleasant, and his manner remarkably unaffected, gentlemanly and agreeable. I thought that in his whole carriage and demeanor he became his station singularly well."

The winter social season of 1843 in Washington was enlivened by the arrival of the beautiful Julia Gardiner from New York. Julia, who at the age of twenty-three had already cut a wide swathe in the elite circles of Paris, London, New York, and Rome, was an olive-skinned brunette, of queenly bearing and impeccable background. When she lifted her soft gray eyes in a frank gaze, the most eligible gallant was said to forget all other women.

On first arriving in Washington Julia had accompanied her father, David Gardiner, a former New York State Senator, to the White House to meet President Tyler. She noted the "silvery sweetness" of his voice, the "incomparable grace of his bearing," and the "elegant ease of his conversation." Tyler, who had recently lost his wife, was before many months asking Julia to become his second First Lady. Since Tyler was fifty-three and Julia was in no mood for a May-December marriage—they decided to think no more of it. In the early spring of 1844, however, a freak accident aboard the warship *Princeton* started a chain of events which drastically altered the course of their lives.

The *Prineeton* was cruising down the Potomac with a distinguished party on board on a fine day in late February, 1844. The President had brought his Cabinet and numerous other noted gentlemen, many of them from the foreign legations; David Gardiner and his two daughters were also on board. All went well on the trip down, with experimental firing of the guns causing considerable excitement. On the way back, the great gun of the boat, the "Peacemaker," was fired a final time. The gun exploded, killing five men, two of them Cabinet members. Also fatally injured was David Gardiner. The men were given a state funeral in the East Room, and President Tyler, in his efforts to comfort her, had a new reason for spending time with the grief-stricken Julia. Three months passed and in June Julia became Mrs. Tyler in a private ceremony in the Church of the Ascension on lower Fifth Avenue in New York City.

It was the first time any President had been married while in office, and newspaper readers hungrily ate up the stories about the cosmopolitan belle and the aging President. In Washington, former President John Quincy Adams, aged seventy-seven, wrote in his diary that the couple was the laughing-stock of Washington. Down in Virginia, Tyler's and Letitia's seven daughters and sons kept a discreet silence.

Only eight months remained of Tyler's term of office. In that short stretch the White House got a show of ostentation that had the elite of Washington shaking their heads in disapproval. With a flourish Julia set about establishing something very much resembling court life. At her drawing rooms she received while seated on a low dais in front of the great Blue Room window. Twelve "maids of honor" stood around her. In purple velvet with a train, and a headdress of bugles which was perilously close to resembling a crown, Julia bestowed a queenly smile upon the guests who were announced at the door before entering, exactly as at Windsor Castle.

Julia's younger sister, Margaret, was staying at the White House, and every mail brought admonishments from the girls' mother to go slow and not to do anything that would draw attention to them. The younger

Julia Gardiner Tyler had always been daring. In 1840, when a lady's name
got into the newspapers only at her marriage and her death, Julia appeared
in an advertisement for a department store. In this lithograph, called
"The Rose of Long Island," she carried a placard which read, "I'll purchase
at Bogert and Mecamly's. . . .Their goods are beautiful and astonishingly
cheap." It was the beginning of testimonial advertising in this country.

daughter she advised to be "agreeable and not too smart" and, knowing Julia, she sent her the wise suggestion to "avoid display for the present." Julia promised to do so, but there was no perceptible letup in the social show at the White House. And Julia's elaborate carriage, drawn by four horses, remained the talk of the town.

No matter what was being said behind her back Julia Tyler was enjoying every minute of her reign. She was delighted with the State dinners and receptions and the constant parade of men whose names she had heard all her life. When she was toasted by Daniel Webster or John Calhoun as "Mrs. Presidentess," Julia loved it and waited for more. In long letters to her mother, she effused over the attentions paid her by noted gentlemen of the world: "The British Minister Pakenham was here with his Secretary, and devoted to me . . . fifty members of Congress paid their respects to me, and all at one time."

It was Julia who instructed the Marine Band to play "Hail to the Chief" whenever her husband made an appearance at formal affairs. Her admiration for him was sincere and constant; she admired his manners, his calm; she even thought him handsome. She enjoyed his musical voice and found his eloquence "inspired," writing home of the style of one of his speeches, that it was "supernatural." "I never had any idea of the power of true eloquence till then," she boasted to a friend. Hers was a total appreciation, and the pomp which she conjured up so facilely was for the President's profit as well as her own.

In Julia's hands John Tyler underwent a transformation. Soon he was smiling on Julia's love of the quadrille and the polka as danced at White House balls, and learning to approve of the waltz, that "vulgar" dance he had warned his daughters against a mere fifteen years before. The White House was having a social whirl like nothing Washington had seen since the days of Dolley Madison.

President Tyler's official life in the White House came to an end with the signing of the bill which admitted Texas to the Union. James K. Polk of Tennessee had won the election and in early March the Polks attended a dinner party at the White House; Julia wore her "black blonde over white satin." At the inauguration ceremonies the following day she finished off her dramatic costume by wearing on a chain around her neck the gold pen which Tyler had used when he signed the Texas Annexation bill.

The official leave-taking of the Tylers on the afternoon on March 8, with farewell speeches punctuated by sobs and sighs, was gravely enjoyable. A crowd of friends and acquaintances gathered in the Blue Room to bid the Tylers farewell. The President made a parting speech entirely without preparation and his enraptured wife described it for her mother: "He raised his hand, his form expanded, and such a burst of beautiful and poetic eloquence as proceeded from him could only be called *inspiration*. His voice was more musical than ever; it rose and fell, and trembled, and rose again. The effect was irresistible." The devoted friends of the Tylers were truly sorry to see them depart, for "as they shook us by the hand when we entered our carriage, they could not utter farewell."

A romanticized White House pictured in a romantic era, with the still adjacent swamps prettied up in the foreground.

67

"I yielded to the request of an artist named Brady of N.Y. by sitting
for my daguerreotype likeness today," wrote President James K. Polk
in his diary on February 14, 1849. "I sat in the large dining-room."

Some quiet times

Wine had been banned and card-playing declared taboo at the White House. There was no more dancing at evening parties, and the populace crowding the parlors at the big receptions came and went unrefreshed by any food or drink. A new order had begun in the White House the day James Polk became President, and was to continue throughout the three administrations which followed.

President James Polk looked with profound distaste upon "time unprofitably spent" in simple fun or diversion, but it was his proudly pious wife, Sarah Childress Polk, who was actually responsible for the new austerity which enshrouded the White House. She could not, to be sure, banish frivolity from the city—it still existed at the embassies, in some of the wealthy private homes, and in one house just across Lafayette Park, where the eighty-year-old Dolley Madison still filled her house on reception days with the choice of the official and social worlds. But in the White House itself, Sarah Polk's stern Calvinism, outlawing the deadly sins of dancing or card-playing, held sway.

Paradoxically it was the card-playing, snuff-taking Dolley Madison who lent a certain distinction to the sober Polk social functions. Mrs. Madison could still enliven any affair simply by making an entrance on the arm of the President.

A contemporary account of a White House levee under the Polks was clearly written by someone who did not have a very good time. "Such introducing," he wrote, "such scraping, such curtsying, such jabbering of foreign compliments and violent efforts of some of our people to do the polite in uncouth tongues—such a wild clamor of conversation rages—the band, too, has become insane and the room is oppressively warm, when the President enters leading a lady—probably Mrs. Madison, and followed by Mrs. Polk and all the great people of Washington."

Mrs. Polk compensated for the lack of buoyancy at her parties by adopting a grand style of receiving. At her receptions, dressed in a style

The strong-minded, handsome Mrs. Polk, who emphasized the earnest side of White House living.

69

The White House in 1848, the year that gas lights were installed.

"rich but chaste" which ran to velvets and satins in somber colors, she remained seated as the guests were presented to her. She was much admired for her quick and clever repartee, her great dignity and courtesy.

While the White House drowsed in the background the westward expansion of the nation to the Pacific raced ahead. By the close of the swashbuckling Mexican War, the United States had over a half-million square miles of new territory. The discovery of gold in California in January, 1848, brought hordes of new settlers into the area.

President Polk was a hard worker and had already worn himself out in the conduct of the Mexican War. With the growing problems of an expanding country, he assumed more and more responsibility for the workings of government, cutting short his hours of sleep in his zeal to perform his duties. In Polk's first year in office, an observant visitor had already noticed that the President was far from robust and had suggested that measures be taken to improve his health: "We think a visit to the salt water—Piney Point, Old Point, or any other point accessible or convenient for sea-bathing, soft crabs and oysters would fatten him up a little and be a great help to him—we want him to live out his term."

Polk never took the advice. He was in harness from the day of his inauguration until his departure from the White House, almost without pause. During his first year there he allowed himself three social calls—two to members of his Cabinet and one to the venerable Mrs. Madison across the park. So busy was the President that Mrs. Polk came to his aid in the role of confidential secretary—the first time a First Lady had served in that capacity. It was not until the summer of 1848, his last year in office, that Polk enjoyed a much needed vacation in the Pennsylvania mountains.

The White House got a major improvement in 1848 when gas lights were installed, replacing the old oil lamps and candle-burning chandeliers. Mrs. Polk insisted that one chandelier, the one in the reception hall, be left untouched, and guests at the first reception had reason to thank her for her idea. They had just assembled when the gas lights flickered and died. The rooms were left in darkness—all, that is, but the reception hall which continued to shimmer in the soft light shed by wax candles.

Inauguration Day for the incoming President, Zachary Taylor, fell on Monday, March 5, and Polk rode up to the Capitol with the old soldier whom he judged "of very ordinary capacity." Polk's trip back to his home in Nashville, Tennessee, began immediately afterward.

For the enfeebled Polk, worn out by his conscientious labors of four years, the trip turned out to be the last straw in a series of health-breaking exertions. Feted and cheered on the long roundabout journey, the former President arrived in Nashville in a state of exhaustion. He survived his term of office by only three months, and died in June, 1849, at the age of fifty-three.

WHITE HOUSE LIFE proceeded from the sedate to the placid as Zachary Taylor, the popular "Old Rough and Ready" of the Indian and Mexican Wars, began his unpretentious occupancy. Mrs. Taylor, who was an invalid, secluded herself in an upstairs bedroom and turned over the responsibilities of hostess to her twenty-two-year-old daughter, Betty Taylor Bliss.

Mrs. Taylor had not wanted to go to Washington in the first place. She had opposed her husband's running for the Presidency and when he was elected had said bitterly that it was all a plot "to deprive her of his society." Reluctantly she left her home in Baton Rouge, Louisiana, to go to Washington. While she remained in her room, appearing only at the family dinner table, the gossips of Washington amused themselves by repeating choice anecdotes about the crudity of her background, saying that she was kept out of sight because she liked to smoke a pipe. Mrs. Taylor, a Maryland-born aristocrat, never answered the charges.

The White House functions under the Taylors were delightfully hostessed by Mrs. Bliss, whose husband, Captain Bliss, was President Taylor's secretary. Betty Bliss was described by one guest as presiding "with the artlessness of a rustic belle and the grace of a duchess."

The President himself was pictured as friendly and easy to approach, receiving his guests in a grandfatherly way. At summer receptions on the grounds of the mansion, the short, swarthy Taylor would stroll among his guests, shaking hands and saying a kindly word to each while the Marine Band boomed out from the veranda.

Old Whitey, Taylor's campaign horse, knock-kneed and uncurried and described as being of the type known as a "family horse," cropped grass on the grounds and gave up souvenirs in the form of hairs from his tail to an admiring public. The old charger, nosing about the lawn, contributed to the air of homely simplicity the Taylor family had brought to the President's home.

Taylor's administration came to a sudden end with the President's illness and death in the summer of 1850. The story goes that after attending Fourth of July exercises at the site of the uncompleted Washington monument, the President returned to the White House nearly prostrated from the heat. After refreshing himself with ice-cold milk and fresh cherries, the President became ill with what was diagnosed, perhaps mistakenly, as cholera. Five days later he was dead. Hurriedly, the handsome and greatly admired Vice President, Millard Fillmore, was sworn into office in a short ceremony in the House of Representatives.

Mrs. Taylor, lying in her upstairs bedroom, was forced to hear all the agonizing sounds accompanying her husband's funeral arrangements—the carpenters and drapers in the East Room, the comings and goings of a multitude of officials, relatives, and friends, and finally the heavy music of the bands as they blared out the mournful dirges. For the remaining two years of her life, Mrs. Taylor remembered the White House only in relation to this tragic period.

Zachary Taylor—
"Old Rough and Ready"—
from a daguerreotype
by Brady.

71

MILLARD FILLMORE said he passed the first sleepless night of his life when he learned that he was to become President. Fillmore was not accustomed to nervous upsets. To the President's boundless good health and serenity, as well as to his pleasing appearance—"stout but not corpulent"—could be attributed much of his personal magnetism.

Good health was not the lot of the President's wife. Abigail Powers Fillmore, another in the line of fragile, retiring Presidents' wives, was little inclined to enter into the energy-sapping White House social routine, and the Fillmores' eighteen-year-old daughter, Mary Abigail, shouldered many of her mother's duties.

Mrs. Fillmore's work in behalf of her husband had, in a way, already been done. As a young schoolteacher in western New York, she had given much encouragement to a pupil named Millard Fillmore, who was belatedly starting his education in late youth. She had continued to give him excellent advice throughout his career.

Perhaps President Fillmore paid more than ordinary attention to his health because his predecessor had met such a sudden end. He neither drank nor smoked, regulated his life so that Sundays were always free of work, and slept long hours.

He could not, however, expect his surroundings to contribute greatly to his well-being. Following Zachary Taylor's death, the White House, with its damp walls and basement and proximity to the malarial Potomac River, was generally looked upon as little more than a breeding ground for disease.

The changes Fillmore brought to the White House kitchens may have offset some of the failings of the big, cold house. In place of the picturesque manner in which food had formerly been prepared—in an open fireplace, with its forest of hooks, cranes, pots, pans, and frying pans—there now stood in the basement kitchen a brand-new cook stove, of "small hotel size," bewildering and infuriating to the black cook who had managed very well for many years without it. Since the cook could not get the hang of the thing, President Fillmore himself was forced to go to the Patent Office and find out how to operate the stove's drafts and pulleys.

Mrs. Fillmore is remembered especially for her efforts in obtaining the first library for the White House. When the Fillmores entered the mansion in 1850, she learned, to her horror, that not even a Bible or a dictionary was to be found. An appropriation was secured from Congress for books to be purchased in New York City, with Thackeray and Dickens particularly in demand.

On the morning of March 4, 1853, the Fillmores accompanied the incoming President, Franklin Pierce, to the Capitol and remained through the post-inaugural reception in the parlors of the White House. Present at the reception were two famous literary personalities—William Makepeace Thackeray and Washington Irving, the latter of whom had begun his visits to the White House nearly forty years before when Dolley Madison was the First Lady of the land.

Millard Fillmore was considered one of the
handsomest and most charming of Presidents.

President Franklin Pierce.

GLOOM DEEPENED in the White House with the entrance of President Franklin Pierce and his wife, Jane Appleton Pierce. For four years they fought a daily battle with melancholy in a city which Mrs. Pierce had always detested, in a house she had never wanted to occupy. A family tragedy following Pierce's nomination for the Presidency had destroyed all chance for personal happiness.

Two months before Pierce became President, he and Mrs. Pierce had seen their only surviving child killed in a train wreck which had left them unharmed. The child was eleven-year-old Benjamin, and it was the third time the Pierces had endured the loss of a small child. Mrs. Pierce, in her desolation, morbidly related the child's death to her husband's rising fortunes. She was too ill to attend his inauguration.

In order that at least a partial social program might be carried out, Mrs. Pierce brought her aunt, Mrs. Abby Kent Means, from Amherst, Massachusetts, to act as official hostess while she herself stayed out of sight, resting in an upstairs sitting room or going for a carriage drive.

Although Pierce was the son of a New Hampshire governor, Washington society under his administration was Southern in feeling. Southerners and abolitionists avoided the increasingly urgent subject of slavery, however, when they met in the parlors at the White House or at private homes in the city. The Secretary of War, Jefferson Davis, encouraged his wife in maintaining a gay salon, the most popular spot in the city.

The New Year's reception had always been the most important public affair of the year at the Executive Mansion—a day on which the populace could wander at will through the White House and shake the President's hand. It was at such a reception, nearly two years after coming to the White House, that Mrs. Pierce finally appeared as hostess at a large function. There were no refreshments, no punch bowl, and no eggnogs, but still the crowd was glad to see the President's wife.

Mrs. Pierce's unfamiliar appearance in the East Room ushered in no wild round of gaiety in the White House. She did appear frequently at state dinners each week—ceremonial affairs for which the Monroe gold plate was brought out and stiffly wired bouquets placed at each of the ladies' plates—but the sad-eyed lady was still under a cloud and continued to be, in the words of one guest, the "very picture of melancholy."

Pierce was defeated for renomination by James Buchanan of Pennsylvania. One of the interesting details of that election was the knowledge that Buchanan was going to have for his hostess, once in the White House, his niece, Harriet Lane, who was young, chic, of worldly background, and above all, brimming with health.

For three administrations the White House had hidden away on an upper floor fragile First Ladies who could take little part in the strenuous social whirl that Washington expected at the White House. Now at last there would be a hostess who embodied all the qualities demanded by the exacting position. All Washington waited to welcome with open arms the distinguished President James Buchanan and his fair niece Harriet.

The "very picture of melancholy"— Jane Pierce.

*James Buchanan prepares to leave
his hotel for the inaugural ceremonies.*

THERE WAS A LEGEND that James Buchanan had never married because many years before he entered politics his young fiancée had suddenly died. Whether true or not, when Buchanan entered the White House in March, 1857, he was still a bachelor—sixty-five years of age and distinguished for his courtly manners.

After the lugubrious tone set by his immediate predecessors, President Buchanan had a rare opportunity to make a social splash in the White House. The suave President had no intention of letting his opportunity slip by without results. Perhaps more than any other man before or since, Buchanan anticipated the Presidency and his entry into the Executive Mansion. Just as important as his assets of personal wealth and experience at the courts of England and Europe was the hostess he brought to the White House.

From the age of nine, when she had come under the guardianship of

The veteran politician James Buchanan, whose White House years were both socially successful and politically disastrous. By Brady.

Harriet Lane, credited with returning gaiety to the White House.

James Buchanan, Harriet Lane had been reared for the job. Every detail of her education and training in the social arts had been carefully supervised. She had been sent to the most fashionable schools and had known only the circles looked upon as correct. While still a very young girl Harriet had had a season in London, where Buchanan was minister. Queen Victoria had been very gracious to her.

The blue-eyed, blond Harriet presided at the President's state dinners and stood beside him at receptions, "in all the freshness of rural health," as one visitor put it. There was little in her poise and tact to suggest the rural, however. With amazing sagacity the young girl said the right thing to each guest, offending no one, Northerner or Southerner, and soon became so popular that a song, "Listen to the Mockingbird," had been dedicated to her. It was largely Harriet's doing that the White House once again became a worthwhile place for fashionable women to parade their finery. She set many of the fashions shown off in the White House drawing rooms: lace berthas, lower necklines, and skirts that became fuller and stiffer.

A rarely seen engraving of the White House during Buchanan's tenancy.

To provide flowers for the White House parlors and dinner table, a spacious conservatory was added on the west side of the Executive Mansion. It was the start of the great clutter of greenhouses which would endure until the time of Theodore Roosevelt. New furniture valued at $20,000 was bought to replace the old, some of which had been imported by the Monroes forty years before. The old French pieces disappeared.

In spite of his urge to establish an imposing regime, Buchanan had a few homely habits. Often he invited friends in for the afternoon like any ordinary citizen. Daily he took a walk on Pennsylvania Avenue, allotting exactly one hour to it, and meeting and greeting old acquaintances in the most informal way.

White House functions had a touch of the exotic in the late spring of 1860, with the arrival in Washington of the Japanese ambassadors, the first ever to visit America. The Japanese envoys insisted upon addressing President Buchanan as "Emperor" and "Your Majesty" and were astonished when they saw the President mingle with the visitors at a Saturday afternoon band concert on the White House grounds. Only Harriet Lane and the wives of Cabinet members were considered of high enough rank to be presented to the Japanese officials, and this ceremonious affair was carried out in the Blue Room at the request of the Japanese.

In the fall of 1860 the Buchanan regime scored another social triumph with the arrival of Edward Albert, Prince of Wales, later Edward VII of England. Traveling under the incognito of Baron Renfrew, the young prince was received in the White House with ceremony and given spectacular parties.

The Prince was traveling with a large entourage and because of the limited space in the White House, most of his party were housed at the British Embassy. Even so, the President was forced to sleep in a hallway in order to put up the Prince and his attendants in decent style.

During his week's stay, the Prince was given a public reception in the East Room, and the populace accepted the invitation, printed in a morning paper, with enthusiasm. All ages, sizes, and stations of American life were represented at the noontime affair. "The rush at the doors was terrible. Confusion reigned. The Royal party have certainly seen Democracy unshackled for once," wrote a correspondent of a New York newspaper.

It was at this huge levee that the youthful prince exhibited his remarkable tact. He noticed that the President was not wearing gloves, so he immediately removed his own. That afternoon he endeared himself further to all who met him by accompanying Harriet Lane to a school for young ladies, where he played ten-pins in the gymnasium to work up an appetite for dinner.

When the Prince had departed, President Buchanan wrote to Queen Victoria that her son had ingratiated himself with the American people. Queen Victoria reciprocated with a grateful, motherly letter and sent Miss Lane a set of engraved likenesses of the royal family.

The agitation over the slavery question had now reached the danger point, and some last-minute efforts to patch up the quarrel between North

Buchanan received the first envoys ever sent from Japan to the United States.

Some of the more important members of the first Japanese embassy to visit America were photographed with their American hosts in 1860. Seated at center are the deputy ambassador, Muragaki Awaji-no-Kami and the chief ambassador, Shinmi Buzen-no-Kami. Whenever the Japanese appeared in the streets, crowds battled policemen and soldiers in order to get a close look at their strange and beautiful dress. "What immense crowds there were!" wrote Muragaki after a visit of the embassy to the White House. "The streets were like seas of human beings . . . I could not help smiling at the wonder in their eyes." Below are sketches made on the scene by a "vassal" of Shinmi. They show an ascending balloon, "a view from the President's garden," and a White House chandelier.

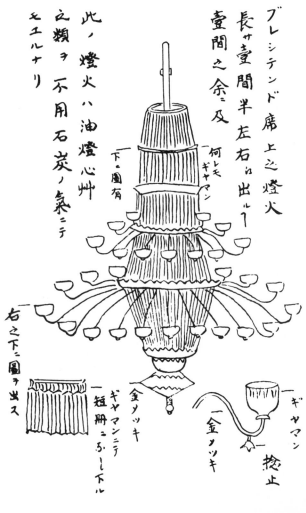

and South took place in Washington. On February 4, 1861, the Peace Convention, a conclave of delegates from the border slave states, met in the Capitol to seek means of staving off war. When the delegates went in a body to the White House to talk to the President, all of Buchanan's perplexities over the issue came to a head. The President talked to the delegates with tears streaming down his face.

As the time approached for the inauguration of Abraham Lincoln, General Winfield Scott, over Buchanan's strong protests, filled the city with troops to prevent its being taken over by the secessionists. Scott, who was positive there was a plot on foot to kill Lincoln, also planned a military parade for Inauguration Day.

While President-elect Abraham Lincoln prepared to travel eastward from Illinois, President Buchanan gave his last White House reception. Five thousand people poured through the White House that evening. The Marine Band, booming forth music from the vestibule, began a set program with "Dixie." But before they picked up their music to go home, they played "Yankee Doodle."

An East Room reception under Buchanan, drawn by a Harper's Weekly artist.

Crisis and tragedy

PRESIDENT ABRAHAM LINCOLN and Mrs. Lincoln were holding a reception. It was in no sense a routine White House affair, admitting all who wished to come. The smiling guests at this elaborate party had been carefully selected and were the most sought-after figures in Washington society in this first winter of the Civil War.

To Mary Lincoln the success of the evening was proof that she had made the White House the center of Washington's social life in spite of the hostility of the entrenched aristocracy. On this occasion she had at last reached the apex of her longings for position and acclaim.

Only one flaw marred the brilliant evening. Upstairs, the Lincoln's two little boys, Tad and Willie, lay ill—and only that day Willie's condition had grown worse. Again and again as the Lincolns met the blur of faces, the thought of Willie intruded.

An array of statesmen, admirals, and diplomats and their wives paid their respects to the tall President and his wife in the East Room and then moved on to the lively chatter in the crowded parlors. General McClellan and General McDowell were each the center of a group of admirers, and the rooms were spotted with other distinguished Union generals—Heintzelman, Blenker, Hooker, Keyes, and Hancock. The handsome young Comte de Paris and his brother, the Duc de Chartres, were there in the uniform of the Union army, and Lord Lyons, M. Mercier, and the Chevalier Bertinatti raised their voices in a variety of accents above the music of the Marine Band. Miss Kate Chase, the ravishing auburn-haired daughter of Salmon Chase, Lincoln's Secretary of the Treasury, and Mrs. Lincoln's avowed social competitor, was as usual holding her own court in the Blue Room.

The reception had been criticized in the press from the beginning; Mary Lincoln had been viciously attacked for daring to give an extravagant party in wartime. Already characterized as a spendthrift and countrified shrew, she was now charged with heartlessness.

The supper at Mary Lincoln's splendid party had to wait while the White House steward searched for the key to the dining-room door.

83

Mary Todd Lincoln.

Willie Lincoln.

Tad Lincoln.

Robert Lincoln.

A Brady photograph, said to be the first made of the White House. The Jefferson statue stood on the grounds from 1841 to 1875.

Nevertheless, demands for invitations had flooded the White House offices. The original guest list of five hundred swelled to twice that figure. When, in the late hours of the party, the President and Mrs. Lincoln led the promenade around the East Room, the ladies in their bell-shaped dresses had a hard time moving in the crowd.

By the time the last guest had left, the Lincolns were frantic with worry over Willie's condition. Their concern was well founded; his "cold" proved to be typhoid fever. For nearly two weeks, the distraught Lincolns took turns watching at his bedside while his condition was successively reported as very low, slightly improved, much better, worsening, and finally on February 19, as hopeless. On February 20, Willie Lincoln, who had been the greatest pride of his parents' lives, died at the age of eleven.

The heartbroken President tried hard not to give way to his grief, but Mrs. Lincoln was completely prostrated. She was too ill to attend the funeral services in the East Room or to pay any attention when Tad, too, came down with the disease. Mrs. Lincoln refused ever again to enter the room in which Willie had died or the Green Room where he

Lincoln reading to his son Tad.

85

had been embalmed. Mary Lincoln's grief continued to be so agonizing that Lincoln, despairing of bringing her out of it by loving kindness, tried a more drastic means of saving her. According to Elizabeth Keckley, the former slave who became Mrs. Lincoln's modiste and companion, Lincoln one day led his wife to the window and pointed out the insane asylum in the distance. "Mother," he said to Mrs. Lincoln, "do you see that large white building on the hill yonder? Try and control your grief, or it will drive you mad, and we will have to send you there."

Since, according to the newspapers, Mary Lincoln could do nothing right, her grief was now labeled excessive and ostentatious. One paper printed a letter written by the mother of a Confederate soldier slain on the battlefield expressing envy of the President's wife; she had at least been permitted to be with her son when he died.

Calling up all his resources of mind and character, President Lincoln turned once more, in his big office over the East Room, to the business of directing the persistently unsuccessful war. Though the President's private secretaries, John Hay and John G. Nicolay, tried to protect him, his waiting room was jammed day and night with office seekers demanding everything from postmasterships to Indian agencies.

Since the White House had no telegraph of its own, Lincoln went several times each day to the War Department to get the latest news. The

Office-seekers plagued Lincoln from his first day to his last in the White House. They jammed the hallway leading from his bedroom to his office.

telegraph office, next door to that of Secretary of War Stanton, became a sort of retreat where the harassed President could get away from the constant press of the crowds and have a few minutes to think. Once in a while he even spent the night on a couch in Stanton's office.

Lincoln was aware early in the war that the emancipation of the slaves would give the North a fresh purpose for fighting the war to a finish. By August, 1862, Lincoln was looking for an encouraging moment in which to put forth his Emancipation Proclamation already discussed with his Cabinet. After the debatable victory at Antietam in September, he issued a preliminary proclamation, and on New Year's Day, 1863, the slaves were finally given their freedom.

The first day of January, 1863, dawned cold and sunny. For the first time since Willie's death the Lincolns shook hands with the public at a large morning reception in the East Room. The public rooms were still filled with callers when just before noon members of the Cabinet made their way through the crowd and up the stairway to the President's office. Less than a dozen men witnessed the signing of the proclamation.

Lincoln was fully aware of the importance of the moment. After he had twice dipped his pen in ink in preparation for signing the document, he turned to Secretary of State Seward and said: "I have been shaking hands since nine o'clock this morning and my right arm is almost paralysed.

Long after the event, Francis B. Carpenter made this detailed painting of Lincoln reading the Emancipation Proclamation to his Cabinet.

Ambitious and arrogant Kate Chase, who longed to live in the White House.

Lincoln's first Vice President, Hannibal Hamlin, and his wife.

If my name ever goes into history it will be for this act and my whole soul is in it. If my hand trembles when I sign the Proclamation, all who examine the document hereafter will say, 'he hesitated.'" Lincoln then slowly and carefully wrote his name.

Mary Lincoln's shopping sprees, the subject of much ridicule, came to a brief halt after Willie's death. In her first year in the White House she had spent seven thousand dollars more on redecorating than she was supposed to, and had been forced to ask the affable B. B. French, Commissioner of Public Buildings, to go to the President for more funds. Tearfully, Mary Lincoln had pleaded with French to explain to the President that the rugs, drapes, wallpaper, curtains, and china had eaten up the money before she realized what was happening. More money must be obtained from Congress. Above all, French must not permit the President to pay the bills out of his own pocket.

For once Lincoln completely lost patience with his wife. Where in the White House, he asked, could a rug costing $2,500 be placed? The idea of asking for more money for "flub-dubs for this damned old house" in a period when every cent was needed for the army filled him with distress. In the end he had to give in and a bill was rushed through Congress which would take care of Mary Lincoln's over-buying.

Mrs. Lincoln was soon attacked on grounds more serious than those of extravagance. With one brother, three half-brothers, and as many brothers in-law in the Confederate army, the Kentucky-born Mary Todd Lincoln was inevitably accused of having Southern sympathies, and even of using her position to gain information to be passed on to the Confederacy.

Fortunately Mrs. Lincoln had one champion to help her. He was William O. Stoddard, a secretary who became a third with Hay and Nicolay, who thought him a humorless, unimaginative sort. With the President's wife, however, he was the soul of tact and understanding. He was at once put to work opening all the mail that came addressed to her at the White House, even letters from her sisters. Mrs. Lincoln told him she did not mean to open a single letter or package until he had looked it over.

Meanwhile, the state dinners, the audiences for delegations and committees, the arrangements for receiving military personages, and more than ever, the receptions for the public went on, in spite of fatigue, anxiety, and illness.

Not the least remarkable of the entertainments at the wartime White House was the reception given in honor of General Tom Thumb, the latest P. T. Barnum exhibit, and his tiny bride, Lavinia, while they were in Washington on their honeymoon. While an invited audience looked on amused and delighted, the Lincolns shook hands with the tiny couple in the East Room. Robert Lincoln, home from his classes at Harvard, remained upstairs in disapproval.

In 1863 twin victories for the Union forces at Gettysburg and Vicksburg inspired the nation to dream of the war's end. November found Lincoln journeying up to Gettysburg to play second fiddle to the flamboyant orator, Edward Everett. Tad was ill again, and Mrs. Lincoln there-

*The Clay Battalion, in civilian dress and shouldering muskets,
lines up at the start of the Civil War. The citizen's militia
was headed by Cassius Clay. Lincoln is said to be standing at center.*

fore did not hear the dedicatory speech her husband made on that occasion in a tired, high-pitched voice.

Shortly after his return to Washington, Lincoln's illness, which had come on him on the train, was diagnosed as a mild form of smallpox. Business went on as usual in the President's shabby office, and even in these luckless days, Lincoln managed to find a humorous side to the picture. "Now let the office-seekers come," he said, "for at last I have something I can give all of them."

In the fall of 1863 the disasters of war came home to the White House in a personal way. Ben Hardin Helm, husband of Mrs. Lincoln's "little sister," Emilie Helm, was killed while serving in the Confederate army in Alabama. Emilie went from Kentucky to the South for his funeral, taking along her little girl, Katherine. On the return trip she was stopped at Fort Monroe and told she could not continue her journey unless she took the oath of allegiance to the United States. Emilie refused. The Union officer responsible for her welfare wired the White House for instructions, and the President answered, "Send her to me."

In having the widow of a Confederate officer come to the White House, Lincoln knew that he was laying himself open to criticism. But the benefit his sick, unhappy wife would gain from her companionship overbalanced the dangers. That summer Mrs. Lincoln had been seriously injured in a fall from her carriage and lain ill in her bedroom for weeks. Her headaches

89

and depression had increased. Worry over Robert Lincoln's plans to enlist seemed to remove her last hope of happiness.

Emilie was received with tears of joy by both the Lincolns and settled with her daughter in the great State Bedroom, decorated with pride by Mrs. Lincoln in light and dark shades of purple. The sisters sat together and wept over their bereavements but dared not mention the war which reared up between them, Emilie wrote, "like a barrier of granite closing our lips." Emilie shared the President's concern about his wife, whose nerves, he told her, had gone to pieces. She did not tell him that Mary had visited her room one night, her eyes shining in a peculiar way that terrified her. Mary had told Emilie that Willie Lincoln stood at the foot of her bed nightly, smiling in his sweet familiar way. Sometimes, Mary said he brought little Eddie, the son who had died in Springfield. Twice he had had with him Alec Todd, their young brother who had been killed at Baton Rouge the year before. Such consolation she could not live without.

Emilie was aware that Mrs. Lincoln had consulted spiritualist mediums after Willie's death and that one, Mrs. Nettie Colburn Maynard, had held a séance in the Red Room, with the skeptical President also present. A second medium had been exposed as a fraud. Emilie was surprised that her sister could take consolation from such flimsy sources and thought Mary's behavior "unnatural and abnormal."

Emilie also noted Mrs. Lincoln's concern over the President's health and the remarkable way she had of trying to hide her nervousness for his sake. At his approach she would mechanically change her demeanor, taking on a lightness of behavior that she in no way felt.

In general Emilie's stay with the Lincolns was unhappy and depressing. She hated the heavy, dreary State Bedroom and hated being questioned by White House callers on the subject of former friends now lost to the Confederacy. Little Katherine Helm contributed her share to the general tension when she had an argument with Tad over who was truly President. Tad said it was Abraham Lincoln, but Katherine held out for Jefferson Davis. "Hurrah for Jefferson Davis," she shouted when the excitable Tad persisted. Lincoln settled the question by taking the children, one on each knee and telling them: "Well, Tad, you know who is your President, and I am your little cousin's Uncle Lincoln."

After a week Emilie and her daughter left for Kentucky, equipped with a special pass signed by the President. When Lincoln begged Emilie to return the following summer and live with them at the Soldiers' Home retreat she declined.

In early March, 1864, General Ulysses S. Grant came to Washington to receive his commission of lieutenant-general. His fourteen-year-old son, Fred, was with him. When they arrived at the White House for the presentation, the gentlemen of the Cabinet, who had met for the occasion, thought the hero of Vicksburg and Chattanooga could not have appeared a more unlikely candidate for such an honor. Small and seedy, he seemed embarrassed by the attentions paid him and read the brief speech he had written on a torn sheet of note paper as though seeing it for the first

In the South, the overconfident Confederates danced on the American flag.

Lincoln reviews Union troops from the North Portico.

time. Greater honors were to follow within a few days. Even while Grant was on his way back to his troops, the rank of commander-in-chief was being readied for him.

The war was about to enter its final year and the President was growing more haggard and sick-looking every day. Francis B. Carpenter, the portrait painter, had been commissioned to paint a large canvas of President Lincoln and his Cabinet, arranged as they had been at the first reading of the Emancipation Proclamation, now long past.

As Carpenter moved freely about the White House, making studies for his painting, he saw Lincoln in every mood. During the battles of the Virginia Wilderness the President hardly slept at all. Carpenter wrote how he had met Lincoln, "pacing back and forth a narrow passage leading to one of the windows, his hands behind him, great black rings under his eyes, his head bent forward upon his breast,—altogether such a picture of the effects of sorrow, care and anxiety as would have melted the hearts of the worst of his adversaries, who so mistakenly applied to him the epithets of tyrant and usurper."

The White House had become a popular spot after the Federal victories of 1863. The harassed, sad-faced President carried out his ordeals of public handshaking, "working like a man pumping for life on a sinking vessel," according to the journalist, Jane Grey Swisshelm. Mrs. Lincoln stood a little behind the President in order to escape as much handshaking as possible, wearing a succession of costly, beautiful gowns, made of

91

As Union victories increased, receptions became more and more popular.

velvet or brocade, and dipping now and then in a curtsy to some special friend or acquaintance. Soldiers stood at the entrances to handle the crowd.

All day long and into the night at times, sightseers were allowed to make themselves at home. Intent on collecting souvenirs, they tramped over the flowery East Room carpet that Mary Lincoln had seen installed with such pleasure, ripped off strips of the velvet wall covering, and attacked the lacy Swiss under-curtains with scissors and knives.

In spite of the almost public aspect of the White House at this time, protection for the person of the President was haphazard until the autumn of 1864. At that time two policemen armed with .38 Colt revolvers took up their stations at the doors of the room currently occupied by the President. At night two other members of the city police force guarded his bedchamber or walked beside him on his trips back and forth to the War Department. There was a sheaf of crank letters threatening the President's life on file in his office.

Although Mary Lincoln's shopping trips to New York had always received their full share of publicity, no one, least of all the President, knew to what lengths her passion for finery had led her. Articles of clothing she would never wear were delivered to the White House and put away in her closets in boxes. In four months she purchased three hundred pairs of gloves. Five hundred dollars went for a lace shawl, another $5,000 for three evening dresses.

During the presidential campaign of 1865, Mrs. Lincoln confided to Elizabeth Keckley that her debts for clothing amounted to $27,000. She was in terror lest her husband be defeated. "I do not know what would become of us all," she told Mrs. Keckley. "If he is re-elected I can keep

92

him in ignorance of my affairs; but if he is defeated, then the bills will be sent in and he will know all."

In her addled brain there bloomed the idea that the Republican politicians, who had grown rich "off the patronage of my husband," should pay her debts and save the Lincolns and the Republican Party from embarrassment. She told Mrs. Keckley that she had ways of influencing certain politicians in order to assure her husband's reelection.

On November 8, however, when the election returns made it plain that Lincoln had been chosen for a second term, Mrs. Lincoln told Mrs. Keckley she was sorry he had won. "Poor Mr. Lincoln is looking so broken-hearted, so completely worn out," she said. "I fear he will not get through the next four years."

On the evening of Inauguration Day, March 4, 1865, the last reception of the winter season was given at the White House. When at midnight the President had shaken the last hand and gone to bed exhausted, his bodyguard, William Crook, noted that the parlors looked "as if a regiment of rebel troops had been quartered there—with permission to forage."

In late March, as victory for the Union armies appeared certain, President Lincoln decided to accept an invitation from General Grant to visit his headquarters at City Point, Virginia. The President was plainly in poor health, and the trip, in addition to affording Lincoln a chance to see actual warfare, was intended partly as a vacation. For thirteen days, Lincoln remained with Grant, and on April 8 began his trip back to Washington on the river steamer, *River Queen.*

That same day John Wilkes Booth checked in at the National Hotel in Washington. Plans had already been perfected for the murder of the wartime President.

It was not long after his return from City Point that President Lincoln had a dream which disturbed him deeply. In the dream he heard the sound of weeping throughout the White House rooms, rose from his bed, and went down to the East Room. There he saw a catafalque on which lay a corpse, with soldiers standing on guard and a weeping crowd filling the room. He asked a soldier who it was who had died and the soldier said it was the President and that he had been assassinated.

A theatre party had been planned for the night of Good Friday, April 14, with General Grant and Mrs. Grant as guests of the Lincolns. They were going to Ford's Theatre to see the popular Miss Laura Keene in a performance of a light comedy, *Our American Cousin.* That afternoon Grant withdrew from the engagement, giving the excuse that he and Mrs. Grant must go to visit their children. A young, engaged couple, Clara Harris and Major Henry R. Rathbone, were invited to go instead.

The President was sitting in a rocking chair in his box at Ford's, his wife at his side, when a pistol shot rang out. The sound of the shot was so minor amid the audience's laughter over some antic on the stage that it was not the shot but Mary Lincoln's screams that first announced the tragedy. The murderer, his ankle injured as he leapt to the stage, escaped through a back exit.

At the theatre, the President's party was left unprotected in the flag-draped box, while his bodyguard visited a tavern.

John Wilkes Booth, gun in one hand, knife in the other, assassinates Lincoln in this imaginative lithograph. His leg broken in a fall to the stage, Booth limped to the wings and escaped on horseback.

Lincoln was carried to a house across the street, where he died the next morning.

Mortally wounded, the President was carried by soldiers across the street and into a small lodging house. The narrow bedroom where he was placed filled with dignitaries and doctors. Mrs. Lincoln alternately wept and fainted, or pleaded with her dying husband to speak to her or to take her with him. At dawn, when all hope was gone, she again fainted, was revived and led moaning to her carriage. "Oh, that dreadful house! that dreadful house!" she cried when for the last time she looked on the façade of Ford's Theatre.

Bells of mourning tolled throughout the city and the murdered President, with a military escort, was taken back to the White House. Wrapped in the American flag, his body was carried to the State Bedroom while Mary Lincoln lay convulsed with grief in a room nearby. Elizabeth Keckley came at once to care for her.

Meanwhile there was a new President of the Union. Andrew Johnson, Vice President for only a few weeks, had been speedily sworn into office in his hotel room, while guards stood outside the door.

On Tuesday the President lay in state on the catafalque which had hastily been erected in the East Room. Soldiers stood at either end. The sound of weeping was heard throughout the house. Black hung at the windows and veiled the chandeliers, bringing to the room the gloom of a sepulcher. Mirrors were masked with white cloth. A sad-faced procession passed through the room the entire day, mounting the steps of the catafalque to look once more on Lincoln's face, then exiting over a platform leading from a window.

Mary Lincoln did not leave her bed. While the funeral services went on in the East Room and while the black-canopied hearse bore the President's remains to the Capitol for one more day of lying in state, the grieving widow kept to her bed, seeing only her beloved Tad and her friend, Mrs. Keckley. When the Lincoln funeral train began the long trip back to Springfield, Mrs. Lincoln remained in her room, shattered and ill.

94

The catafalque upon which the murdered President lay. Artist Alfred Waud of Harper's Weekly made the above sketch in the East Room. Below, the engraving based on the sketch, as it was printed. As Waud included a mourning woman, he apparently expected Mary Lincoln to come downstairs.

Andrew Johnson.
Photograph by Brady.

Mrs. Johnson, who
longed for Tennessee.

Martha Patterson, the
President's daughter,
who ran the White House
with a capable hand.

THE WHITE HOUSE had not been put in readiness to receive the Johnsons, but the President's family—his wife, two sons, two daughters, and five grandchildren—made their tardy entry anyway in the summer of 1865. Coming from Tennessee, two carriage loads of Johnsons disgorged at the White House entrance and spread out over the denuded, shabby house, delightedly hunting and choosing their own rooms and cheerfully overlooking the dirt and discomfort.

Eliza McArdle Johnson, ailing and elderly at fifty-eight, picked for her own use a small bedroom facing south. In that room she was content to remain, knitting, reading, and sewing, while her elder daughter, Martha Johnson Patterson, wife of a Senator from Tennessee, took over the responsibility of making the house livable once more.

In spite of being an invalid, Mrs. Johnson, by the strength and benevolence of her character exerted a strong influence over the lives of the entire Johnson clan, keeping three separate families in harmony under the White House roof for nearly four years. For much of that time Andrew Johnson was to look to his family for sustenance as he fought a bitter battle with Congress over reconstruction policies.

Martha Patterson, a paragon of housekeepers, had been horrified by some of the sights in the public rooms—the bugs in the furniture in the East Room, the tobacco juice freely sprayed here and there, and the grimy state of all the rugs, drapes, and upholstery. With inadequate funds, tardily given by Congress for the purpose, she carried out a thorough housecleaning and refurbishing, acting as agent for all expenditures. Never had a housekeeper stretched money so skillfully. The Red, Blue, and Green parlors soon came alive in their new wallpaper and linen slipcovers. At large receptions Martha Patterson had the carpets in the public rooms covered with muslin.

The White House had a destructive fire in January, 1867, when a large part of the conservatory went up in flames. Nearly one-third of the rare plants, including a sago palm imported by George Washington, were lost. Fire crews kept the fire from spreading to the main structure, where the only damage was from smoke.

The picture presented by the Johnsons in the White House was in general one of pleasing simplicity; inevitably it was contrasted with the ill-managed stay of Mary Lincoln, to the credit of the Johnsons. Mrs. Patterson bought two Jersey cows so that the family could have choice milk and butter, and the public gazed approvingly at the beasts grazing on the mansion grounds. According to a contemporary journalist, Martha Patterson arose every morning at dawn and would quickly "don a calico dress and spotless apron, then descend to skim the milk and attend the dairy before breakfast."

Her mother, meanwhile, took no delight in the loftiness of her position but yearned to be back in Tennessee. To Colonel W. H. Crook, a mem-

President Johnson's big office upstairs in the White House.

The upstairs Oval Room, used as a library under the Johnsons.

ber of the White House staff, she once admitted: "Crook, it's all very well for them who like it, but I don't like this public life at all. I often wish the time would come when we could return to where I feel we best belong."

When Martha Patterson described the Johnsons as "plain people from the mountains of Tennessee," adding, "I trust too much will not be expected of us," it was generally taken for granted that the White House was due for a boring four years. Martha's remarks had been misleading. Without ostentation but with charm and finesse the President and his daughters entertained in the best White House tradition, receiving the unimportant and the distinguished impartially.

In an era when feminine dress for evening wear exposed as much flesh as possible, the Johnson girls appeared in the drawing room in dresses cut high around the neck, finished off with little collars fastened with a brooch.

97

The Radicals in Congress had been hot for Andrew Johnson's removal from office for two years when they finally found what they thought were unbeatable grounds for impeachment. Here, the summons to appear before the high court of impeachment is served on President Andrew Johnson in his White House office by the sergeant-at-arms of the Senate.

Their frocks were lent elegance by exquisite detail—embroidery, pleating, puffing, and tucking. The lack of chic seemed only to add to the popularity of the Johnson sisters. Against this harmonious background, Andrew Johnson engaged in a fight to the finish with the rebel-hating Radicals of the Republican party.

Johnson had been in office only a short while when he made it clear that he believed the war had been fought for the purpose of saving the Union and that he stood for a moderate, lenient plan of reconstruction for the ruined South. The Radical Republicans in Congress opposed him with their own program under which the South was to be treated as a conquered nation, kept in check by military government, and they passed oppressive laws over Johnson's veto again and again.

When the Congress enacted the Tenure of Office Act, making it impossible for the President to remove any civil official or Cabinet member

98

Johnson never appeared at the impeachment trial but conferred with his counsel daily at the White House. He was ably and passionately defended. Wild accusations against the President, even charges of complicity in the murder of Lincoln, tended to weaken the case for the opposition.

without its sanction, it was obvious that its backers—Senator Charles Sumner and Representative Thaddeus Stevens—were trying every method they could devise to ruin Andrew Johnson.

By the summer of 1867 the warfare between the Radicals and Johnson had reached an explosive point and the President, fighting to preserve the prestige and power of his office, decided to test the strength of the Tenure of Office Act by dismissing his trouble-making Secretary of War, Edwin Stanton. Stanton, with the backing of Congress, refused to vacate his post, and early 1868 found him barricaded in his office behind guards.

Johnson's removal of his Cabinet officer provided the grounds upon which his opponents believed they could fight. March 13, 1868, was selected by due process as the day on which the President was asked to appear before the court of impeachment and show cause why he should not be removed from the office of President of the United States.

Two months of argument and oratory led to a hairsbreadth decision in Johnson's favor. Thirty-five votes for removal and nineteen votes against it came within one vote of the two-thirds majority necessary to remove him from office. Here, Senator Ross of Kansas casts a deciding vote of "not guilty."

Johnson received congratulations on his acquittal with the same stubborn composure with which he had faced the harrowing weeks of the trial. His wife, who had never for one moment believed her husband would be removed, said simply, "I knew he would be acquitted, I knew it," when she was told of the outcome.

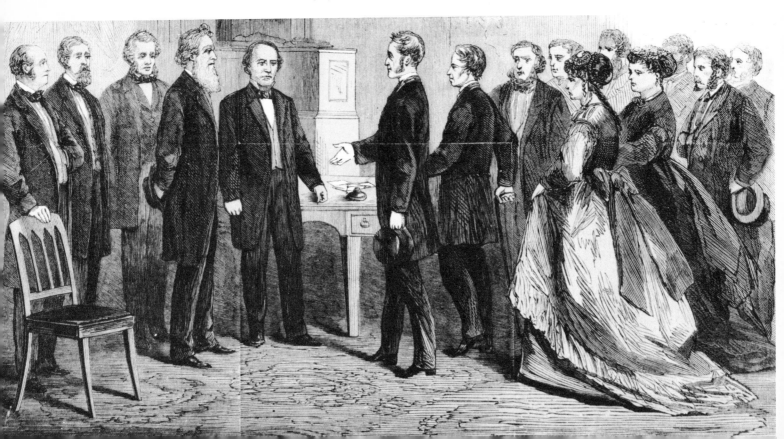

After the happy outcome of the trial, the Johnsons, as if in celebration, planned an extra round of entertainments. Parties for children, for friends, the Washington public, officialdom, and as much of the country as could get to Washington were given, all with great success. Andrew Johnson's popularity was definitely on the rise.

The East Room, very much as it had been since the time of Monroe
and before the radical changes of the 1873 renovation. Four
white marble mantelpieces, two on each side of the room, were
topped by mirrors; portraits of Presidents filled the spaces
between the windows and over the doors. When the crystal chandeliers
were lighted they "blazed like mimic suns" behind the closed shutters.

7	Ulysses S. Grant	1869 - 1877
	Rutherford B. Hayes	1877 - 1881
	James A. Garfield	1881 - 1881
	Chester A. Arthur	1881 - 1885

Four family circles

WHEN PRESIDENT ULYSSES S. GRANT, on his first evening in the White House, dismissed the military guard which had been posted there since the start of the Civil War, the gesture seemed to wipe out the last vestige of military atmosphere. His presence in the White House, however, was entirely due to his fame as a military leader—plus a simplicity of personality found very appealing by most Americans. It was as a popular hero of rare proportions that Grant entered the Presidency in the spring of 1869.

The President's family was an engaging one, with great diversity of youth and age, charm and interest. Two young children, Jesse and Nellie, were still at home. Fred was soon off to West Point, and Ulysses, Jr., to Harvard. The President and Mrs. Grant also had with them Mrs. Grant's aging father, "Colonel" Frederick Dent, a former slaveholder from Missouri, who held on to his role of Southern gentleman with mulelike tenacity and liked to discourse, over a mint julep, on the differences of opinion that existed between his renegade son-in-law and himself. The President's father, Jesse Grant, came to Washington frequently but always stayed at a hotel, since, as he scornfully said, the White House was full to overflowing with "that tribe of Dents."

The President's son, Jesse Grant, Jr., had much to say in later years of the rivalry between his two testy grandfathers, one a Confederate and the other a hard-bitten Unionist. Grandfather Grant was growing somewhat deaf and on one occasion Grandfather Dent announced in a loud voice to Mrs. Grant: "You should take better care of that old gentleman, Julia. He is feeble and deaf as a post, and yet you permit him to wander all over Washington alone." Grandfather Grant, who had heard every word, said to young Jesse: "I hope I shall not live to become as old and infirm as your Grandfather Dent."

The elderly Mr. Dent occupied a somewhat loftier spot in the White House than did the older Grant. A special niche had been set aside for him in the office section on the second floor, where he entertained the poli-

A fabulously popular general enters the White House as President.

A locket containing a picture of her husband was a personal touch Mrs. Grant added to her fashionable attire.

ticians and news writers who sought him out, according to Jesse, to talk about "the life and times of forty or fifty years ago." Dent was also considered a source of good material on life in the White House, and many a story told by him was retold at the club or used in a colorful news story.

President Grant was happiest when he had men around him he had known in earlier circumstances, and if they were not relatives—like Gen. Frederick Dent, Mrs. Grant's brother—they were friends or military associates, particularly former officers from his wartime staff. Most important of these was the handsome, young Colonel Orville E. Babcock, Grant's private secretary, who soon exercised a power greater than most Cabinet members.

Mrs. Grant, an enthusiastic helpmeet, was thwarted at the start in carrying out two plans she thought conducive to her own and the President's social success and comfort. The first was to have her crossed eyes remedied by an operation newly developed by a surgeon in the South. Grant would not have it. He said he had fallen in love with her with those eyes, and he wanted them to stay as they were. The plan for the operation was dropped.

Mrs. Grant's second idea concerned the discomforts of living in the White House, especially with such a retinue as the Grants'. She wanted to remain in their I Street house and use the White House only for official and public affairs.

It was true that the White House was not adequate for a large family. Of the living quarters on the second floor, only six rooms, on the north side, were in use as bedrooms. The other seven rooms on that floor were given over to offices, the Cabinet Room, and a ladies' parlor. All kitchens, pantries, and butlers' rooms were in the damp and gloomy basement.

This second proposal, however, was also rejected. The Grants moved into the run-down, dingy mansion that had seen few changes since the time of President Monroe.

The periodical renovation, which took place during the Grants' early months in the White House, made it almost presentable, and soon the kindly Mrs. Grant was having teas and receptions and standing in the Blue Room to receive all who cared to stop by for a moment. If the public did not know already that it was welcome it could read in a daily newspaper: "In the Blue Room the President's wife holds her morning receptions. Here, with the daylight excluded, soft rays falling from the chandelier above, . . . one day in each week of the season, from three to five P.M., the President's wife receives her critic—the public." Mrs. Grant carried out her duties with warmth and sincerity.

The President's social duties were also heavy. Grant could not escape the receptions given once a week for the diplomatic corps, the Cabinet officers, the Supreme Court justices, or the Senators and Representatives. When inviting members of Congress, however, Grant put on the list only those he really wanted to see. Up to that time Senators and Representatives had been entertained in alphabetical order, thirty-six at a time. Under Grant, wives were included and of necessity many Congressmen

104

The Grants' seaside cottage at Long Branch, New Jersey, was the scene of this picture, in which Grandfather Dent joined the Grants and their friends.

omitted. The preparation of such lists demanded considerable social tact.

After the strain of the war years and Johnson's unpretentious occupancy the White House took its rightful place in the world of glitter and extravagance. Society was ready for a fling, and the Grants, for all their plainness, were its unmistakable leaders. Before the mirrors of the East Room there strolled a strange cavalcade of diplomats in full regalia, war profiteers and their over-dressed wives, and gently bred aristocrats, and the public, if excluded, could at least read of the event in the torrent of descriptive copy that appeared in the daily press.

Social doings had suddenly become a leading department in the newspapers. The female society writer made her appearance in important numbers and furthered the significance of society. No detail of flowers, dress, or deportment escaped the ladies of the press. Adjectives spilled from their pens; events became "gala," "brilliant," "elegant"; current belles "ravishing," "ethereal," or "stately."

After a New Year's reception in the White House, one writer produced the following: "The gorgeous costumes of the diplomats and the elegant dresses of the ladies formed a picturesque and animated 'coup d'oeil'." The French phrase had been popularized. Paragraphs in magazines and newspapers were devoted to Mrs. Grant in "Lyons silk velvet, with high bodice, trimmed with black lace and satin," or in "pink grenadine, with flounced over-skirt, hair ornaments of fresh flowers, and diamond necklace."

At one of Mrs. Grant's fashionable afternoon receptions the Paris gown worn by the beautiful wife of a Senator enchanted the reporter for *Harper's Bazaar*. "The first skirt is of Mexican blue," she detailed, "with over-dress of French blue, open in front; then a basque and shorter skirt of turquoise blue, with a vest of Mexican blue. The fringe is knotted in a narrow hem on each skirt—French blue on the Mexican, turquoise on the French, and all mingled in the most delightful confusion. . . ." A little confused herself by this time, she added lamely, "Mrs. and Miss Boutwell should have had precedence except for that lovely dress. They are ladies who impress you more by their cultivated minds than by gorgeous array."

State dinners were elaborate and expensive during the Grant period and the Italian steward, Melah, delighted in serving between twenty-five and thirty courses at these affairs. When Prince Arthur, third son of Queen Victoria, dined at the White House in January, 1870, the cost of the dinner was said to be about two thousand dollars. The guests sat around the horseshoe-shaped table in the State Dining room, feasting on soup, fish, game, and meats, and ending with frozen punches and nuts. There were six wine glasses at each plate and the wines served were the best from France.

While dinner could consume two or three hours, the conversation which followed afterwards in the Blue Room and the Red Room was brief indeed. When the large gilt clock on the mantelpiece in the Red Room had ticked off fifteen or twenty minutes, the President would give the signal to end the evening.

Although the wine flowed freely on State occasions, certain employees around the White House were being deprived of their holiday stimulants by the year 1873. A report on the New Year's festivities of that year read: "It has been the habit heretofore to furnish the policemen and attendants with refreshments, which have included something to drink as well as something to eat. Today the President directed that refreshments be furnished as usual, with coffee substituted for liquors." Teetotalism had once again showed its homely face in the White House.

In 1871, Grant's secretary, Orville Babcock, was made Commissioner of Public Buildings and Grounds, and his report on the "condition, capacity, and adaptability" of the Executive Mansion, made at the request of Congress, gave a dismal and alarming picture of the state of the aging residence. The timbers in the floors and roof were decayed; the basement "damp and unhealthy." "It hardly seems possible to state anything in favor of the house as a residence," Babcock continued. "There is hardly a ceiling which has not cracked. . . . One large ceiling fell last year, but fortunately when the room was unoccupied. . . . No closets or clothes-presses, which are now considered indispensable."

Babcock's report produced the first drastic changes in the White House interior since President Monroe had moved into the rebuilt President's House after the fire of 1814. In the renovation of 1873 the old simplicity

Mrs. Grant's practice of inviting several women of prominence to assist her at receptions was looked upon as typically gracious.

Early in Grant's first term, Harper's Weekly published drawings of his horses and stable. Egypt and Cincinnati are in the center, and two ponies, Reb and Billy Button, in the foreground. Reb had been captured at Vicksburg. Below, Reb and Billy take Jesse to school.

Grant leaves the
White House for his
second inauguration.

The lovely
Nellie Grant.

was replaced by a florid ostentation, similar to that of the "public salon" in large hotels or on Hudson River steamers.

The East Room suffered most from the general overhauling. It became an overdecorated horror in the "Greek style," its ceiling broken into three panels by heavy beams supported by columns. From each section of the ceiling was suspended a colossal chandelier of cut glass, imported from Germany at great cost. Wallpaper gilded "to bring out the figures" and white and gilt woodwork in great profusion completed the destruction of the once stately room. New furniture of ebony and gold was placed around the fringes of the room. A vogue for the gaudy had been given a boost that would carry it through several decades.

A large part of the social excitement of Grant's second term centered on his daughter Nellie, by far the most delightful member of the Grant family. An effort had been made to force some advanced schooling on Nellie, but a single day at a New England boarding school had been enough for her. A frantic wire had brought President Grant north to take her home again, and from that day on her life was one long round of parties and beaux.

Nellie's winning personality and lovely face were enough to assure her social success in Washington, and these led to even greater triumphs when she was taken abroad by old friends of the Grants. She was a sensation at English balls and parties, was feted and petted and on one occasion introduced to Queen Victoria.

On the ship bringing Nellie home was Algernon Sartoris, the nephew of the noted actress Fanny Kemble. It was love at first sight and President Grant's warnings on the perils of a hasty marriage were without effect. Elaborate plans were started to give Nellie a spring wedding before her nineteenth birthday. The wedding took place on a May morning in 1874.

Over the Grant regime there hung an aura of the sporting life. A lifelong lover of horses, Grant had the stables enlarged and filled with racing and carriage horses. A new walk was laid between the White House and the stables and down this walk Grant strolled daily to visit his horses. His rather ostentatious display of them and the rank, black cigar which he smoked constantly caused Grant to be labeled vulgar in some quarters.

Another mild indication of the sporting life was the billiard table which Grant installed at government expense. Times had changed since John Quincy Adams and his modest billiard room, paid for out of his own pocket, had caused such a rumpus in Congress.

Contradictions in Grant's character sometimes made him difficult to grasp and hard to deal with. He was gay and talkative with intimates but could freeze an unwanted visitor with what John G. Nicolay called his "terrible accusing silence."

So long was the string of scandals in the Grant administration that its successes were more or less lost sight of. Shenanigans involving Secretary of War Belknap and Grant's trusted confidant, Orville Babcock, touched the personally honest President in the most painful way. But the Grants left the White House still very much the darlings of the nation, the luster of the General's name hardly dimmed in the public mind.

Wedding presents poured into the White House when Nellie Grant married Algernon Sartoris. In the heavily floral atmosphere of the East Room the young couple exchanged vows under a wedding bell made of roses and babies'-breath. Eight bridesmaids attended the bride, whose white satin gown carried $4,000 worth of Brussels point lace. From her stiff little bridal bouquet a tiny banner flaunted the word "Love."

President Rutherford B. Hayes receives the acclaim of the crowds in front
of the White House on the night after his inauguration. The election
contest was one of the most unpleasant in American history.

W HEN RUTHERFORD B. HAYES and Mrs. Hayes boarded a train for Washington and the inaugural ceremonies of March, 1877, they still did not know whether Hayes had been elected President.

In a highly competitive race with the Democratic candidate, Samuel J. Tilden, Hayes had lost the popular vote by half a million but had squeezed by with one vote in the electoral college. Charges of trickery and fraud in the carpetbag-governed states of South Carolina, Florida, Georgia, and Louisiana followed, and a delegation of Congressmen traveled south to investigate the election proceedings. The inquiry was still in progress when Hayes and his wife left Ohio. At Harrisburg, Pennsylvania, they learned that the commission had decided in Hayes's favor.

Inauguration Day fell on a Sunday in 1877. After such a close call, it seemed the height of folly to President Grant to leave the nation executiveless for an entire day, as would have normally been the case. Arrangements were made to circumvent any kind of incident.

A distinguished group of thirty-six guests, including Cabinet members and Chief Justice Waite, assembled at the Executive Mansion on the evening of Saturday, March 3, for what appeared to be a typical White House dinner. Just before going in to dinner, Hayes, Grant, and Chief Justice Waite, accompanied by Secretary of State Hamilton Fish, went quietly into the Red Room, where the oath of office was administered to Hayes by Waite. The entire ceremony took about three minutes and some of the guests did not even know it was happening. On Monday the ceremony was repeated before a huge crowd at the Capitol.

Following the brief swearing-in the party sat down to a twenty-course dinner, with six wine glasses at each plate. Ropes of smilax and roses festooned the ceiling. Behind Mrs. Hayes stood a pink azalea ten feet high.

Perhaps it was the air of luxury run wild during the Grant era that made the Hayes occupancy of the White House seem by contrast strait-laced and puritanical, for no President and First Lady had ever brought more enthusiasm to their official duties. With their entrance, however, extravagance and empty show made an exit. It was as though a fresh breeze swept through the old rooms, clearing out the scent of champagne and costly perfumes.

Both President and Mrs. Hayes were persons of positive character and broad interests. Mrs. Hayes was the first college-trained woman ever to become First Lady; after a distinguished career as soldier and Congressman, Rutherford B. Hayes had served three terms as governor of Ohio.

In the Hayeses' first spring in the White House, two Russian Grand Dukes, Alexis and Constantin, were given a state dinner by the President. Gossip had it that a drunken incident at that affair brought about Hayes' decision to bar the serving of wines altogether. True or not, shortly thereafter a dinner for the diplomatic corps saw the first wineless table since the days of President Polk. The party broke up with amazing punctuality, some of the guests making for the State Department building opposite, where a thoughtful Secretary of State had made provisions for the occasion.

Their stand on alcoholic beverages placed President and Mrs. Hayes on

President Hayes turns his piercing gaze to the camera and, below, steps over the threshold of the White House.

111

In the conservatory Mrs. Hayes, with her children, Scott and Fanny, and a friend, posed for the New York photographer, Pach. The conservatory was a favorite spot for the early portrait photographers, probably because of the abundant light there.

The Hayes servants posed for this picture in May, 1877.
It is the first photograph ever taken of a White House staff.

a moral pedestal in some quarters but drew a volley of ridicule from others. The dignified, motherly Mrs. Hayes was dubbed "Lemonade Lucy," and the Hayes setup known as a "cold-water regime." "Water flowed like wine," gibed one guest who had had what he considered a dull evening. While Mrs. Hayes received most of the praise or blame for this, her husband was actually responsible. Hayes had been caught up in the temperance movement as a young man and had got much of his early training in public speaking by making speeches for the Sons of Temperance.

The Hayeses' official receptions were sedate indeed, with "Home, Sweet Home" played by the Marine Band as a signal for dispersing at ten o'clock sharp. The Hayes family was at its best under more informal circumstances. They all enjoyed living in the White House, and unlike some of her predecessors, Mrs. Hayes found the old building charming and perfectly adequate. She once said to a friend who was being shown around for the first time, "No matter what they build, they will never build any more rooms like these!"

Early in 1878, Austine Snead, whose news letters were published under the name Miss Grundy, got permission from Mrs. Hayes to inspect the

President and Mrs. Hayes celebrated their silver wedding anniversary in December, 1877 by repeating the original ceremony. Mrs. Hayes wore her old wedding gown.

113

The home life of the Hayes family set an example widely imitated in that Victorian era. Here the President and Mrs. Hayes with three of their children and some close friends have a musical evening in the upstairs sitting-room. Carl Schurz is at the keyboard.

family quarters, with a view to describing them in the press. "Miss Grundy" treated her readers to an imaginary tour of the private rooms on the White House second floor, a part of the mansion seldom seen, before or since, by any but relatives and close friends of Presidential families.

"On the second floor," wrote Miss Grundy, "the business offices take up half the house, leaving only the western portion for family rooms. A broad corridor runs through the house from east to west on this floor, and just beyond the President's office large double doors divide the private section of the house from that which is open to all desiring to see him or any of his secretaries. . . .

"There are only eight bedrooms, a library and a bathroom in this part of the house, three of which are of quite moderate size, and the others very large. Quite a small room in the southwest corner the President keeps as his *sanctum sanctorum*, retreats there when he wishes to be absolutely uninterrupted. . . .

"The interior views upstairs are as handsome, in their way, as those below. The prettiest of the bedrooms, though not the one most elaborately furnished, is used by the President and Mrs. Hayes. It has windows opening south and commands a fine view, as do all the rooms upstairs, but es-

114

A few weeks after moving into the White House Mrs. Hayes held a reception for ladies, greeting them in the Blue Room with a word and a smile. Flaunting the grotesquery of the bustle and carefully practicing the "Grecian Bend," all the ladies of Washington who had the proper finery to display put in an appearance at the White House to meet the First Lady. Even the conservative Mrs. Hayes wore a modified bustle, but her hair style remained her own. There were no rats or puffs or purchased hair on Mrs. Hayes's head.

Described by a visitor as "Frenchy and pretentious," the Green Room nevertheless had a gracefulness it was soon to lose.

pecially those looking south, from which the gardens, the river and the Virginia shore can be seen. The walls of Mrs. Hayes' room are tinted pale blue, with panels of light gray and pink, divided by bands of gilt. . . . The mantel is white marble, as are most of the mantels in the house, and above it is a large, square mirror. The fireplace is a beauty, with nickel-plated setting, fender and andirons, on which rests a gas log. The bed is a low one. At its foot is a marble-top table, on which is a lamp communicating with the chandelier above, and books lie nearby, showing that the luxury of reading in bed is sometimes enjoyed by one or the other of the occupants of the apartment. . . .

"Next this room is the grand State Bedchamber, usually called the President's room, 'but I never slept in it,' adds President Hayes. . . . The present incumbents of the White House never live in state, or encourage ceremonious observances when they can help it. . . .

"The library, which is next, is over the Blue Parlor, and is an equally beautiful room, oval in shape. Its walls are covered with green velvet paper,

116

An uncluttered
Presidential
bedroom.

paneled with light coffee-color and gilt bands. Low bookcases line the walls. . . . A very inviting looking table, with reading lamp and books upon it, is in the center of the room. A Bradbury piano is in this room, which is used more especially as a family sitting room. . . . By day or night this room is the most inviting in the house.

"On the north side of the hall are five bedrooms, three of them small. The first in the northwest corner is now known as 'the boys' room,' and is used by the President's sons when at home. . . . The first large room on the north side is a spare bedchamber, handsomely furnished with black walnut. . . . Next this is a large bathroom finished in oak. . . . Fannie Hayes' room is of suitable proportions for a little maiden. . . . There is a cabinet piano in the room to give Miss Fannie an opportunity to practice undisturbed. A large globe is also here . . . .

The upstairs Oval
Room used as a
library.

"The shabbiest furniture in the house is that in the President's cabinet room. This is a large, bright, cheerful apartment, with handsomely painted ceiling and walls, the latter a light coffee color. The chairs and sofas, of which there are an abundance, are very faded and soiled; they were once a bright maroon rep, but are now a dirty brown. The chair backs are the shape of the United States shield, the woodwork of the sofa has the United States coat-of-arms on it, and on the cornices at the windows and surmounting the mirror frame of dark wood, are carvings of the United States shield.

"The cabinet table which stands in the center of the room is of dark wood covered with red morocco. There are seven drawers in the table, with locks and keys, and each member of the cabinet has one of his own. The President, at all times during office hours, sits at the head of the table with his papers in front of him, and every morning a large, fresh bouquet is placed before him, an indication of the gentleness and refinement so characteristic of him. . . .

The Blue Room
under Hayes.

"On the walls are large maps and a photograph of this city. . . . This is where the cabinet meetings are held and where the President is daily persecuted by countless bores and office-seekers. . . . While invariably courteous, President Hayes knows how to free himself from those disposed to linger too long. He does this usually by discountinuing replies to his persecutors. Only as a last resort does he terminate an interview by the broad hint of rising from his chair. His gentle manner can be ruffled, however, when occasion demands, and his mild voice assume the sternness necessary to rebuke those deserving it. . . . One detects, lying underneath the mild face with its serene expression, which might in some denote weakness, that greatest of all human strengths, which springs from the moral courage that never fears to face the right."

Chiefs of the Sioux Indian Nation came to Washington to meet the President and had their photograph taken by Brady.

Hayes greets the delegation in the East Room.

Although she was a warm and capable hostess, Mrs. Hayes regarded the White House primarily as a family house and her chief interest lay in the welfare of her children. Webb Hayes, who had just graduated from Cornell University, acted as his father's private secretary. Two other sons, Birchard and Rutherford, were still in college but visited the White House frequently. Fanny and Scott, aged nine and six, completed the family group.

The President and his wife were regular churchgoers. Every Sunday they could be seen going on foot to services at the Foundry Methodist Episcopal Church. Daily family prayers followed breakfast and many an evening was spent singing hymns. Sometimes Representative McKinley of Ohio joined the circle of Cabinet members and old friends that clustered around the piano to sing the ancient tunes.

Hayes earnestly wished to unify the country still suffering the effects of the Civil War, and made numerous personal appearances throughout the South and East. While in Providence, Rhode Island, on one such trip, Hayes was given a demonstration of the telephone by Alexander Graham Bell, was delighted with the new device and installed both the telephone and the telegraph in the White House.

118

Toward the end of his term, the President and Mrs. Hayes took a long trip through the West, visiting all the principal towns from Omaha to San Francisco and traveling as far north as Seattle. Hayes thus became the first President ever to go to the Pacific coast.

Both the President and his wife were innate politicians. The coolness which attended Hayes's early weeks in Washington soon vanished, and he was looked upon as a rare President of great gifts and his wife as a model of womanly virtue. One news writer referred to Mrs. Hayes as "the most idolized woman in America." To the W.C.T.U. she became a veritable heroine. Through their offices a portrait of Mrs. Hayes, wearing maroon velvet and holding three cream-colored roses, was painted by Daniel Huntington and presented to the White House.

Mrs. Hayes's evenings at home, when anyone who wished could call on her, became a heartwarming symbol of the Hayes hospitality. A minor coup was brought off when the Easter Monday egg-rolling, suddenly taboo on the Congressional grounds, was brought to the White House and became the most publicized of customs.

In his constructive moves in Civil Service reform and his liberal stand on the problems of the South, Hayes had acted in direct opposition to the interests of the New York political machine and its leaders, Roscoe A. Conkling and Chester A. Arthur, both Grant men. By removing Arthur from the important post of Collector of Customs in New York City, he wrecked his own chances for renomination, had he wanted it.

The Republican party, however, had produced a number of other potential candidates. The most promising aspirant was former President Grant, his popularity still intact. James Blaine was avid for nomination, and high among the potentials was the Secretary of the Treasury, John Sherman.

In the early summer of 1880 delegates to a prolonged Republican convention haggled over the selection of a candidate. Thirty-five ballots produced only a stalemate. From the complexities of the meeting one fact stood out; the Grant backers were giving in to no man. On every ballot their vote was the same, and someone came up with an appropriate name for them—the Stalwarts.

On the thirty-sixth ballot a compromise candidate was agreed upon. He was James A. Garfield, a handsome, forty-eight-year-old Congressman from Ohio, present in his capacity as campaign manager for Sherman. During his years in Congress, Garfield had not been closely identified with any of his party's feuds. His reputation for moderation and his experience and high character made him acceptable to all factions. A gesture of appeasement was then made toward the Stalwarts in the selection of one of their favorites, dapper Chester A. Arthur, for Vice Presidential candidate.

Differences within the party were patched up long enough to bring off the election of Garfield and Arthur. But the curtain had actually been raised on a patronage fight of unprecedented bitterness. It was this battle which would lead directly to Garfield's assassination—the second of a President of the United States.

The Blue Room was the scene of Hayes's meeting with Chen Lan Pin, the first Chinese Minister to the United States, in 1878.

James A. Garfield, whose qualities of mind and personality took him to the White House.

The bookish, serious-minded Lucretia Garfield.

The office-seekers were waiting for President Garfield when he walked into his office on the day after his inauguration in March, 1881. Anyone who had so much as handed around a circular during the campaign felt he was entitled to an interview and the promise of a lucrative job.

Daily they tramped up the stairs to the crowded waiting room, each hoping for a pay-off. A visitor described it: "As I go up the stairs, the atmosphere is heavy and close on this stairway and affects one singularly. Perhaps the sighs of disappointed office-seekers, who for more than half a century have descended the steps, have permeated the walls and give to the air a quality that defies ventilation. Crowds in ante-room and crowds in the upper hall. All these people are eager-eyed, restless and nervous. They want something which the great man in that well-guarded room across the hall can give if he chooses, but which they fear they will not get."

The Stalwarts, under the leadership of Senator Conkling, had already discovered that Garfield's appointments were not favoring them. The choice of James G. Blaine as Secretary of State and other Cabinet members not picked from the Grant-worshiping Stalwarts brought down thunderous abuse upon the President. He was accused of going back on promises to award them exclusive New York patronage. The Stalwarts maintained it was only through their efforts that he had been elected at all. Vice President Arthur joined in the charges.

Garfield, caught between two camps and trying to be impartial in his distribution of offices, was labeled a weakling and a tool of the brilliant, ambitious Blaine. Every move brought fresh charges of favoritism. Exhausted by the demands of persons in both high and low positions, Garfield began to suffer from insomnia. To his secretary he said: "These people would take my very brain, flesh and blood if they could. They are wholly without mercy."

There was a serene side to the President's life, evident to all who had known him in the years he had been a Congressman from Ohio. It involved his wife, Lucretia, and his five children. The two oldest boys, Harry and James, were preparing to enter college. Three younger children—fourteen-year-old Mollie and Irwin and Abram, aged eleven and nine respectively—made up the remainder of the family.

The Garfields were learned persons who took a major part in their Washington literary society. They hoped to transplant to the White House the quiet, scholarly life they loved. An evening of reading was their favorite pastime and, according to a close friend, the President continued his children's education even at the dinner table, skillfully drawing them into conversation on worth-while subjects.

The Garfields knew what was expected of them as tenants of the White House. The customary routine of official dinners and receptions began immediately. Using strictly classified lists, they entertained members of the diplomatic corps, important figures from the Army and Navy, Congressmen and their wives. Mrs. Garfield was "at home" twice a week.

Toward the first of May 1881, Mrs. Garfield became seriously ill with malaria, then prevalent in Washington, and Garfield, forgetting his own fatigue, would often keep vigil by his wife's bedside long into the night.

By the middle of June Mrs. Garfield had recovered sufficiently to leave Washington for a holiday. The entire family went to the ocean resort of Elberon, New Jersey. A few days later Garfield returned alone to Washington to finish the business of the fiscal year.

His plans were made to attend the commencement exercises at Williams College, his alma mater, and at the same time to enroll his two older sons for the coming year. Once the pleasant business of seeing old classmates was over, he would rejoin his wife at Elberon.

Garfield was enthusiastic about his coming trip to Williams. On the morning of July 2, 1881, he had recovered some of his normal lighthearted-ness as he climbed into a State Department coupé with Secretary Blaine for the short ride from the White House to the railroad station. It was nearly twenty minutes after nine when they arrived at the Baltimore and Potomac terminal, ten minutes ahead of departure time. As the President and Blaine sauntered across the waiting room in the direction of the tracks, a short, thin man dressed in black and wearing a wide-brimmed hat, watched them closely from his place near the wall.

When the President and Blaine had nearly crossed the room, the man quickly moved near them and fired two shots point-blank at Garfield. The first bullet struck Garfield in the back, the second barely missed his arm. The President staggered and collapsed, and after a few of the stunned people in the station had regained their wits, he was carried into an adjacent office

room. The would-be assassin, Charles Guiteau, made a dash for the door but was stopped by a policeman. "I am a Stalwart of the Stalwarts," Guiteau shouted. "I did it and I want to be arrested. Arthur is President now." Cries of "Lynch him!" came from the crowd. Evidently Guiteau had thought of such a possibility, for a letter he handed to the policeman, addressed to General William Tecumseh Sherman, asked that troops be sent immediately to guard the jail. A copy of the New York *Herald* found in his coat pocket contained an article calling Garfield's treatment of the Stalwarts double-dealing and his appointments dishonest. The paper was worn with handling and inflammatory passages had been underscored. When the ambulance arrived to carry the President to the White House, he seemed near death.

Physicians were certain he would not live through the day. Members of the Cabinet were notified and Vice President Arthur summoned to the White House and told to be ready to assume office at any time. At noon Mrs. Garfield left Elberon, New Jersey, on a train specially routed over connecting railroad tracks. An operation to remove the bullet, which had lodged behind the pancreas, was deemed impossible. There was little left to do but wait.

By nightfall rumors had spread over the entire country that the President had died. But the crowds gathered at the White House gates knew there had been little change in his condition. Newsmen rushed every scrap of information to the waiting papers. As the night wore on it became clear that the doctor's predictions had been wrong. Instead of reporting his death, the bulletins coming from the sickroom spoke of Garfield's cheerfulness and courage. At 4 A.M. it was reported that his doctors had been greatly encouraged when he told them a funny story from his youth.

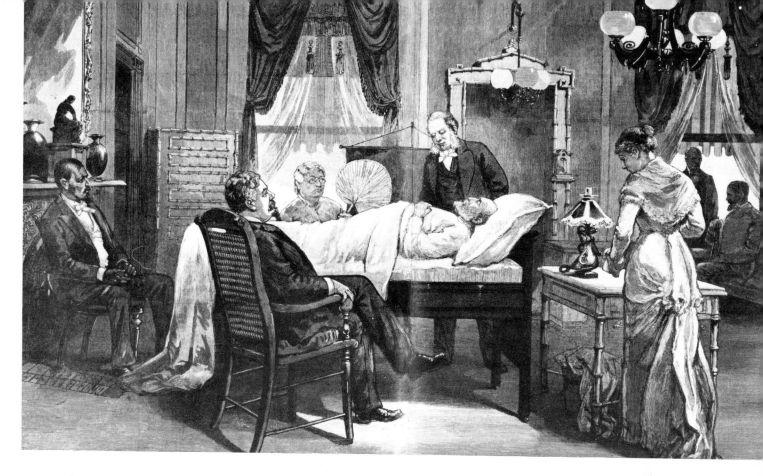

In the morning the President was told he had a chance of recovery and the situation was taken in hand with a new spirit. Wives of Cabinet members who had acted as nurses were replaced by Dr. Susan Edson, who had once been an army nurse. The atmosphere in the patient's room became more cheerful and Mrs. Garfield appeared, smiling and calm, several times each day. Even the children managed to come into the room in a lighthearted manner. Garfield's detached interest in his own case astonished the doctors. He wanted to know the "central velocity" of the bullet still imbedded in his back and what the people were saying about the whole affair. The man Guiteau he would not discuss. He knew that only an unbalanced mind could have conceived the attack.

Callers at the White House were given the latest news of President Garfield's condition by a member of the White House police. Word of his bravery in the face of unknown developments had reached every corner of the country and had brought forth a rush of pride in the man who lay helpless in the White House. Hopes for the President's full recovery rose and fell throughout the long, hot summer.

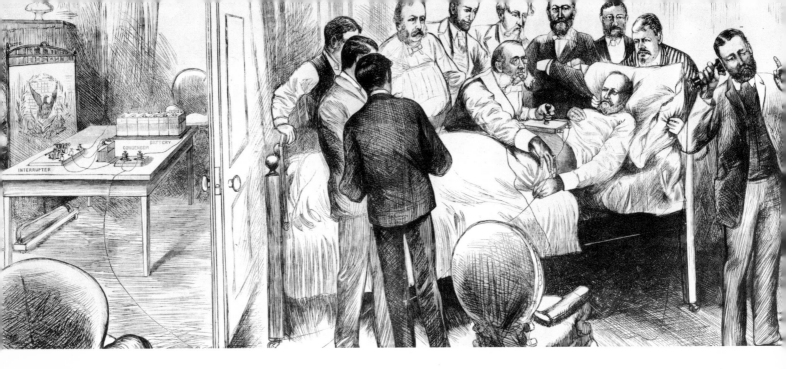

In late summer a new electrical contrivance created by Alexander G. Bell was used in an effort to determine the exact location of the bullet. The experiment failed because the President had been placed on a steel-spring mattress, although Bell had expressly asked that there be no metal near the bed. Newspaper reporters gleaned every shred of interest out of this experiment. The entire nation became familiar with the problems of infection caused by gunshot wounds. Garfield was heard to say, "I should think the people would be tired of having me dished up to them in this way."

Throughout a series of crises which continued through the summer, the Garfield family maintained an outer calm which concealed a terrible foreboding of tragedy to come. Garfield's daughter, Mollie, was permitted to see her father on his better days. Mrs. Garfield often went to the White House kitchen to prepare the patient's food herself.

By the end of August the doctors once again considered Garfield's condition nearly hopeless. His strength was declining daily and a newspaper headlined a story from the White House THE END EXPECTED. In New York City, the street bulletin exhibited on Broadway by the New York *Herald* drew crowds day and night. But once more the remarkable patient rallied and once more hope was held for his recovery. President Garfield had many times expressed the desire to get away from Washington and go to Elberon. His doctors decided the move was feasible and plans were made to move him to the seashore with the least possible disturbance.

On September 6, 1881, the President was carried through the door of the White House on a cot. The cot was placed in an express wagon for the trip to the railroad station.

From the express wagon, Garfield, still lying on his bed, was placed on a special train. It sped across Maryland, Delaware, parts of Pennsylvania, and New Jersey, to the fresh breezes of the sea coast. A track had been laid right to the door of the cottage in Elberon. Members of the Cabinet with their wives settled down in a hotel in nearby Long Branch. Robert Todd Lincoln, Secretary of War, later said that during the sad, tedious days, no mention was made of anything except the President's condition. No government business of consequence was carried out and no move made to place Arthur in the Presidency.

126

In the fresh sea air Garfield seemed to be gaining until September 17, when a distinct change for the worse occurred. All that day and the next he grew steadily weaker. On the evening of September 19, President Garfield fell asleep shortly before ten o'clock, but was awakened a short while later by an agonizing pain over the heart. With Mrs. Garfield beside him, he died at 10:35 P.M. In New York City, Vice President Chester A. Arthur, the Stalwart favorite, received the news of the President's death and prepared for his own inauguration.

127

The White House draped in black for a dead President.

WHEN PRESIDENT CHESTER A. ARTHUR decided to engage a decorator to rejuvenate the White House, it was typical that his mind settled on Louis Comfort Tiffany, artist and originator of the exotic tastes in interior decoration then in vogue. A man of modish and elegant preferences and something of a social butterfly, Arthur could not bear the sight of the White House as he found it in September of 1881. "A badly kept barracks" was the phrase he used as he moved to the home of a friend so that workmen could take over.

While they plastered and painted under Tiffany's direction, Arthur kept a sharp eye on every detail. Every evening after dinner he drove to the White House to see how the work was progressing and to give instructions for any changes. The Blue Room was painted a gay robin's egg blue, the Red Room acquired a frieze of eagles and flags, a pattern later to embellish the famous screen which Tiffany designed for the rear of the vestibule. Everything was sprayed with gold paint in a manner typical of the era: "Even the heavy iron railings in front of the house," one account stated, "are tipped with gold." Practical additions to the White House at this time included two new bathrooms and an elevator.

128

Arthur's attention to the decoration of his private dining room showed where his real interests lay; he intended to do a great deal of unofficial entertaining. Heavy gold paper covered the walls as a background for the pomegranate plush which hung in heavy folds from the windows and draped the mantelpiece. The wall lights were of crimson glass. It was in this hushed, snug room, in the glow of an open fire, that Arthur celebrated his arrival in the White House on December 7, 1881. A French chef prepared the meal.

In the early spring the citizens of Washington were given a rare treat. Twenty-four wagonloads of broken-down furniture and assorted junk were hauled away from the White House and put up for auction. A variety of old stoves, cuspidors, moth-eaten carpeting, and hair mattresses that had been stashed away since the days of Buchanan were eagerly bought as precious relics. A globe from which Nellie Grant had learned her geography brought an exorbitant price. A man from Baltimore purchased all the lace curtains that had enhanced the ground floor parlors. Two highchairs for small tots, originally presented by President Hayes to his wife's niece on the occasion of her marriage, were also among the prizes.

President Arthur needed pleasant surroundings for reasons of morale. From the day of the attack on President Garfield's life until the day of his own inauguration he had been a very dejected man. Already on bad terms with Garfield because of the factional fight, Arthur had been forced to face the seriousness of his situation.

The day after Garfield was wounded, Arthur, after paying his respects to Mrs. Garfield, was shown to the room where Garfield's Cabinet was meeting. At the doorway he hesitated, waiting for an invitation to enter. Cold stares and silence stunned him. Arthur would have left, but at that instant a visitor at the meeting happened to see him, came forward to greet him, and brought him into the room. The ice was broken and others rose to welcome him.

During the harrowing months that followed, Arthur went through his own ordeal. He was aware of the consternation in the country over the possibility of Garfield's death. Former President Hayes was only expressing popular opinion when he wrote in his diary: "The death of the President at this time would be a national calamity . . . Arthur for President! Conkling the power behind the throne, superior to the throne!" A writer in *The Nation* put it bluntly: "Out of this mess of filth Mr. Arthur will go to the Presidential Chair in case of the President's death." Vilification in the newspapers forced Arthur into seclusion. His health suffered from the constant tension and worry.

As the fateful summer wore on and Garfield's death was only a matter of time, the press changed its tune. Arthur was no longer presented as a vulgar politician with rapacious tendencies, but rather a weak-willed man of good intentions, still a helpless tool of the ruthless Conkling.

Those who expected the White House to be a loafing spot for the old New York political crowd were astonished by the developments during Arthur's early months in the White House. Arthur, instead of bring-

An official portrait of the modish, society-loving Arthur.

129

*Joseph Pennell made these
White House sketches in 1881.*

The north entrance.

Entrance to the East Room.

In the Blue Room.

The Red Room.

ing in the spoils system, vigorously encouraged Civil Service reform. His former associates were furious. Roscoe Conkling, angriest of all since he had the most to lose, hung the insulting nickname of "His Accidency" on Arthur. Meanwhile other measures, notably Arthur's moves toward the development of a modern navy, built public confidence in his ability.

President Arthur was an extremely methodical man, capable of long sessions of hard work, but he had definite ideas about the rights to worldly pleasures due men in high positions. In addition to demanding the best of everything in the way of food, wines and service, he was the first President to employ a valet, and every occasion saw him dressed in impeccable taste. His orders for suits and coats from his New York tailor were large and frequent, once amounting to twenty-five coats at one time.

Arthur's love of flowers was also well known. At all State dinners and receptions flowers and plants from the White House conservatories were used extravagantly, with additional flowers sometimes ordered from New York. When, late in his administration, he had improvements made in the greenhouses, they became the showplace of the White House. Visitors could go directly from the State Dining Room into the palm house and on into the wing where tropical plants were grown. In the rose house alone over a hundred varieties were to be found. This plethora of flowers was destined to produce some awe-inspiring creations.

At a State dinner in the winter of 1884 the guests were struck by the appearance of the showy centerpiece. A floral temple over four feet long and a foot and a half high, it had even been given a title: "The Swinging Garden of Babylon." Built up from a mirror base, it utilized roses, carnations, honeysuckle, and blossoms of the nun plant. To indulge his guests further, Arthur had had bouquets of roses prepared for the ladies and boutonnieres of rosebuds for the gentlemen.

President Arthur's wife, Ellen Herndon Arthur, had died only a few months before his nomination for Vice President, and Arthur had persuaded his younger sister, Mary A. McElroy, to come from Albany to act as hostess for the winter months. Although she temporarily left be-

The south entrance.

hind a devoted husband, Mrs. McElroy brought her two young daughters along. She also looked after the motherless Nell Arthur, the President's daughter; his young son was away at school.

Night after night Mrs. McElroy stood with the President under the gas chandeliers and received a never ending stream of guests. Mrs. McElroy was well liked and brought to formal affairs an unusual degree of warmth. Two former First Ladies often graced Mrs. McElroy's well-ordered teas —Julia Gardiner Tyler and Harriet Lane Johnston, belles of the forties and fifties respectively. On State occasions, as many as forty ladies of position were frequently invited to receive with Mrs. McElroy, thus putting down any complaints concerning precedence.

Mrs. McElroy often acted as a buffer between the President and those he did not wish to deal with, and she helped him retain some semblance of private life. Arthur was frequently seen dining at private homes in Washington. Daily he went for an airing in his dark-green landau "picked out in red," and drawn by a pair of mahogany bays. These numerous appearances in public and at social functions, both in Washington and Newport, along with his easygoing manner, fostered the belief that the President did little but play.

Since Arthur had enemies in all quarters, gossip about him was constant during his four years in the White House. The talk usually dwelt on his extravagance with public funds, his frivolity and foppishness, and quite often on some new infatuation. The ladies supposed to be romantically linked with the President covered a wide range in both age and quality. Perhaps the strangest name to be connected with Arthur's was that of Frances Willard, a passionate temperance leader—very strange in view of the fact that Arthur's high color was often attributed to too many visits to the punch bowl.

Even without gossip, Arthur's chances for renomination were slight, for with his old friends, the Stalwarts, turned against him, he finished out his term without even a faction to support him. Arthur had paid dearly for his four elegant years in the White House.

Entrance from the east.

President Grover Cleveland.

8	Grover Cleveland	1885 - 1889
	Benjamin Harrison	1889 - 1893
	Grover Cleveland	1893 - 1897
	William McKinley	1897 - 1901

A walk through the mansion

THE RESULTS of the Cleveland-Blaine contest were not announced until three days after the election. It had been a campaign marked by exposures of scandal on both sides. A Buffalo newspaper had uncovered an old story about Cleveland's illegitimate son; for a while it looked as if he would not be able to survive this damaging revelation. Fortunately for Cleveland, his opponent also had a tarnished reputation from his connections with some old railroad scandals. Blaine's woefully mismanaged pre-election campaign also turned over to Cleveland large blocks of votes he had not expected .

Cleveland could not have approached his office with more humility. Once in the White House he set to work with an ardor and efficiency completely in keeping with his excellent record as reform Mayor of Buffalo and Governor of New York State.

The world of society did not expect very much from the White House after Grover Cleveland took possession of it. His reputation as a blunt man of practical leanings had preceded him, and although he was not the boorish, beer-swilling plebeian his enemies delighted in picturing, it was true he did not enjoy large social gatherings and would have avoided them althogether if possible. But the White House, he felt, should represent a high level of taste and decorum, and he was fortunate in having his younger sister, Rose Cleveland, as hostess to help establish it.

Rose was eminently qualified to maintain a tone of dignity and refinement in the White House. A former teacher in private schools for young ladies and an experienced lecturer, she was most at home with people of intellect and background. She was said to have appeared a bit formidable to certain Congressional wives from the backward areas of the country, and this was scarcely remarkable for one of her scholarly attainments. It was said that she dared to relieve the boredom of long stretches of handshaking by conjugating Greek verbs as she stood smiling in a receiving line. During her first summer in the White House there

Albert Hawkins, a figure at the White House from the days of Grant, drives outgoing President Arthur and Cleveland to the inaugural exercises.

133

appeared a little volume called *George Eliot's Poetry and Other Studies* of which she was the author. Her essays demonstrated a strong feminist view, a profound belief in the potentialities of the female mind and soul.

In general there was no fault to be found with Rose Cleveland's style as hostess in the White House, although her brother was irked by her attitude toward the serving of wines, which was almost as severe as that of Mrs. Hayes. Wines continued to be served at the White House and Rose carried out her arduous duties through Cleveland's first season.

By June of 1886, Miss Cleveland's services were no longer needed and she returned to the old home place in Holland Patent, New York, and to her writing. In that month there took place in the White House a totally unprecedented event: the stout, middle-aged bachelor President took as his bride the lovely Frances Folsom of Buffalo.

It was no sudden romance that transformed the beautiful twenty-three-year-old girl into the country's First Lady. Frances Folsom was the daughter of Oscar Folsom, Cleveland's former law partner in Buffalo. Cleveland had known Frances from babyhood, had helped, in fact, to buy her first baby carriage. When Folsom was killed in the summer of 1875, Cleveland became administrator of the estate and took a keen interest in the welfare of his friend's widow and twelve-year-old daughter. Considering himself Frances's guardian, Cleveland had written her and sent her flowers through her college years and had arranged her European trip when she graduated from Wells College in 1885. Cleveland always called her by her nickname, Frank.

The President himself wrote out short invitations to the wedding, which was scheduled for the evening of June 2. At 5:30 in the morning of her wedding day, Frances Folsom, accompanied by her mother and a cousin, arrived at the railroad station in Washington and was met by Rose Cleveland. At eight o'clock they were breakfasting in the family dining room.

Even on his wedding day President Cleveland changed his routine very little. While he labored as usual on pressing problems, a crew of florists turned the Blue Room into a bower as a setting for the wedding ceremony. Amid banks of roses and pansies were floral monograms of the bride and groom and the date of the wedding spelled out in flowers. In the fireplaces there blazed masses of fire-red begonias, fancifully simulating the glow of an open flame.

The curiosity about the young bride was intense. The White House grounds were crowded long before the hour of the ceremony, and at 7 P.M. the gathered crowd heard John Philip Sousa lead the Marine Band in the strains of the Mendelssohn wedding march.

The President and Frances Folsom appeared on the grand stairway unattended. A society writer present, awestruck by the dexterity with which Miss Folsom handled the fifteen-foot-long train, wrote: "The train was a marvel of graceful arrangement, and it was marvelous how she handled it in a small well-filled room, for it was nearly as long as the room itself and would have reached easily, during the ceremony, from the spot

Thomas Nast comments on the bachelor in the White House.

134

Statuesque Frances Folsom Cleveland in
formal attire, which was so becoming.

Two great weeklies, Leslie's and, below, Harper's, pictured the Folsom-Cleveland wedding in much the same way but with striking differences in the bridal gown.

where the vows were pledged into the corridor through which the bridal party had come, but for the bride's deft management, whereby it lay in a glistening coil at her feet." As the short marriage ceremony came to an end a salute of twenty-one guns roared in the distant Navy yard, and church bells sounded throughout the city.

The Cleveland honeymoon was made miserable by the prying of newspaper reporters. Every move in the Maryland resort where the President and his bride had gone to spend a few days was written up and sent to the large Eastern newspapers. Newshawks armed with spyglasses settled down in an open pavilion near their rented cottage and waited for the bride and groom to appear. So enraged was Cleveland that he wrote a long letter denouncing sensational journalism and permitted it to be published in the New York newspapers.

136

Mrs. Cleveland continued to be hounded by reporters and to be the center of enthusiasm whenever she appeared in public. When the youthful First Lady appeared at her first Saturday afternoon reception, so much excitement was generated that a panic resulted. Crowds did not move on as systematically as necessary under such conditions. Several hysterical females were the center of a disturbance when they decided to turn back for a second look at Mrs. Cleveland's lovely face and charming gown. Caught up in the maelstrom of the mass reception, they could neither come nor go, lost their bearings altogether and rushed headlong into a screen of palms behind which the red-coated Marine Band was sheltered. White House guards had to be called to restore order.

By 1886 the proportions of the public reception were completely out of hand. At some affairs the President and Mrs. Cleveland might shake hands with six or eight thousand callers and the crowds would stand four abreast outside the White House entrance patiently waiting to enter. Sometimes the First Lady would have to have her arms massaged, even the left arm aching after the strain of shaking so many hands.

Life at the White House was brightened remarkably by the advent of Mrs. Cleveland. Her unaffected charm warmed the atmosphere at the routine receptions and was a delight at the luncheons and teas where there was more time to spend with her. Mrs. Cleveland usually gave two receptions each week, one of them on Saturday afternoon so that working women, employed during the week, could meet her.

As Cleveland's administration wore on, the Clevelands tended to spend more and more time at Oak View—or Red Top, as the newspapers dubbed it—the country place which the President had bought just before his marriage. It was a comfortable old farm near Georgetown, well stocked with animals and having a kitchen garden and coachhouse. Best of all it commanded a magnificent view of the city and the Potomac.

In the close political contest of 1888 Cleveland lost to the Republican candidate, Benjamin Harrison, grandson of William Henry Harrison. Cleveland's delayed low tariff message, his poorly organized campaign, and every conceivable kind of political fraud on the part of his opponents contributed to his defeat, as did a whispering campaign based on Cleveland's alleged drunkenness and brutality toward his wife, even to the point of his driving her out of the White House into a storm.

Cleveland took his defeat with the greatest calm. In reality he looked forward to a period of rest and change and freedom from the eternal grind of public duty. For the first time since his early youth he faced a time of comparative leisure and quiet.

Clearly Mrs. Cleveland was in a different mood when she left the White House. As she said good-by to the servants on March 4, she gave some definite and unusual orders to an old Negro servant, Jerry Smith: "Now, Jerry, I want you to take good care of all the furniture and ornaments in the house, for I want to find everything just as it is now when we come back again. For we are coming back just four years from today." That her prediction was correct is a matter of history.

Oak View, the country home of the President and Mrs. Cleveland during his first term.

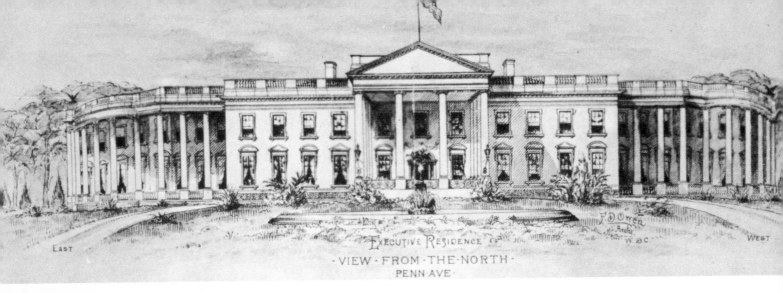

The north and south fronts of the most complex of
Mrs. Harrison's three plans for an enlarged White House.

Mrs. Benjamin Harrison was not the first First Lady with a large family to complain about the discomforts of living in the White House while it was used also as a public building for official business. She was the first, however, to come forth with detailed ideas for correcting the situation. The only solution, she said, was a new Executive Mansion, and that was exactly what she intended to have. Mrs. Harrison went to work on her campaign for a new White House soon after President Harrison took office.

Perhaps Mrs. Harrison's rigorous background had much to do with her ability to act with authority. The daughter of the President of Oxford Female Seminary in Ohio, she had led an active public life with her lawyer husband long before he entered politics. During Harrison's Civil War services, she had visited the war camps, ready to take over any duties of

138

nursing and feeding soldiers for which she was needed; she had become flexible and efficient under the necessities of the times.

In the White House Mrs. Harrison did not limit her building campaign to a single plan; three were drawn up by the architect, Fred D. Owen, with Mrs. Harrison's aid. One plan was for a separate residence to be built on Sixteenth Street. Another was for minor additions to the White House as it stood. But the third commanded considerable attention.

Using the White House as a starting point, the grandiose design called for a wide range of structures to be erected around a hollow square. To the west would stretch the "official wing," attached to the Executive Mansion by corridors and a rotunda to be filled with statuary. To the east would lie its counterpart, the "historical art wing," or national wing. Across the southern base of the White House grounds there was drawn a huge conservatory for foliage plants and flowers, with circular palm houses at each end to match the rotundas of the wings. In the court thus provided, there would stand an allegorical fountain, commemorating Christopher Columbus's discovery of America, and the laying of the White House cornerstone exactly three hundred years later.

An architectural writer, no doubt bearing in mind that delight of the era, the formal stroll, wrote approvingly of the whole project: "The entire tour of this uninterrupted series of salons, anterooms, corridors, rotundas, conservatories and winter garden . . . would afford for the comfort and enjoyment of the throng of distinguished guests a promenade of 1,200 feet from point of departure, making the entire circuit, thus avoiding the confusion of returning by the same way." Mrs. Harrison greatly desired to have the building completed in time for the centennial of the White House on October 13, 1892.

Fortunately, in the opinion of many, the campaign for a new White House got nowhere at all; but it did have at least one champion in the person of Senator Stanford of California. Stanford planned to bring his bill favoring Mrs. Harrison's plans before the Senate on the morning of March 4, 1891, and spent the night before in the Senate Cloak Room, expecting to have the bill brought to him after it had been passed by the House. The measure failed to pass in the House, however, and Speaker Reed later told Senator Stanford why. President Harrison had not appointed Reed's candidate to the Collectorship of the Port of Portland, Maine; Reed could not therefore be expected to do anything for the Harrison family. On such a small political blunder did the fate of the White House hang, at least for a while. It was to have other narrow escapes later on.

Although the exterior of the White House remained the same under the Harrisons, dramatic changes took place indoors. Methodical extermination of rats was undertaken; the engine room was rebuilt; the old, rotting floor boards, five layers of them in some places, were removed from the ground floor and new floors laid. The kitchens were modernized and the greenhouses rebuilt and enlarged. Most important of all, electric lights and bells were installed throughout the White House.

The capable, busy Mrs. Harrison.

The smiling boy is Baby McKee, much-publicized child of the White House.

139

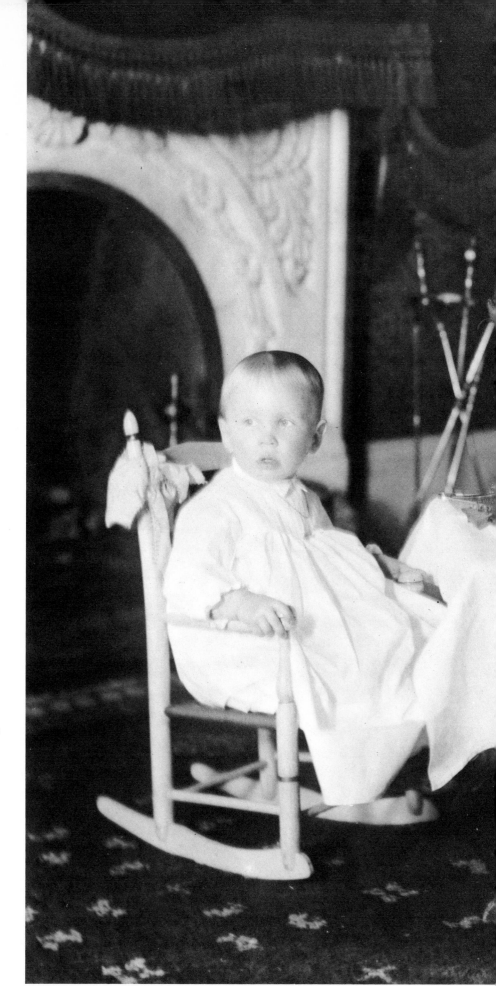

The President's
grandchildren,
Baby McKee,
Marthena Harrison,
and Mary McKee,
in the upstairs nursery
with their nurse.

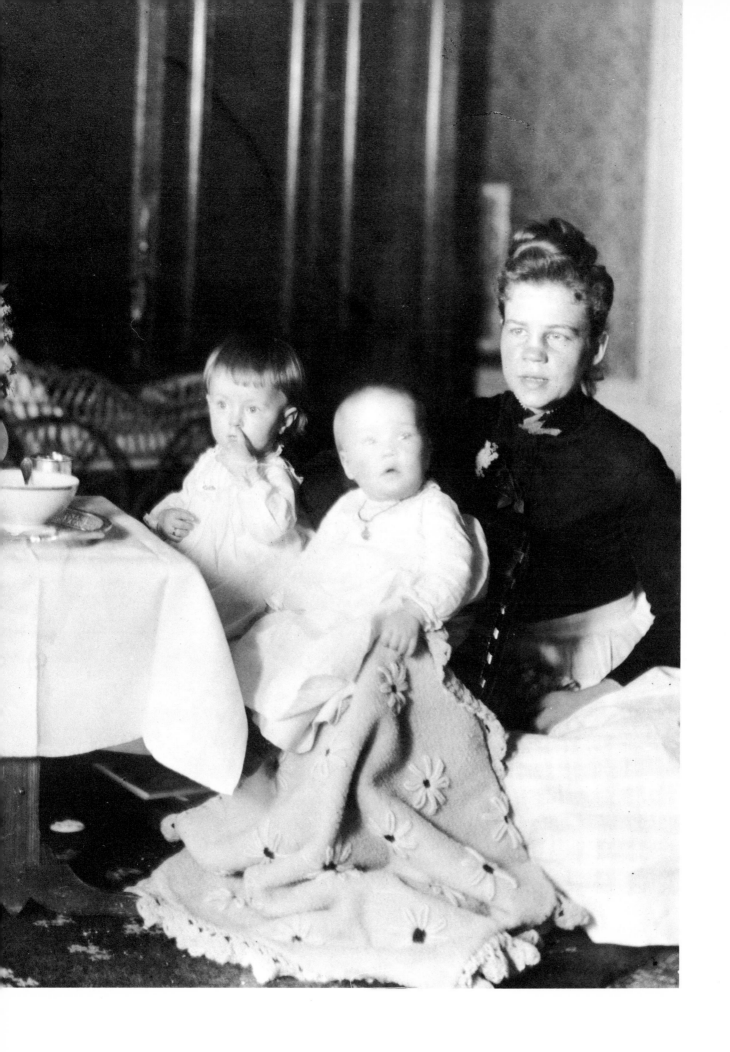

President Harrison with his daughter,
Mary Harrison McKee, and his grandson.

Mrs. McKee, young and dignified
in a then-fashionable "boa."

When the job of wiring the White House was begun in May, 1891, some help was requested of the Edison Electric Company. The company sent Ike Hoover, who, coming into the Executive Mansion as an electrician on a temporary job, stayed for forty-two years and acted as chief usher from Taft's tenure to that of Franklin D. Roosevelt. In his book *Forty-two Years in the White House*, Hoover remembered how the White House had looked to his youthful eyes: "In the kitchen of the original house . . . could be seen the old open fireplaces once used for broiling the chickens and baking the hoecakes for the early Fathers of our country, the old cranes and spits still in place. Out of the door to the rear there yet remained the old winevault, the meathouse, and the smokehouse. . . . The west wing was hidden almost wholly by the old conservatory where the couples would roam during parties and be lost among the tall palms and ferns! Here were all the funny kinds of plants and the tropical fruit trees whose dwarf fruit we were all so proud of. There were bananas, oranges, lemons, figs and nuts of various kinds. . . ."

The wiring of the White House took over four months. The gas chandeliers throughout the house were converted into combination lights, burning either gas or electricity, and an elaborate bell system was placed throughout the house, replacing the mechanical system of wires and pulleys hitherto used to summon the servants.

The Harrisons were eager for the new lighting to be finished, but once it was installed and the current went on, they did not trust the magic

142

A family group snapped on the south lawn.

Baby McKee directs an imaginary band.

stuff, and, afraid of getting a shock from a switch, continued to use the gas lights. Hoover, himself, would turn on the lights in the downstairs rooms at dusk and on his return to the White House the following morning would find them still burning.

Mrs. Harrison loved the conservatories and especially the orchid house, where she would spend long periods gazing at the blooms. Since she was quite proficient at china painting, one of her many hobbies, she enjoyed combining two interests and often painted orchids on china plates.

Mrs. Harrison's interest in china was not entirely frivolous, for it was she who first thought the china used by past Presidents to be of some historical value. She became interested when she was having a new china closet installed, and a collection of the better pieces from the Monroe to the Cleveland eras was begun under her guidance.

When President and Mrs. Harrison came to the White House they brought along a considerable entourage. Most of the time a son, Russell Harrison, and a daughter, Mrs. J. R. McKee, with their families occupied some of the rooms. Even nieces and nephews came for long stays. Mrs. Harrison's elderly father lived with the Harrisons until his death toward the end of the President's term in office. Another relative was Mrs. Mary Scott Dimmick, a niece of Mrs. Harrison's, who was her secretary. Mrs. Dimmick, an attractive young widow, was destined to become the second Mrs. Benjamin Harrison some time after the White House was far behind.

The most publicized member of the household was Benjamin Harrison McKee, always called Baby McKee, the small son of the Harrison's only daughter. Along with his sister Mary, and his cousin, Marthena Harrison, Baby McKee occupied the nursery in Nellie Grant's old room. Publicity stemming from the White House built up the relationship between the President and his grandson as one of remarkable proportions and presented the two as inseparable companions; actually, according to Ike Hoover, the two were seldom together.

In the summer of 1892 Mrs. Harrison became hopelessly ill. After her death that autumn, the sorrowing family spent its last months in the White House impatiently waiting to leave the scene of their grief. In March Harrison welcomed into the Executive Mansion the same man who had seen him take residence four years before. Mrs. Cleveland's prediction had come true; the Clevelands had returned, just as happy to be there as the Harrison family was eager to leave.

Dash has his picture taken.

While Benjamin Harrison was living in the White House, picture-taking was fast becoming a popular hobby. In the above snapshots, two "sports" cover the 1889 Easter egg-rolling on the White House grounds with one of the first Eastman Brownies. It was simple to take a perfect picture. All you had to do, according to the little folder of directions which accompanied the new Kodak, was: "Point the camera, push the button, turn the key, and pull the cord." The factory would do all the rest. Then, as later, there were certain subjects which appealed strongly to the amateur. High on the list were pretty girls, children, crowds, the photographer holding his camera, and, of course, the White House.

Professionals, too, were taking pictures. This photograph of a wet holiday
crowd in the park south of the White House, with the Washington Monument
rising in the background, was made by Frances Benjamin Johnston. Miss
Johnston, the first important woman news photographer, between 1889 and
1901 also took the thirty or so pictures which follow. They represent the best
photographic coverage ever to be made of the old White House—which stood
from 1817 to 1902 with only minor changes in its appearance. The pictures,
many of which have never been published before, have the unique quality
of suggesting to the viewer that he is taking a stroll through the White
House in the 1890s, and can best be looked at with that in mind.

A White House watchman and watchdog with their respective houses, at the south entrance.

Russell Harrison, the Harrison grandchildren, and two of the family's menagerie make an appealing group on the south grounds of the White House.

Mrs. Russell Harrison with two of the three White House babies.

White House messenger service
was more picturesque than speedy.

A policeman and staff members
pose manfully on the north porch.

More of the White House
staff, at the main entrance.

Visitors "hold it" for the photographer.

The table in the State Dining Room is adorned with the surtout de table from the days of Monroe.

Potted plants add a homey note to the profusion of velvet, fringe, screens, and floral patterns in the Red Room of the nineties.

Close-up of the Red Room fireplace.

The Blue Room in its most ornate period.

The steamboat-palace décor of the
East Room in 1893. Frances Benjamin
Johnston photographed it in a wide
range of circumstances. Above, the
big room appears icily formal, and below, it
is luxuriantly decorated for a wedding.
At right, in use as a reception hall.

The office staircase, so well trodden by favor-seekers.

One of the upstairs offices which occupied the space coveted by First Ladies. Below, a telegrapher sits at his machine amid cramped executive quarters.

Major Lewis of the White House police.

A crowded office in the days

...ectric light was new.

The Cabinet Room on the second floor.

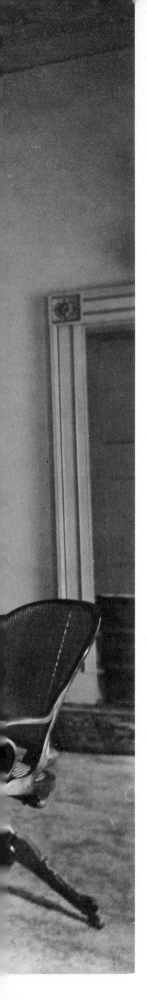

The upstairs Oval Room in use as an office for the President,
and below, the same room, furnished as a family sitting room for the Harrisons.

The northwest corner bedroom.

The State Bedroom in the Harrison era.

A workman in the basement.

Old Jerry displays his feather duster.

The conservatories, which leaned against the White House. Below, an interior view.

The East entrance
of the White House.

IN SPITE OF their elation at being back in the White House, the Clevelands probably spent less time there, during their second stay, than any other Presidential family. They were off to their rented suburban house on Woodley Lane as soon as the weather was fine, driving into town for a few hours each day. Their summers were spent in Maine.

There were good reasons for the insistence upon privacy during the early part of Cleveland's second term. The President had always looked upon the prying of newspaper reporters with loathing, and in 1893, the year of the panic, there were new grounds for seclusion when it was discovered that Cleveland was suffering from cancer, localized in the roof of his mouth. It was decided to keep Cleveland's illness a secret, and the details of the operation that followed—to remove the President's entire left upper jaw—were so carefully carried out that the public and indeed many of Cleveland's close friends did not know about it for twenty-five years. A yacht putting to sea from New York harbor with a full quota of surgeons served as hospital. Sitting upright in a chair propped against a mast, Cleveland went through the ordeal with magnificent fortitude, endured a long period of convalescence, and emerged to carry on his arduous duties once more.

The Clevelands were particularly harassed by the amount of attention paid their only child, Ruth, who had been born in New York. While at first it was possible to take the baby for an airing on the White House grounds, before long an inquisitive crowd began to gather whenever the nurse and her charge appeared out of doors. One day Mrs. Cleveland found that the crowd had taken over, and while a distraught nursemaid stood by helpless, the baby was being fondled by strangers who were passing her around as if she were a toy.

The White House gates were closed and gossip began that the baby was half-witted and deaf and dumb. Tales of her supposedly malformed ears were passed around. The Clevelands began to spend more and more time at the Woodley Lane house.

A second daughter, Esther, was born that fall, the first time a child had been born to a President in the White House.

During his second administration, Cleveland received so many threatening letters that his wife became alarmed for his safety. The President took her advice and increased his Secret Service force from three to twenty-seven, with extra guards brought in for large public gatherings. It was a vast change from the days when President Benjamin Harrison had strolled where he pleased, day or night, without protection. As a Washington newspaper put it, "Mr. Cleveland not only keeps off the sidewalks, but seldom goes driving, and when he is seen abroad in one of the White House carriages, he is under the protection of two detectives, who follow in another vehicle."

Since the Clevelands spent so much time in their private house, the question of better arrangements in the White House was not so urgent as

168

Inevitably there was a new plan for enlarging the White House.

it had been for the large Harrison family. Nevertheless, by the year 1896 full plans for proposed additions to the White House had been prepared. They attracted as much attention as though they were a brand-new idea.

The architects of the Cleveland plan provided a wing for social affairs and a wing for offices, leaving the original White House for residential quarters. Uninspired as the project was, it won approbation from *Harper's Weekly:* "The point is this, that it is perfectly proper to take the White House and extend it in length, using all the motifs that it possesses, and to create a perfect architectural composition. . . . It seems that in placing so large a space around the White House. . . , the original projectors of it must have conceived the very plan that is here presented . . . the fact is that we have before us the very soul and substance from which to frame as beautiful a building as the Capitol or the Treasury."

The Cleveland campaign for additions to the White House fortunately got no further than that of Mrs. Harrison.

On their last evening in the White House the Clevelands entertained the incoming President, William McKinley, at dinner. McKinley arrived alone since Mrs. McKinley had suffered an attack of her malady, epilepsy, at the last moment and was unable to come. Cleveland was deeply impressed by McKinley's earnestness and awareness of the responsibilities of the office he was ready to assume. They talked about what most people were talking about—the threat of war with Spain.

In a thoroughly domestic scene, Frances Cleveland writes at her desk in an upstairs sitting room.

169

*At William McKinley's inauguration his wife and
mother sit directly in front of the speaker's stand.*

The threat of war and then war itself were to dominate the entire
McKinley administration. Cuba's uprising against the tyrannical rule of
Spain had already aroused deep feeling throughout the United States and
had focused attention on Spain's brutal treatment of Cuba and the Philippines. For over a year McKinley stood firmly against intervention. Pres-
sures brought to bear on him by Congress, certain members of his own
Cabinet, the press, and public opinion left McKinley sad and oppressed.

Some of McKinley's mental agony over his responsibility was evidenced
in the story told by his old friend, H. H. Kohlsaat. Kohlsaat, on a visit to
the White House, was talking with the President on the South Porch when
McKinley spoke of "being forced" into declaring war on Spain. "As he
said this," Kohlsaat reported, "he broke down and wept as I have never
seen anyone weep in my life. His whole body was shaken with convulsive
sobs. . . . He asked me when we got into the light if his eyes were red,
and I told him they were, but if he blew his nose very hard just as we
entered where the others were, the redness of his eyes would be attributed
to that cause."

Events were taken out of the President's hands when on the evening of
February 15, 1898, the United States' battleship *Maine* was blown up while
lying in the harbor of Havana. The heavy loss of lives sent a wave of fury
across the country: Congressmen threatened to go over the President's

170

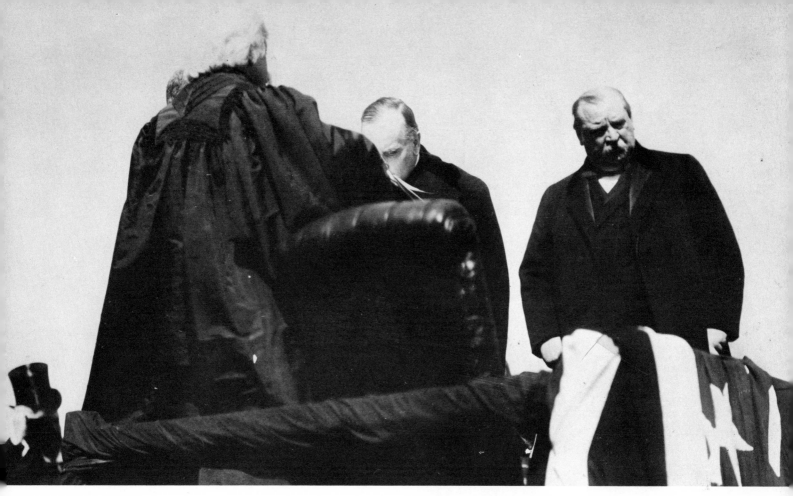

*McKinley kisses the Bible at his inaugural
exercises, as Cleveland stands by.*

head and act without his approval. The entire nation was on the warpath. McKinley at last was forced to declare war on Spain. The young and combative Assistant Secretary of the Navy, Theodore Roosevelt, who had been urging the President to declare war, was satisfied and was soon organizing his famous Rough Riders.

The conduct of the war found McKinley spending the day and much of the night in his White House office, in conference with a stream of officials from the War and Navy departments. If he had a free moment he spent it in the map rooms next to his office, where tiny flags stuck into wall maps showed the positions of each land and sea campaign. McKinley followed every move made by the American forces. He was on hand when word came that Admiral George Dewey, the commander of the Asiatic fleet, had sailed into Manila Bay, destroyed the Spanish fleet, and taken the harbor of Manila. He was standing by for news when in July word came of the naval victory off the shores of Santiago de Cuba which meant the war was near its end.

The peace protocols of August and the treaties that followed brought the United States new responsibilities in the form of Puerto Rico and other islands in the West Indies. The Philippines became colonial duties of the United States. A young judge from Ohio was sent out to the Philippines to set up a civil government; his name was William Howard Taft.

171

President McKinley as photographed by Frances Benjamin Johnston.

Miss Johnston's portrait of Mrs. McKinley.

The McKinley bedroom.

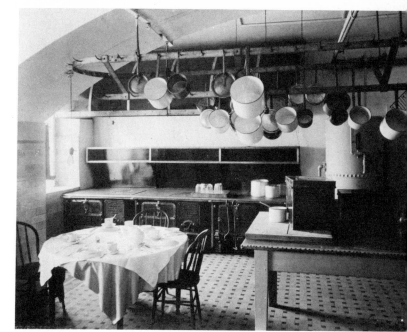

The kitchen.

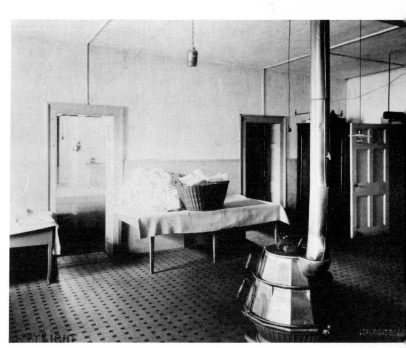

The laundry.

McKinley dictates to his secretary, John Addison Porter.

Added to his worry over the war was McKinley's constant concern over Mrs. McKinley's health. An invalid for many years, she took no part in the running of the White House but was, because of the nervous condition accompanying her frequent attacks of epilepsy, entirely dependent upon her husband for companionship. She ate her meals alone in the upstairs sitting room, but unless completely indisposed often attended the larger social functions. The President had had matters arranged so that she always sat at his right at the table. If an epileptic seizure came on, a handkerchief or napkin was thrown over her face until she was herself again. She did not faint but sat rigidly in her chair until the attack subsided.

Nothing was permitted to separate the McKinleys for more than a few hours at a time. The busy President would often slip away from an important meeting to see how his wife was faring. "To her he is far more than a perfect man," wrote a friend of Mrs. McKinley's. "He is divine."

His devoted treatment of his wife was typical of McKinley's kindness and courtesy. Ike Hoover wrote of him: "It was his one idea in life to make those around him feel he was their friend." McKinley's tact and grace when meeting callers at the White House was made much of in *McClure's Magazine* in an article published in 1898. In a private room on the second floor of the White House McKinley might find waiting for him a large cross-section of American citizens, each with his special problem and request.

The map room next to the President's office.

Coaches wait for guests to emerge from a New Year's reception.

"He moves from one to another, as it pleases him, shaking hands with each," wrote the correspondent for *McClure's*. "His hand grasp is quite up to date; he holds his hand high and touches the ends of the fingers rather than clasps the palm. He is a most interesting figure as he stands with his left hand in his trousers pocket, pushing back the skirt of his long coat and slowly whirling his eye-glasses in his right hand.

"As the President passes about the room from one group of visitors to another, he takes in, from the corner of his eye, everybody who is waiting for him. His quick side glance is one of the most interesting things about his calm, immovable face; he sees everything in going about the room, though only a keen observer would notice that he saw anything."

In his 1898 message to Congress, McKinley spoke of erecting some "handsome, permanent memorial" for the capital's Centennial Celebration in 1900. This was the cue for yet another campaign to rebuild and expand the White House. This time the scheme was in the hands of Colonel Theodore A. Bingham, McKinley's Superintendent of Public Buildings and Grounds.

As the initial event of the Centennial fete, on December 12, 1900, a model of the projected improvements was shown in the East Room of the White House before a distinguished gathering. Although the model was actually a revised plan from the days of Mrs. Harrison, the showing was successful; everything seemed to be going well for Colonel Bingham.

On the day following Bingham's victory, however, the American Institute of Architects, calling the model a monstrosity, passed two resolutions. One recommended that no changes should be made until a commission of architects had examined the plans. The second urged that the city go back to the L'Enfant plan and that Congress should set up a commission for that purpose. The white House remained unchanged.

President McKinley was scheduled to speak at the Pan American Exposition in Buffalo, New York, in September, 1901, the first autumn of his second term in office. In Buffalo on the late afternoon of September 6, Mrs. McKinley was resting after the trip, at the home of the Exposition president, and McKinley was greeting the public at the Buffalo Music Hall, as part of the preliminaries to his speech. In the line approaching the President stood a commonplace-looking young man, his right hand bandaged in a handkerchief, making it necessary for him to extend his left to the President. As the President shook his hand the man fired two shots point-blank at the President from the gun hidden in the bandage. His name was Leon Czolgosz and he was later termed a follower of Karl Marx.

President McKinley's concern for others was evidenced even at the moment when he had been fatally shot. "My wife—be careful, Cortelyou, how you tell her!" he begged his secretary. He then asked bystanders not to harm his attacker. For a week McKinley lay between life and death.

Theodore Roosevelt, Vice President of the United States, was characteristically indulging in strenuous exercise when word reached him that

178

*A picture of President McKinley taken fifteen minutes
before he was shot, on the afternoon of September 6, 1901.*

President McKinley was thought to be dying. On that September day,
Roosevelt, on vacation in the Adirondack mountains of New York, had
climbed to the summit of Mount Marcy with a party of friends. On the
return hike a messenger handed Roosevelt a telegram. It came from Secretary of War Elihu Root and read: THE PRESIDENT APPEARS TO BE DYING,
AND MEMBERS OF THE CABINET IN BUFFALO THINK YOU SHOULD LOSE
NO TIME IN COMING.

It was nearly dark when Roosevelt reached his cottage. Other telegrams
repeated the tragic news. One said that a special train was waiting for Roosevelt at North Creek, thirty-five miles away.

Later that night a horse-drawn buckboard tore along the rain-washed
mountain roads toward the railroad station. At breakneck speed a series
of drivers and horses drove Roosevelt relay-fashion over the pitch-black
roads on the first lap of his trip to Buffalo.

On reaching the station at dawn, Roosevelt sent his wife a one-line
telegram: PRESIDENT MCKINLEY DIED AT 2:15 THIS MORNING.

That evening, in a private house in Buffalo, Theodore Roosevelt took
the oath of office in the presence of McKinley's Cabinet.

179

President Theodore Roosevelt strides jauntily down the street for an early newsreel camera.

Gentle ladies and stubborn men

The American public was astonished and then entranced when President Theodore Roosevelt staged a Chinese wrestling match in the elegant old East Room. It looked on, further amused, when the President, interested in the relative merits of conventional wrestling and jujitsu as a means of protecting oneself, arranged a contest between an American wrestler and a Japanese jujitsu artist. The vision of two muscle men sweating and grunting before Cabinet officers, Senators, and a President of the United States was diverting even to a nation already familiar with the eccentricities of the young President.

Roosevelt on the south lawn with one of the many White House pets.

The White House was a lively place under the regime of Theodore and Mrs. Roosevelt and their six children, who ranged from the seventeen-year-old Alice to Quentin, the baby of the family. Although Theodore, Jr., was usually away at school, Archie, Kermit, and Ethel were noisy youngsters who considered the White House a superb setting for their fun. The upstairs corridor was ideal for roller skating, and the high-ceilinged rooms were perfect for walking on stilts. In time, as the children drenched each other in water fights or jumped over the satin upholstered furniture, it all came to seem perfectly normal to the White House employees.

New pets were constantly appearing, for the Roosevelts were all attracted by animals. The zoo got some of them, but even so whole menageries were collected and pampered. Dogs, cats, a black bear, and a kangaroo rat which Archie liked to carry in his pocket—to the horror of some squeamish persons—formed the backbone of the animal collection. A calico pony named Algonquin was a great favorite; once when Archie was ill with measles, the pony was smuggled into the basement and taken upstairs in the elevator. This was considered a sure cure for Archie.

When Quentin became old enough he was sent to a public school, and it was there that he found the half-dozen friends who romped with him through the White House. Parts of the house no one had seen in years rang with their shouts and laughter. From the flagpole on the roof to the basement

181

Roll-call of the White House police . . . including Archie and Quentin.

President and Mrs. Roosevelt, with all the children,
at the summer White House, Sagamore Hill, in 1903.

every corner was explored by the White House Gang, as it was called. Their favorite haunt was the attic, huge, rambling and filled with mysterious boxes and trunks from another era. An imagined ghost or two made it all even more hilarious.

Often when the President, after a day in the Executive Office, joined in the roughhousing, the commotion would become too much for Mrs. Roosevelt, who would take a book and disappear into her sitting room. She possessed a great talent for letting each member of her family develop his own individuality.

Mrs. Roosevelt, the former Edith Kermit Carow, had been brought up according to the strictest moral and social rules and the behavior of all who entered the White House had to conform with her standards. She acted as hostess at hundreds of social events, all of which found the same calm, poised, smiling lady, charming everyone with her natural manner.

The President's wife also directed the well-known Tuesday morning meetings of the Cabinet wives when the female connections of the Roosevelt inner circle gathered in the Green Room. While the ladies knitted or embroidered, the fine points of protocol were made clear and personalities and reputations rather deeply explored.

Theodore Roosevelt truly believed that everyone in the world needed more exercise. One of his favorite forms of exertion was the long tramp, a sport long popular at Sagamore Hill, the Roosevelt summer home at Oyster Bay, Long Island. On these jaunts Roosevelt and his party would make a beeline for some point four or five miles distant, the objective being not merely to arrive at the point, but to cross any hurdle that lay in the path, whether it was haystack, fence, river, or mountain. On one occasion the group was seen clambering over a beach house.

In the city the President's walking companions on his obstacle hikes were usually his close associates or sometimes a foreign ambassador, often very dignified gentlemen, who were used to nothing more taxing than climbing into carriages. Roosevelt, still much younger than the average Congressman or Cabinet officer, seemed to enjoy the sufferings of his victims.

From fencing to medicine ball the President went through his paces daily. Lawn tennis was his favorite game and for this he could choose as his partner any of fifty or so Cabinet members, ambassadors, Army men, or personal aides. The men most often called upon formed a group known as Roosevelt's Tennis Cabinet. Roosevelt enjoyed selecting his opponent for the game. When he was feeling unusually well he would take on an expert player and on his bad days one of the aides would be invited. Poor players were never asked to return.

A few months after the Roosevelts were settled in the White House Alice had her coming-out party. The newspapers treated her debut as though it were a national event, for the attractive volatile daughter of the President was already the darling of the country. Although Alice complained that the evening was flat because the guests had only fruit punch to drink, no party could have launched a more spectacular social career.

No princess was ever more feted and adored. Every move of Alice Roose-

183

Theodore Roosevelt, Jr., poses with one of the more exotic of the White House tenants.

Quentin with a friend.

velt's long day was examined and served up to the reading public. Her elegant tastes, her choice of clothes, friends, beaus, and her incredible social activities were subjects of interest across the nation and even in Europe. A French publication solemnly predicted a breakdown of her health unless she slowed down.

A few weeks after her debut, Alice widened her scope to include European royalty and enjoyed it thoroughly. The Emperor of Germany, long aware that his relations with America could benefit from personal cultivation, purchased a yacht, the *Meteor*, from an American shipbuilder and sent Prince Henry, his brother, to take possession of it. On February 24, 1902, the Prince came to the White House to meet the President. Late in the morning the Marine Band, stationed outside the White House, struck up a lively German tune, announcing the approach of a procession of carriages carrying the Prince and his suite. Between lines of saluting Marines, the party entered the Executive Mansion, traversed the Red Room, and passed into the East Room.

There then took place a series of moves which showed the height of social tact. There was no one in Washington of sufficiently high rank to present the Prince to the President of the United States, but a solution had been found. The Prince was ushered into the Green Room by an aide. At the same moment President Roosevelt stepped into the Blue Room. Immediately Prince Henry entered the Blue Room by another door and they introduced themselves. Later in the day the President repaid the call at the German Embassy.

No women were invited to the elaborate state dinner given in honor of the Prince that evening. At a crescent-shaped table set up in the East Room, important members of the State, Navy, and War departments

The President and the Prince introduce themselves in the Blue Room.

The stag dinner party for the German prince.

toasted the Prince, who sat at the President's right. His nautical leanings had been kept in mind when the decorations for the evening had been planned. Seafaring emblems in the form of stars, canopies, ropes, and anchors made of thousands of electric light bulbs swayed from the ceiling and from every window, mirror, and post in the great room. The menu, which was in French except for the wholly American item of hominy, displayed a picture of the *Meteor* along with flags of the two countries and American and German eagles. The next day in Jersey City, Alice smashed a bottle of champagne on the *Meteor's* bow, and it slid down the ways.

Theodore Roosevelt succeeded in carrying out the idea cherished by other White House residents, notably Mrs. Harrison, the Clevelands, and the McKinleys, of separating the living quarters from the executive offices, giving each enough space for comfort and future expansion. In the summer of 1902, the White House finally got its much needed enlargement. Extensions in the form of colonnaded one-story wings stretching east and west, much as they had been planned by Thomas Jefferson and his architect, Benjamin Latrobe, provided space for offices, cloakrooms, and storage rooms. The vacated areas on the second floor were turned into private rooms.

The architectural firm of McKim, Mead and White had the complicated job of transforming the White House. Charles F. McKim gave the interior a thorough going over before he decided just what improvements it would need. His report stated that for the sake of "comfort, safety and necessary sanitary conditions" the entire interior would have to be rebuilt. In early summer, therefore, the Roosevelts moved into a private home on Lafayette Square. Between June and November the old White House was treated to some dramatic changes.

Alice Roosevelt.

In 1902, the old greenhouses were torn down to make room for offices.

The ornate Tiffany screen installed by President Arthur
was removed from the vestibule.

Excavations were made for a new boiler room and conduits laid, as
part of the big job of replacing plumbing, heating, and electrical systems.

An Executive Wing replaced the rambling greenhouses.

By December, 1902, everything was ready for a second round of official social functions, beginning with a dinner for the Cabinet, which was actually an unveiling of the new White House interior. Reactions to the radical changes were mainly flattering; it was a mere gadget that aroused the most excitement. The ingenious device was the electrical "carriage call," a contrivance for summoning carriages when guests were ready to leave. A punch-card system which flashed out numbers in sequence corresponding with the importance of the visitors brought carriages rolling to the White House entrance with an alacrity never before seen.

Disputes over matters of social precedence were always expected in the White House. The President had each case written up for the social record and the instruction of future tenants. That no one was ever too famous to ignore rank was apparent when Admiral George Dewey took exception to the seating arrangements planned for a diplomatic dinner. Dewey, who had just been commissioned "Admiral of the Navy," felt that his position below the foreign ministers at the table was unfair. His argument was founded on the fact that he rated a seventeen-gun salute, while a foreign minister had to get along with fifteen. The Admiral did not win this particular battle.

In all the rooms modernization was the keynote.

187

*Alice, with her
father and new husband,
Nicholas Longworth.*

As the months went by and the next election approached, Theodore Roosevelt wanted more than ever to be elected to the Presidency in his own right, and by 1904 his accomplishments in office made his nomination and election practically certain. Although he was jubilant over his victory in November, an incident at the time of his inauguration moved him especially. On the night before the inaugural ceremonies, Secretary of State John Hay sent Roosevelt a present which he would cherish as long as he lived. It was a ring containing hair cut from President Lincoln's head on the night of his assassination. The ring was engraved with Roosevelt's and Lincoln's initials. Hay wrote, "Please wear it tomorrow. You are one of the men who most thoroughly understand and appreciate Lincoln."

Secretary Hay was a constant source of strength on which Roosevelt could draw when the going got difficult. Hay, who had been Lincoln's private secretary in his youth, had had a long and distinguished diplomatic career, which Lincoln had launched. On his way home from church on Sundays, it was Roosevelt's habit to visit John Hay in his house on Lafayette Square. The tie with Lincoln sustained and encouraged Roosevelt, who somehow felt that Lincoln's spirit still lived in the White House. To a friend he once wrote, "I think of Lincoln, shambling, homely, with his strong, sad, deeply-furrowed face, all the time. I see him in the different rooms and in the halls. For some reason or other he is to me infinitely the most real of the dead Presidents."

On Inauguration Day some of Roosevelt's beloved Rough Riders, who had fought with him in Cuba, rode in the inaugural parade. That evening they rode up to the White House portico and leaned from their saddles to shake hands with the thrilled President waiting on the steps.

In June, 1905, Secretary of War William Howard Taft and a large Congressional party were sent on a junket to the Orient. Alice Roosevelt went along, as did a young bachelor, Representative Nicholas Longworth of Ohio. His name had already been linked romantically with Alice's and the fact that they were both making the trip to the Far East lent interest to the stories reaching the United States. Rumors that they were engaged appeared almost daily in the newspapers. In Japan Alice was presented to the royal family and in China was received with great ceremony by the old Empress Dowager Tz'u Hsi. She returned home laden with gifts. Newspaper reporters had about given up on the engagement when the official announcement was released.

Preparations were begun weeks in advance of the wedding day. Presents poured into the White House from the highest and lowliest sources. A huge table encrusted with mosaic arrived as a gift from the King of Italy. The Republic of Cuba sent a string of precious pearls and the French Government a Gobelin tapestry. The Empress of China sent rolls of rare brocades, jewelry, and jade carvings. Freak presents came in large numbers—mousetraps, a barrel of popcorn, a box of snakes. The most inappropriate gifts of all, at least for Alice, were brooms, feather dusters, washing machines, and other household helps.

The wedding on February 17, 1906, put in the shade any White

For Alice's wedding, flowers were used sparingly in the East Room.

House event that anyone could recall. Not since Nelly Grant's wedding to a handsome Englishman more than a generation before had there been an occasion so exciting. The setting was one of austere elegance. An improvised altar stood on a platform at one end of the East Room. White satin ribbons roped off sections for the use of Cabinet members and the diplomatic corps, and formed an aisle leading from the State Dining Room to the altar. At exactly noon the bride, on her father's arm, walked down the aisle to wedding music played by the Marine Band. Although the groom had a best man, Alice shared the honors of the occasion only with her father. Her bridal veil was pinned firmly to a high pompadour and behind her swept six yards of silver brocade train. She carried a bouquet of orchids.

Nearly seven hundred guests had a close look at the lovely bride and later strolled through the Green Room, Red Room, and the Blue Room, all lavishly adorned with pink carnations, red roses, and Easter lilies. After the ceremony the bridal pair and the President stood on the platform and posed for official photographs. Alice had laid aside her bouquet of orchids but had retained her long white kid gloves.

There were actually two receptions after the wedding, one in the private dining room for the bridal party and close friends, the other in the State Dining Room. It was at the former that Alice, in the process of cutting her wedding cake, found the whole business much too slow and took action as only Alice would. She borrowed a sword from a gentleman in full military dress and sliced away with that. The White House was still riotous with celebration when the newlyweds left for their honeymoon, with the family waving from the South Portico.

189

". . . seven years in the White House without making a mistake," Archie Butt wrote of the charming Mrs. Roosevelt.

During Roosevelt's second term, Sagamore Hill continued to serve as a summer White House. Daily during the hot months, carriages and an occasional new-fangled motorcar wound their way slowly up the curving road, bringing diplomats, statesmen, or politicians to discuss weighty propositions at the dinner table or in the famous Trophy Room, which was adorned with buffalo heads and elk antlers, souvenirs of Roosevelt's Western hunts.

Warlike remarks meanwhile were emanating from Berlin, and relations between Japan and the United States were extremely touchy, with the Hearst press deliberately stirring up anti-Japanese feeling. European leaders regarded every Japanese move with suspicion. Roosevelt had built the Navy to a formidable strength and in 1907 he decided that a good look at the American fleet might have a staying effect on any militant power. In November of that year he saw the American battleship fleet steam out of Hampton Roads for the first leg of its voyage around the world.

In the spring of his final year in office, President Roosevelt took as his personal aide Archibald Butt, Southern gentleman and avid Roosevelt worshiper. Butt performed every conceivable White House duty, from arranging parties to acting as confidant to Mrs. Roosevelt. He also recorded, in long newsy letters to his mother and later to his sister-in-law, the daily doings of the White House. We get from Butt's letters, for example, a picture of Roosevelt's strong belief in the rightness of his selection of Taft and his later doubts about his choice of candidate.

In Butt's self-assumed role of chronicler of the Roosevelt family life,

he presented in detail the domestic problems of the President's wife. If Mrs. Roosevelt objected to discussions of prize fights during dinner, Archie Butt recorded the occasion with relish. If she reprimanded Kermit for eating with his elbows on the table, the incident went into a letter. Archie's admiration of Mrs. Roosevelt was summed up in his adoring phrase about her: ". . . seven years in the White House without making a mistake."

It was Archie Butt who acted as Mrs. Roosevelt's agent in settling an *affaire de coeur*. Gossip concerning the wife of a high official in Washington and a member of the diplomatic corps finally reached Mrs. Roosevelt and she acted with a firmness that surprised Butt. He was sent to talk to the erring lady and to give her a choice of ending the romance at once or of foregoing any further invitations to the White House. The affair came to an abrupt finish.

The Roosevelt administration was touched with glory when in February, 1909, the United States fleet returned to Hampton Roads, Virginia. According to Butt, Roosevelt at sight of the ships gave a shout of joy, exclaiming, "Here they are. That is the answer to my critics . . . I could not ask a finer concluding scene to my administration." And soon after, as he neared the actual end of his administration, he said, ". . . When you see me quoted in the press as welcoming the rest I will have after March the 3rd, take no stock in it for I will confess to you confidentially that I like the job. The burdens of this great nation . . . will be laid aside with a great deal of regret, for I have enjoyed every moment of this so-called arduous and exacting task."

Freezing weather sent the inaugural proceedings indoors on March 4, 1909.
Here, Roosevelt and Taft ascend the steps of the Capitol.

THE WEATHER BRIGHTENED and the sun shone on the Tafts as they arrived at the White House, and Mrs. Taft savored her husband's triumph as she entered the vestibule. She wrote of her first reaction: "I stood for a moment over the great brass seal, bearing the national coat of arms, which is sunk in the floor in the middle of the entrance hall. 'The Seal of the President of the United States,' I read around the border, and now—that meant my husband!"

For a more trivial reason, too, the day had been a pleasant one for Mrs. Taft. Two years before William Howard Taft became President, Theodore Roosevelt had said that after the next inauguration he would not observe the custom of riding back to the White House with the incoming President. Immediately after the inaugural ceremonies on March 4, Roosevelt said good-by to the Tafts. Since rules were being changed Mrs. Taft saw no reason why she should not contribute to the pattern and she blithely took Roosevelt's place in the carriage. In a becoming

192

President Taft at his desk. Taft believed quiet, concentrated work was the chief contributor to success in the White House.

costume of purple and mauve, and wearing an egret feather in her hat, Mrs. Taft happily set a precedent for other Presidential wives.

For Taft, however, a shadow lay over his entrance into the Presidency. Gossip about a crack in the Taft-Roosevelt friendship had already been heard before the inauguration. When the Roosevelts extended an invitation to the Tafts to spend the night of March 3 in the White House, their acceptance was considered an answer to malicious talk.

A rather small group attended a dinner in honor of the Tafts on the evening before the inauguration. Present, among others, were President Roosevelt's sister and her husband, Admiral W. S. Cowles, Alice and Nicholas Longworth, and Archie Butt. Archie Butt's services to the new administration had already begun when the Tafts came to Washington after a post-campaign vacation in the South, and under his efficient direction a new order was to go into immediate effect in the White House.

A housekeeper, Mrs. Elizabeth Jaffray, replaced the White House

The talented Taft family. President and Mrs. Taft with Charles, Helen, and Robert.

steward—since Mrs. Taft believed only a woman could cope with the job. The refurnished State Bedroom got twin beds and the Blue Room a Victor talking machine. The Oval Library was decorated with Oriental tapestries and teakwood furniture the Tafts had brought from the Far East. Mrs. Taft had vaults installed to hold the White House silver, formerly kept in old trunks, and a cow named Pauline Wayne was kept in the stables, with fresh milk for the White House kitchen twice a day.

Mrs. Taft encountered some criticism when she placed uniformed doormen at the main entrance of the White House. Six Negroes in blue livery spelled each other in receiving visitors and giving information. Visiting cards fell on their small silver trays instead of being collected by a policeman as before.

Less than a decade had passed since William Howard Taft had settled his wife and three children in Manila, where he was Civil Governor. The Tafts had loved the life in the Philippines and there was one feature of it Mrs. Taft wanted to transplant to Washington. This was the outdoor meeting place, an oval driveway with grandstands at each end for band concerts, called the Luneta. Mrs. Taft conceived the idea of turning a part of Potomac Park into such a spot, a place where on certain evenings band concerts would be given for the public. With Archie Butt's help the idea was successfully carried out, and there was a grand opening at which the President appeared on horseback. Concerts continued to be given at five o'clock on Wednesdays and Saturdays.

194

Pauline Wayne, the Taft cow, before the State-War-Navy Building.

During their first weeks in the White House, President and Mrs. Taft carried out an enormously heavy social schedule. The strain on both the President and his wife was serious, and for Mrs. Taft it had grave consequences. During an outing aboard the Presidential yacht, the *Mayflower*, she suffered a slight stroke and for over a year was unable to take part in social affairs. Her four sisters took turns coming to the White House to take over the duties of hostess.

Anxiety over his wife's illness and the pressure of work combined to make the conscientious President a harassed man. Butt said the President "would be about three years behind when the fourth of March, 1913, rolls around" unless he could speed up his program.

Butt himself was forced to go through some painful days. He missed what he called "the marvelous wit and gaiety" of the Roosevelts. At times he imagined that Taft missed Roosevelt even more than he did. "He always speaks of him as 'the President,'" wrote Butt to his sister-in-law a few days after Taft took over. To a friend Taft confided, "When I hear someone say Mr. President, I look around expecting to see Roosevelt."

Butt worried also over the President's relations with the press. Newsmen complained that Taft was not giving them any material for stories, and when the complaint was carried to Taft he merely said that he hoped to accomplish as much as Roosevelt had, and "without any noise." Eager for news, reporters turned to any possible source, often to bitter opponents of the administration. Determined to popularize President Taft, Butt ar-

195

*President Taft
tots up his
golf score.*

ranged for public appearances in appealing spots and won Taft away from his beloved golf so that he could show up at a baseball game.

Mrs. Taft needed no coaching in public relations. She was much admired for bringing to Washington streets the beauty of the Japanese cherry trees she had seen in Tokyo. The mayor of Tokyo, Yukio Ozaki, heard of Mrs. Taft's wish to embellish the capital and had two thousand saplings sent as a present from Tokyo to Washington. Unfortunately the consignment was diseased and had to be burned. Again two thousand trees were shipped to the United States, this time special growths that had been raised under more careful conditions. They were planted around the tidal basin and in the Capitol grounds.

Every day the President, accompanied by Archie Butt, went for a horseback ride or for an airing in his motor car. If the weather was right for it, they might go around the golf course. Butt, who had his own private affairs to keep up with, was kept on the run day and night.

President Taft was particularly upset when he heard that the White House servants were talking about ghosts. Through Butt he sent word that they were not to mention ghosts in the White House again. Once his anger had subsided, however, he was as curious as anyone else and asked Butt what the current ghost story was. It was the ghost of a young boy with light hair and sad, blue eyes, he was told, who made his presence known by a "slight pressure on the shoulder" as if he were looking over the terrified victim's shoulder to see what he might be doing. Butt found that the servants were taking it all quite seriously. Privately, he hoped they did not know how interested he was.

Even before former President Roosevelt returned from his year-long African trip in June, 1910, his followers had been doing some clever maneuvering with a view to giving their favorite a third term. Taft was driven more and more to siding with Roosevelt's enemies in the Old Guard.

*This fire escape
with its unwinding cable
would have given Mr. Taft
a fast ride down.*

*Four men in Mr. Taft's tub. This tub
was manufactured for the White House.*

By early fall of 1910 the newspapers were full of stories about friction between the two men. One story in *The New York Times* went so far as to quote Roosevelt to the effect that he would take the nomination in 1912 because Taft had not carried on his policies as promised. Taft, worried and confused, still could find no way of dramatizing his accomplishments or of making them popular. As the Roosevelt backers in the Republican party grew stronger, Archie Butt confided to his sister-in-law: "The Colonel hangs over him like a big, black cloud and seems to be his nemesis. He frets under it, I can see."

As Taft worried, his weight rose to new heights and stayed there, in spite of walks, horseback riding, golf, and medicine ball. He was so constantly fatigued that he fell asleep in church and on one occasion at a funeral. While the Victor in the Blue Room poured forth the Sextette from *Lucia di Lammermoor* for his guests, the exhausted President snored in his chair.

Butt thought Taft had the gout but when he suggested as much, the President "loomed up with such an indignant denial" that Butt dropped the subject. Taft liked to think that his foot pains were caused by a new pair of shoes, but Butt was proved right when he finally got the President to a doctor.

As the rift between the President and Roosevelt became greater, Butt began to feel the strain of being loyal to both of them. The Roosevelt followers considered him a fool for sticking by Taft. Alice Longworth re-

197

Taft with the overworked Archie Butt.

layed a warning from her father to sever connections with Taft while there was still time.

Butt remained loyal, however, and Taft, seeing that his aide was on the verge of collapse, suggested that he go abroad for a rest. Tired and depressed, Butt sailed for Europe and a month later sailed for home. His ship was the *Titanic*, and he was not one of the survivors.

As time for the Republican convention neared, it became clearer every day that Taft would be renominated only over violent protests from Theodore Roosevelt. When the nomination came, Roosevelt's answer was the Progressive Party, a third party which split the Republican vote. The Democratic candidate who won the election was Woodrow Wilson, a Princeton professor, lately governor of New Jersey.

As he approached the end of his four years in the White House, Taft's old gaiety and calm once more returned. "The nearer I get to the inauguration of my successor," he wrote, "the greater the relief I feel."

198

The judicial Mr. Taft.

The Wilsons and their three daughters, Margaret, Eleanor,
and Jessie, posed on the lawn of their Princeton home, the
year Woodrow Wilson ran for President.

Decisions and disillusion

Eavesdropping from her niche in the upstairs sitting room, Eleanor Wilson, the youngest of the three daughters of President Woodrow Wilson, sometimes heard strange sounds emanating from the room where her father was in conference with his Cabinet—loud guffaws which seemed scarcely in keeping with the serious tone of a Cabinet meeting. When she teasingly suggested to one of the august members that she had always believed their meetings were for the solemn settling of the problems of the world, she was informed that her father began all of them with some witticism or a funny story.

Members of Wilson's Cabinet could hardly compete with the President, for Wilson, a talented raconteur, had had long experience in making people laugh. He reveled in dialect stories and tales involving exaggerated character; a devotee of the vaudeville theater, Wilson often bewailed the fact that he had not become a performer.

Usually admired for their intellectual qualities, the Wilsons were also an imaginative and lively crew. And unlike many of their predecessors, they were in love with the White House from the start. Mrs. Wilson, Margaret, Jessie, and Eleanor were especially delighted with the huge bedrooms. Margaret occupied the room in which Abraham Lincoln had signed the Emancipation Proclamation in 1863; never had the room been used by anyone so appreciative of its associations with the past. Jessie and Eleanor shared the big northeast suite, scene of countless moods of public persons.

Mrs. Wilson brightened the upstairs Oval Sitting Room with books, paintings, and a piano brought from their Princeton home. It was in this comfortable room that Wilson carried on his custom of reading aloud to his family, a pastime he had enjoyed since his days as professor at Princeton.

The Wilsons found the family Dining Room, jammed with mahogany furniture, depressing, and the State Dining Room, decorated with enormous animal heads, relics of Theodore Roosevelt's hunting career,

Wilson in his White House office.

Mrs. Woodrow Wilson in 1913.

even worse. At last they settled upon having a table placed at one end of the huge State Dining Room, where they could ignore the animal heads and look out upon the beautiful White House lawns and gardens.

Mrs. Wilson turned the attic into badly needed guest rooms. One of the small, oddly shaped rooms had a skylight, and Mrs. Wilson, who was a talented painter, hoped the day would come when she might find time to use it for a studio.

Her understanding of painting was put to use soon after she moved into the White House. She learned that the Watts painting, "Love and Life," which had been presented to the White House by the painter himself, was hanging in the Corcoran Gallery, after having been shuttled back and forth between the gallery and the White House several times since it had been accepted by Rutherford B. Hayes. The painting, depicting two nude figures, was brought back to the White House and hung over the mantelpiece in Wilson's book-lined study.

Woodrow Wilson in his marriage to Ellen Axon nearly thirty years before had achieved his perfect complement. Whatever subtle qualities of tact and understanding were lacking in Wilson's complex nature, Ellen Wilson was able to provide. There was one way in which Ellen Wilson was truly remarkable; she experienced no jealousy over her husband's friendships with women, or if she did, she had a talent for concealing it gracefully. Wilson had always been highly dependent upon the companionship of women. Mrs. Wilson not only seemed to approve her husband's friendships but she shared them warmly; like her daughters, Mrs. Wilson regarded anything Wilson did as right. Wilson's cousin, Helen Bones, who served as Mrs. Wilson's secretary, also had the highest regard for him.

The day began for Margaret, Jessie, and Eleanor with their conference with Isabelle Hagner, their social secretary, who had served in the same capacity for Mrs. Theodore Roosevelt. Upstairs at the end of the long corridor, under the huge fan-shaped window, Miss Hagner sat at her desk, like "the Delphic Oracle" as Eleanor expressed it, dispensing wisdom to the Wilson girls. Miss Hagner, familiar with every phase of Washington social life, realized the importance of correct social observances and advised the girls accordingly.

Mrs. Wilson would have had more time for her easel painting if she had not become so interested in Washington slum clearance. Taking members of Congress along, she trudged the alleys of the city for a close look at the shacks and lean-to's, the squalor and illness that lay hidden in the back streets of Washington. It was largely through Mrs. Wilson's efforts that Congress put through a bill which began to eliminate the city's slums.

Each of Wilson's daughters also had a serious interest in social work. Margaret, in addition, had her singing; but with her two younger sisters it was very shortly evident that their thoughts were mostly of love and marriage. The White House was soon to be the scene of two weddings. In November, 1913, Jessie married Francis B. Sayre. Six months later

Wilson and his early Cabinet. At his left sits William Gibbs McAdoo, Secretary of the Treasury; at his right, William Jennings Bryan, Secretary of State. Josephus Daniels, Secretary of the Navy, faces the camera beyond Bryan's profile.

vivacious Eleanor married William Gibbs McAdoo, Secretary of the Treasury in Wilson's Cabinet.

Wilson received a shattering blow in the summer of 1914 when Mrs. Wilson, long frail and overtaxed, became ill and died. To Wilson her death meant the removal of the strongest prop of his life. "God has stricken me almost beyond what I can bear," he wrote a friend the day after her death. Forcing himself to attend to affairs of State, Wilson soon had the outer look of a man in command of his emotions but privately he admitted he was in complete despair.

Wilson was soon to find the weight of office heavier each day. On August 2, 1914, four days before Mrs. Wilson's death, France had been invaded by Germany and Germany by Russia. The First World War had begun. A confused and alarmed nation read Wilson's pledge of strict neutrality.

On May 7, 1915, a German submarine sank the British passenger liner *Lusitania* with a loss of twelve hundred lives, one hundred and twenty-four of them American. *The New York Times* carried the headline: "Washington believes that a grave crisis is at hand." Wilson was attacked for dragging the country toward war and simultaneously for his "do-nothing policy" of staying out of war.

Among Ellen Wilson's last words had been the often quoted ones spoken to Cary Grayson, the Wilsons' physician and friend: "Promise me that when I go you will take care of Woodrow." Cary Grayson did his best. He saw that the harassed President got out into the fresh air, he took him to the golf course, and inadvertently he placed a new interest at Wilson's disposal when he introduced Helen Bones to a handsome, dark-haired widow, Edith Bolling Galt. Soon Miss Bones and Mrs. Galt were going for daily walks in Rock Creek Park, ending usually at Mrs. Galt's house for tea. On a brisk day in March, 1915, Helen Bones suggested that they go to the White House, since "Cousin Woodrow" would be out playing golf and they would not be in his way. As it turned out the two women had tea in the Oval Sitting Room with the President and Dr. Grayson, who had just returned from their game. For the first time in many months Woodrow Wilson laughed aloud, over some witticism of Mrs. Galt's.

Mrs. Galt was undeniably charming. Vital and positive, her demeanor reflected her careful, conservative background. For added interest she could trace her Virginia ancestry directly back to John Rolfe and Poca-hontas. The lonely President thought her fascinating. A whirlwind courtship followed, carried out under the most discouraging conditions. Surrounded by Secret Service men and accompanied at all times by a friend or relative acting as chaperon, Mrs. Galt and the President went on motor rides and dined at the White House; he sent her orchids and books.

Soon Wilson's melancholy lifted, the strained, harassed look disappeared from his face. On April 28, 1915, Mrs. Galt received her first note—an invitation to go motoring—from Wilson. A week later tactful relatives left them alone after dinner on a White House porch and the President proposed marriage. Mrs. Galt's answer was that if it had to be yes or no at once, the answer would be no. They agreed to see each other, under difficulties, until she could decide.

One day during this period of probation, on a balmy summer afternoon in 1915, Mrs. Galt took her sister Bertha along when she went to tea at the White House. Neither Wilson nor Helen Bones had returned from earlier appointments and the sisters waited on the South Portico, where the tea table was already arranged, with water steaming in the kettle. Presently the President arrived, made apologies for the women of his household, and clumsily set about making the tea himself, at the same time carrying on the typical gay Wilson comment. Mrs. Galt, al-

The President, dressed for golf.

ways correct and realizing the delicacy of the situation, restrained herself from offering to help. His tea brewing being dismally unsuccessful, Wilson quickly suggested that they walk in the garden and as they strolled among the flowers, the President, never at a loss for words, quoted a poem: "A Garden is a lovesome thing, God wot. . . ."

In September Mrs. Galt decided to accept Wilson's offer of marriage. Complications which might have been foreseen arose at once to plague the President, who wanted an immediate wedding. Wilson's political advisers were startled by the idea of his taking a new wife before the 1916 election. They predicted that there would be a mass reaction against Wilson for marrying so soon after Ellen Wilson's death. Wilson's secretary, Joseph Tumulty, dared to suggest as much to Wilson but did not convince him.

A fatal block to the marriage seemed to have arisen when Wilson's confidant and adviser, Colonel Edward House, went to Wilson with the horrifying story that Mary Hulbert Peck, an old friend of Wilson's, with whom he had carried on a long correspondence, was going to bring out embarrassing information about him if the rumors about the engagement proved to be true. Letters she had received from Wilson over a period of seven years were to be made public.

Wilson was shocked into illness by the disclosure. Too shaken even to write to Mrs. Galt, much less go to see her, he sent Cary Grayson to her with the whole story and an offer to release her from her promise to marry him.

After profound soul searching, Mrs. Galt penned a long, passionate letter to the President, pledging her love and loyalty. Three days had gone by without word from the White House when Cary Grayson appeared again to take her to the President. Mrs. Galt found Wilson lying in his darkened bedroom in a state of deep despondency. Her presence had a miraculous effect upon the unhappy President. His recovery was swift and complete. From that moment on there was never any question about their decision to marry.

Much later Colonel House admitted to Mrs. Wilson that the story about Mary Peck had been a hoax, cooked up by Wilson's son-in-law, William Gibbs McAdoo, and himself in order to prevent the marriage.

During the Galt-Wilson engagement, which lasted three months, a direct telephone line connected the White House with Mrs. Galt's home on Twentieth Street. Sometimes the President also sent foreign and domestic information by messenger, for he wanted to keep Mrs. Galt informed on all developments. His war worries seemed less when he could confide them to Mrs. Galt.

Shortly before Christmas the President and Mrs. Galt were married in a ceremony held in her home. Mrs. Wilson, wanting to preserve a little of her personal background, took with her into the White House the furnishings of her own bedroom, her piano and books, and her Wilcox and Gibbs sewing machine. The latter object was treated as a joke by Margaret Wilson and Helen Bones. "When do you think you will ever

Colonel Edward House, Wilson's adviser, who stayed in the background.

205

Edith Galt Wilson comes down the steps in this pre-election picture of 1916. Members of the Democratic Committee are in a confident mood.

get time to sit down and sew on it?" Margaret Wilson wanted to know. A little over a year later, however, it came into use, turning out pajamas and surgical shirts for the Red Cross.

The day began for the newly married Wilsons at eight o'clock sharp, with breakfast served in their private rooms. Then the President got to work, with his bride on hand to help, at routine business. In Wilson's study was the large flat-topped desk which had been a present to the White House from Queen Victoria. Wilson worked at the desk under the light from a green-shaded student's lamp which he had used at the University of Virginia. One drawer of the desk, the large center one, was set aside for urgent papers, and anything that had to be taken care of at once, from the State, War, or Navy Departments, was placed there by his secretary. Each time the President entered the room he looked in that drawer. Later Mrs. Wilson took on the duty of supervising the big drawer, sometimes finding it so full that it could not be closed.

The year 1916 was a critical one for Wilson and for the nation. With the question of neutrality becoming ever more delicate, Wilson had to face a campaign for reelection. During the Democratic convention, the national appetite for peace having become apparent, the slogan "He kept us out of war" was created. The slogan distressed Wilson deeply but

Former President Theodore Roosevelt, cornered by reporters on the North Portico. He had just been refused permission to take an outfit overseas.

probably played a greater part in keeping him in the White House than did the carrying out of his domestic program as outlined earlier in his "New Freedom."

In the months following his reelection, the war-hating President continued to make every effort to end the war by mediation, but with no success. In January of 1917 diplomatic relations with Germany were brought to an abrupt close. On the evening of April 2, Wilson appeared before a special session of Congress and made a speech in which he advised the declaration of war. It followed, four days later.

The White House was soon the center for the management of the war. The day now began at 5 A.M. instead of eight o'clock, and the President sometimes worked until midnight. The strain of mobilizing the nation for war kept Wilson in a constant state of fatigue. "I could go to sleep at an angle of ninety-five degrees," he once said to a member of his "War Cabinet."

Mrs. Wilson realized how much depended on her husband's obtaining some diversion and exercise and whenever she thought the moment had arrived, she would force Wilson to stop work for a while either to go for a drive or to play a round of golf. Going to the theater remained a pastime that delighted the President. Seated in his box at Keith's Theatre, Wilson

The best-known sheep in America grazed on the White House grounds in 1918.

could completely shut the door on his problems as he watched some light-hearted vaudeville skit. Sometimes in the privacy of their upstairs sitting room, Wilson would turn on the phonograph and amuse his wife by dancing a jig in the style of his favorite minstrel dancer, Primrose.

Entertaining was cut to a minimum in the White House during the war. There were wheatless days and meatless days there as in every other home in America. A small upstairs room was turned into a sewing room for the Red Cross with Mrs. Wilson's sewing machine the center of activity. The sheep on the White House lawn produced enough wool—ninety-eight pounds—to bring in $100,000 at auction for the Red Cross. A war garden was put in on the White House grounds.

The Wilsons had just gone to bed in the small hours of the morning of November 11, 1918, when the news of the Armistice arrived at the White House. At noon of the same day, Wilson drove to the Capitol to

Miraculously, the President talks by radio with an airplane overhead.

make the announcement before Congress. The Wilsons celebrated the event that night by going to a ball at the Italian Embassy. There they remained for an hour, then returned to the White House and sat before the fire in Mrs. Wilson's room until early in the morning. Wilson read aloud a chapter from the Bible before going to bed.

In the midst of the herculean task of winning the war, Wilson had not lost sight for a moment of his plans for a just and lasting peace. His plan for peace as embodied in his "Fourteen Points" had been laid before Congress while the war was at its height. When Wilson sailed for France and the peace conference in December, 1918, one part of his program, the formation of an association of nations to maintain the peace, had become the focus of all his thoughts and emotions. Wilson's League of Nations was to become an integral part of the treaty.

In Washington, Wilson's political enemies, under the leadership of

209

Armistice Day, 1918. The crowds would not leave until
Wilson came out on the North Portico and waved to them.

Senator Henry Cabot Lodge, were polishing their plans to kill the League
long before they had seen its Convenant. The necessary Senate ratifica-
tion of the Treaty, including the League Covenant, did not take place.
In spite of warnings from Dr. Cary Grayson that in view of his age—he
was sixty-three—and his fatigue, prolonged effort might kill him, Wilson
decided to lay the issue before the people of the nation, in the belief that
public opinion would sway the Senate.

For twenty-two days Wilson, in hour-long speeches, pleaded the cause
of the League and the Treaty before the people of the United States. Increasingly exhausted and prey to violent headaches, Wilson collapsed
after a speech in Pueblo, Colorado, and was rushed back to Washington.

For a few more days the disheartened President roamed wearily
through the rooms of the White House, his headaches never ceasing.
Then one morning, Mrs. Wilson, making a routine visit to his bedroom
to see how he was sleeping, found her husband groping for a bottle of
water which stood on a table near his bed. "I have no feeling in that
hand," he said, indicating his left hand. "Will you rub it?" A little later
Mrs. Wilson found the President lying unconscious on the bathroom floor.

Suffragettes picket the White House during their campaign for "Votes for Women," finally won in 1920. They gave Wilson no peace for seven years.

The cerebral thrombosis which had struck him down paralyzed his left side.

For weeks Woodrow Wilson was in a critical condition. The White House took on the look and atmosphere of a hospital as doctors and nurses battled for his life. A series of complications then followed. Weeks passed before the President was allowed to sit in a wheel chair, and months before he went for his first short drive in a White House automobile. Mrs. Wilson and Dr. Grayson took on as their first duty the protection of the President from all worries and disturbances. As Wilson's health improved and requests to visit him became more constant, Mrs. Wilson acted as a buffer between the ailing man and his former associates.

For nearly a year and a half the government had no active leader. The White House gates were locked and sentries stationed before them. The White House was as isolated from the world of the Capitol as if it had been on a Pacific island. Critics of the administration said that Mrs. Wilson was running the country. Charles W. Thompson, a White House correspondent, labeled the period "Mrs. Wilson's Regency." Secretary of State Lansing called a Cabinet meeting and was dismissed by the President for his pains.

211

Wilson, in the East Room in 1918, appears strong and determined.

Mrs. Wilson, in her book of reminiscences, *My Memoir*, said that Wilson's physicians told her she must "act as a go-between" in order to save her husband's life. Daily she reported to Wilson, at the hour when his energy was at its highest level, a summary of the problems brought to her attention by Cabinet members and other officials.

By autumn of 1919 it was clear that the Treaty would not be ratified by the Senate unless Wilson agreed to the reservations appended by Senator Lodge. Few visitors were permitted to enter Wilson's bedroom, but Senator Hitchcock of Nebraska was one who gained an interview. Hitchcock hoped to persuade Wilson to modify his unbending attitude toward the reservations. When Hitchcock entered the room, Wilson lay in bed, with Mrs. Wilson and Dr. Grayson at the bedside to protect him from excitement. Under a snowy beard, the President's face was unrecognizable. When Hitchcock suggested that a compromise would be necessary if the Treaty were to be carried, Wilson showed his old stubbornness. "Let Lodge compromise," he said peevishly.

On one occasion, even Mrs. Wilson appealed to Wilson in behalf of a compromise with the Republican Senators. "For my sake," she asked, "won't you accept these reservations and get this awful thing settled?"

212

Wilson's answer put an end to the question. "Little girl," he said, "don't you desert me. That I cannot stand."

With the Treaty and the League voted down, the enemies of Woodrow Wilson still had a few tricks up their sleeves. To the White House and upstairs to Wilson's bedroom came a Senate subcommittee headed by Albert B. Fall to confer with Wilson on a Mexican incident. The committee's real intent, according to Mrs. Wilson, was to ascertain whether Wilson's mental condition had so deteriorated that he could be ruled incapable of administering his office. Senator Fall's insincere remark to Wilson was ill chosen. When he said, "Well, Mr. President, we have all been praying for you," and Wilson shot back, "Which way, Senator?" it was impossible to pretend that Wilson was anything but keen-witted.

Mrs. Wilson, busily taking down every word of the interview, also had an answer for Fall. Noting her activity, Fall observed, "You seem to be very much engaged, Madam." The sagacious Mrs. Wilson answered: "Yes. I thought it wise to record this interview so there may be no misunderstandings or misstatements made."

Very little was seen of Woodrow Wilson in his last months in the White House. A private house on S Street was purchased and the President and Mrs. Wilson were occupied with plans for their retirement there. The President looked forward to years of reading and writing in the seclusion of his private home. Only occasionally could strollers in the Washington streets catch a glimpse of him in a White House limousine, his wife seated beside him.

In the forenoon of March 4, 1921, Woodrow Wilson, gloomy and frail, limped painfully to a waiting automobile and seated himself beside the President-elect, Warren Gamaliel Harding, for the trip up to the Capitol.

A failing Wilson accompanies Harding to his inauguration. On the front seat are "Uncle Joe" Cannon and Philander C. Knox.

Never did any President look the part so perfectly as Warren G. Harding. His charm and affability pleased the nation as deeply as it had pleased his political handlers.

The Hardings had long been a team, and they continued to work together conscientiously while in the White House.

11 | Warren G. Harding 1921 - 1923
Calvin Coolidge 1923 - 1929
Herbert Hoover 1929 - 1933

Three separate griefs

THE WHITE HOUSE GATES, at Warren Gamaliel Harding's request, were thrown open to the public, and the quiet gloom which had settled over the old building during Wilson's last years there vanished overnight. Curious crowds streamed up the walks and driveways, getting a good look at the White House for the first time in years. They photographed each other leaning against the pillars of the North Portico and strolled placidly in the gardens, as if it were all theirs again. The atmosphere, suggestive of a large public picnic, was entirely in keeping with the personality of the genial, benignly smiling man who had just moved into the White House.

President Harding and his wife, Florence Kling Harding, brought to the Executive Mansion the friendly, unassuming standards of Marion, Ohio, where Harding had been editor and publisher of the Marion *Star*, a small-town newspaper on which his wife had been circulation manager. The Hardings would probably have spent the rest of their lives in Marion if they had never met Harry Daugherty, the Ohio political boss, who took a good look at Warren G. Harding, noticed his dramatic and noble bearing, his handsome face and warming smile, and made the famous remark that this man looked the way a President should look.

With Mrs. Harding's help, Daugherty steered Harding into a seat in the United States Senate and later staged the "smoke-filled room" selection of Harding as a dark-horse candidate in the summer of 1920. It was Daugherty, now Harding's Attorney General, who, with his following of Ohio political cronies, was most in evidence around the White House after Harding took office in March, 1921.

Washington was ready for a change of social pace, and under the Hardings the White House seemed to spring into life with parties and receptions in abundance, the first since the beginning of World War I. Mrs. Harding featured large garden parties and intimate dinners and luncheons. Although under the new prohibition law no wine could be served in the dining rooms even on state occasions, upstairs Harding's friends could help themselves to the best bourbon or Scotch.

One of Harding's Ohio friends, eighty-two-year-old Charles Lee Patten, was made a gardener at the White House.

215

A sporting foursome: the
President, Grantland Rice,
Ring Lardner, and Henry
Fletcher pose on the
North Portico.
Below, Billy Sunday,
the acrobatic evangelist,
gets a publicity shot.

*The most distinguished Europeans of the era visited President Harding.
Left, the President escorts Madame Marie Curie down to the south
grounds. Right, Dr. Albert Einstein and his wife are photographed with a
gay party in the White House gardens.*

Mrs. Harding, always impeccably groomed and fashionably dressed,
lent her presence to a variety of public affairs and good works and almost
daily received visiting delegations in the parlors and on the porches of the
White House. Among her favorite activities were her trips to Walter Reed
Hospital, where she visited the sick and wounded veterans of the war.
When she gave a large party for them on the White House grounds, she
thoughfully remembered to wear the old hat in which she had appeared
at the hospital so many times—"so that the boys will know where I am,"
she explained to her secretary.

It was generally believed that the Presidency was more satisfying to
Mrs. Harding than to her husband and she was usually given credit for
actively furthering Harding's career. Certainly, after his election she exercised great influence when he made his appointments to the higher offices.

Although she generally charmed Washington, Mrs. Harding could
also occasionally be very firm. When a bill came up in Congress providing
for the purchase of a fine residence as a permanent home for the Vice
President, Mrs. Harding with some effort managed to prevent its passage.
She had never liked the reticent Vice President, Vermonter Calvin Coolidge, or his wife, and privately admitted killing the bill for that reason:

217

Mrs. Harding made excessive demands on her health in order to perform her duties. Here she takes part in a tree planting on the White House grounds.

"I just couldn't have people like those Coolidges living in that beautiful house."

Strangers seeing Mrs. Harding pleasant and animated could not have guessed that her state of health was precarious and that a flare-up of an old kidney ailment could at any time be fatal. It was known to her close friends, however, and Harding brought from Marion Mrs. Harding's family doctor, bewhiskered little Brig. Gen. Charles B. Sawyer, and his wife to live with them in the White House.

In September, 1922, Mrs. Harding, tired out by her strenuous duties as First Lady, had a severe illness. Her condition became worse and two noted surgeons were called in as consultants. Their decision was that her sole chance of survival lay in an immediate operation. Dr. Sawyer, knowing Mrs. Harding's medical history, stoutly maintained that she could not survive surgery and took upon himself the responsibility of waiting it out. While Mrs. Harding lay unconscious in her bedroom the little doctor strode up and down before the door, in a panic lest she should die, but determined that there would be no operation. Miraculously, Mrs. Harding rallied, slowly improved, and in a few weeks' time was able to sit up in a wheel chair. Her close friend, Evalyn Walsh McLean, took her a present of a lace boudoir cap made in the shape of a crown.

Although the popular conception of Harding was that of a hard-drink-

218

She made constant appearances at public functions, stately and trivial.
Above, she meets a Campfire girl and sends a pigeon off to a poultry show.

ing, woman-chasing President, Edmund W. Starling, chief of the Secret
Service detail at the White House during Harding's administration and
the one man most likely to know, insisted that Harding was a one-drink
man who greatly preferred the companionship of men to that of women
—especially men with whom he could drop all formalities and, with vest
unbuttoned, be his true tobacco-chewing, affable, small-town self. Harding would empty the contents of a cigarette into his mouth in an emer-
gency, if no chewing tobacco was available, a habit, Starling thought,
hardly designed to appeal to women. Wherever the truth might lie, tales
of Harding's extramarital adventures continued to circulate.

An energetic man, President Harding was devoted to his game of golf
and regularly practiced his shots on the south grounds of the White House
with his Scottie, Laddie Boy, acting as retriever. On fair days he played
at the Chevy Chase Club or at the golf course on the estate of Ned McLean,
publisher of the Washington *Post*.

Because of his lack of political experience and his inability to grasp
large problems, Harding was at the mercy of his advisers, all too many
of whom were products of the school of practical politics, with personal
gain their sole aim. The setup for graft could hardly have been better.

Gradually a chain of suspicious and ominous happenings presaged
the end of Harding's "normalcy" and the shattering of his administration.

219

Harding luggage leaves for the Alaska trip, on which they are seen below.

Colonel Charles R. Forbes, placed by Harding at the head of the Veterans' Bureau, resigned in disgrace, leaving a record of misplaced funds; Charles F. Cramer, legal adviser to the Bureau, took his own life, as did Harry Daugherty's crony, Jessie Smith. Rumors of graft and mismanagement gathered momentum. Gossip meanwhile circulated that Mrs. Harding had visited a clairvoyant and had been told that her husband would not live to finish his term.

An empty White House awaits a President who is never to return.

When Harding left on his trip to Alaska in the summer of 1923, he must already have known that his world was crashing into ruin. A code message brought to him there nearly brought on a collapse. He wondered aloud before a group of reporters just what should be done about a President who had been betrayed by his friends. Harding had wanted only to be a helpful friend to the American people.

Distraught and ill, the President began his return trip to Washington.

221

*One of the President's
best friends stares
mournfully down the walk.*

In a San Francisco hotel, as he was resting after an attack of pneumonia, Harding was listening to his wife read parts of a magazine article complimentary to himself when he suddenly died of a stroke of apoplexy. The funeral train sped to Washington and all America grieved for the amiable, well-meaning man who had met such a tragic end.

For a day and a night Warren Harding lay in state in the East Room as had other Presidents before him. Evalyn McLean went to the White House to offer such aid as she could to her friend, Mrs. Harding. She later recalled the singular incidents of that night.

In the middle of the night the two women made their way down the marble staircase to the East Room where Harding lay in his coffin. The dead President, his handsome face touched up with subtle traces of rouge and lipstick, seemed almost alive in the dim light. For nearly three hours Mrs. Harding talked to her husband, eagerly, as though she could not bear the thought of silence. At one point Mrs. McLean heard her say: "No one can hurt you now, Warren." From the masses of wreaths and flowers around the coffin, Mrs. Harding gathered a nosegay of simple blossoms—nasturtiums and daisies—and placed it on the coffin. Then the two women went back upstairs.

222

The flag-draped coffin lies in the East Room and is borne away with military honors. The funeral cortege pauses for a poignant moment in the White House driveway.

Calvin Coolidge was
completely divorced
in the public mind
from the scandals of the
Harding administration.

CALVIN COOLIDGE was on his father's farm in Plymouth Notch, Vermont, doctoring a maple tree when he got the news that President Harding was ill. When the telegram informing him of Harding's death arrived, the Vice President was sworn into office by his father, Colonel John Coolidge, a notary public, in the middle of the night. Afterward, Coolidge, maintaining his habitual calm, went back to bed for a few hours' sleep.

This humble entrance into the Presidency was extremely pleasing to the people of America. The rustic simplicity of a New England inauguration in a primitive farmhouse seemed perfect for a man already widely regarded as highly individualistic.

Washington society had had a taste of the Coolidge taciturnity during his two-and-a-half years as Vice President. When the Coolidges went out to dinner, Mrs. Coolidge charmed everyone with her unaffected gaiety while her husband stared mutely into his plate. He made it plain that he had come to eat, not to entertain. It became a game in some circles to try to draw him out, one woman going so far as to tell him she had made a bet she could make him say more than two words. "You lose," was her reward.

Calvin Coolidge did not permit his personality to change an iota when he assumed the Presidency. He still hid his shyness and sentimentality beneath a façade of restraint and odd-character mannerisms. When the President inspected the White House kitchen or wandered the upstairs corridor in his nightshirt, with his spindly legs on view, or rocked complacently on the North Portico, he was acting as he would have acted in Vermont. He saw no reason to change.

Both the President and his wife felt a deep reverence for the White House and the Presidency. Grace Coolidge spoke of the old mansion as "a home rich in tradition, mellow with years, hallowed with memories." President Coolidge believed his office brought with it so much power and dignity that "pomp and splendor" were unnecessary. "It was my desire to maintain about the White House as far as possible an attitude of simplicity," he wrote later. "There is no need of theatricals."

If, as some believed, Coolidge had missed out on certain social talents, Grace Coolidge amply made up for the lack. The marked contrast between their personalities was never more in evidence than at large, formal gatherings. President Coolidge, who heartily wished the affair to be over so he could get back to his work, would give each guest a little pull past him as he shook hands. Mrs. Coolidge would counteract her husband's tendency to rush things by turning on each guest a warm and interested smile.

The President derived great pleasure from helping Mrs. Coolidge in the selection of her wardrobe, and one of his favorite pastimes in Washington was window-shopping. If he noticed a frock or a hat he thought would be becoming to Mrs. Coolidge, his frugality vanished and he became the most extravagant of husbands.

The President's tastes were not as quiet as those of his wife. He reacted

The Coolidge family gazes into a pool and Mrs. Coolidge gets a May basket.

The President and Mrs.
Coolidge with Rob Roy.

Mrs. Coolidge with her
tame raccoon, Rebecca.

Ezra Meeker, of the Old West, is greeted warmly; and below, some Sioux Indians line up on the lawn.

pleasurably to bright colors and liked to see Mrs. Coolidge in large hats loaded with flowers; he thought the ideal frock one that was loaded with beads and fringe. Mary Randolph, White House secretary, looked on amused as Mrs. Coolidge exercised her tact in keeping most of her husband's choices out of her wardrobe.

The President also found time to go over the household accounts and to check the daily menus. He peeked into the iceboxes and once complained to the housekeeper, Elizabeth Jaffray, that she was providing too many hams —six for sixty guests—for a dinner party. Mrs. Jaffrey was obliged to explain that they were little hams and could not be stretched. "Never did a President save so much money!" wrote Mrs. Jaffray, by way of repayment for the interference. When Coolidge ordered a new breakfast cereal made up in the kitchen, the homely recipe he gave was four pecks of whole wheat to one peck of whole rye.

Although Coolidge kept his finger in domestic affairs, Mrs. Coolidge took no part at all in her husband's political life. She had no press conferences, made no speeches, and admitted that she scarcely knew the members of the President's Cabinet. She saw their wives only rarely.

Mrs. Coolidge liked to carry out her domestic duties early in the morning, to music from the radio or phonograph. After a brisk morning walk she eagerly attacked her arduous social program; the constant teas, receptions, and musicales were a delight to the First Lady, who sincerely loved people. Mrs. Coolidge expressed her true feelings when she wrote: "I have often been asked to name some of my favorite books and my reply has usually been, 'People.' "

President Coolidge had one intimate friend to whom he confided his problems, sometimes after he had already solved them. He was Frank Stearns, a Boston merchant and old friend who knew the value to the President of his quiet understanding. Stearns, with his wife, occupied a two-room suite on the third floor. Stearns would sit without comment, as Coolidge soliloquized, taking on a garrulity rarely heard except by intimates.

Coolidge believed his early morning breakfasts for members of Congress produced a "spirit of good fellowship" which carried through when serious business came up. There were seven of these unusual repasts in the space of one month, at an hour—8: 30 A.M.—considered by some Congressmen to be barbarous.

Edmund Starling of the Secret Service, who had gone riding and golfing with Woodrow Wilson and Warren G. Harding and had seen the pleasure they derived from those sports, was worried about Coolidge's lack of hobbies. Starling, who liked and admired Coolidge, thought the conscientious President would benefit from some light pastime; eventually he interested the President in clay-pigeon shooting and also joined him in taking turns on the electric horse in an upstairs bedroom.

Coolidge had a childlike love of pranks and practical jokes which he played on almost anyone. Once he gave his wife a terrible fright when he marched up the long train of a ball gown she was trying on before her mirror. The President also relished playing jokes on the White House

226

The movie star Tom Mix pays a visit.

Bathing beauties of 1924 at the White House.

employees. He would chuckle as he pushed all the buttons on his desk at the same time, bringing all his aides on the run simultaneously.

When the bearded Charles Evans Hughes was staying at the White House, Coolidge sent a servant to his door in the early morning hours to inquire if Hughes were ready to be shaved. The alarmed servant obeyed the President to the extent of knocking on the door but fled before Hughes could answer his knock.

In the summer of 1924, the Coolidge family experienced a personal tragedy when Calvin, Jr., aged sixteen, died from blood poisoning—the result of a toe infection got while playing tennis with his brother John. In the months that followed, Coolidge tried without success to hide his grief, but Mrs. Coolidge turned a calm, sad face to the world. "When he died, the honor and glory of the Presidency went with him," wrote the President in his memoirs.

Coolidge interrupted his work week as briefly as possible for his inauguration day in 1925. Following swearing-in ceremonies at the Capitol, the President and his wife had sandwiches and coffee on the second floor, while a Presidential aide, Colonel Sherrill, took the Cabinet and the other aides to an elaborate luncheon at the State, War, and Navy Building. When the President came down to make his way to the reviewing stand, he found the lower floors deserted. It was some time before Colonel Sherrill's group arrived at the Presidential grandstand.

On occupying the White House in 1923, President Coolidge had been warned by the office of Public Parks and Buildings that the White House roof was in a dangerous state of decay and would have to be rebuilt. The President had answered wryly that he "presumed there were plenty others who would be willing to take the risk" of living under that roof.

It was not until the early spring of 1927, after extensive surveys, that the necessary alterations on the White House were begun. After the Coolidges had moved into a private house on Dupont Circle in March, the first steps in the restoration—the removal of the roof, the third floor, and the ceilings of the second floor—were carried out.

As work on the White House went on, the Coolidges used the occasion to take a long summer vacation. They went to Game Lodge, thirty-five miles

Three circus performers, George Auger and Mr. and Mrs. Doll.

227

The Coolidges toward the end of their White House years.

from Rapid City, South Dakota, in the Black Hills. It was from Rapid City that Coolidge issued his celebrated decision: "I do not choose to run for President in 1928."

The Coolidges returned from their Western vacation to a White House which had been enlarged to the extent of eighteen modern rooms. The roof had been raised in order to provide space for additional guest rooms and servants' quarters on the top floor; all types of rooms needed for conscientious housekeeping had been added. Mrs. Coolidge—and her housekeeper—were delighted with the sewing room, the pressing room, the storage rooms for blankets, linens, and out-of-season clothing. Above the South Portico, a sun room, called by Mrs. Coolidge the "sky-parlor," gave the family a pleasant meeting spot.

Mrs. Coolidge had the good taste to think that the White House should be furnished at least partially in the period in which it had been designed. Thinking that the American people might like to contribute to the plan, she succeeded in having Congress pass a resolution which would authorize acceptance of "rare old pieces" as gifts to the White House. She admitted they did not come as rapidly as she had hoped, but she did have the satisfaction of seeing the Green Room properly furnished before she left.

Mrs. Coolidge left behind her another contribution to the house when she and President Coolidge vacated it in 1929. It was a bedspread made expressly for the huge Lincoln bed, crocheted bit by bit. Allotting a month's time to each square, she had methodically ticked off, as each piece was completed, another square of the bedspread, another month of the Coolidge tenure.

228

THE INTERIOR of the White House changed markedly in appearance when President Herbert Hoover and Mrs. Hoover moved in early in 1929. The long upstairs corridor lost its bare and homely look with the installation of bookshelves and the appearance of art objects which the Hoovers had collected in the Orient, Europe, and Russia. At the western end of the hall an enormous cage of canaries filled the fan-shaped window; grass rugs from South America and handsome bamboo furniture made an airy, informal gathering place. Throughout, the White House furnishings reflected the active, well-traveled lives of its new occupants.

Mrs. Hoover was greatly interested in White House history and tried diligently to bring the past more significantly into the modern interior. The few pieces left over from the Monroe period she brought together and placed in the room north of the upstairs Oval Room, which had been used by Mrs. Monroe as a parlor. She also visited the Monroe law office in Fredericksburg, Virginia, where other early furniture was carefully preserved, and had some of this copied for the White House. Duplicates of the desk on which Monroe signed the Monroe Doctrine and Mrs. Monroe's tea table were placed in the "Monroe Room," which the Hoovers used for a sitting room.

President Hoover took as his private study the room in which Lincoln had had his office. An old engraving depicting the signing of the Emancipation Proclamation put the Hoovers on the trail of the original furniture used in that room, four chairs of which were discovered in storage and carefully restored.

President Hoover and Mrs. Hoover had come to their high station

President Hoover looks out over the south grounds of the White House.

A gay inaugural parade stand is busily erected on the sidewalk in front of the White House.

The Executive Offices
have a damaging fire;
and below, President
Hoover and secretaries
leave for temporary
quarters elsewhere.

from a remarkably adventurous and useful background. In 1897, as a young mining engineer, Herbert Hoover had gone to the newly discovered gold fields of central west Australia to supervise the building of plants outfitted with American machinery. When he was offered the position of chief engineer of the Bureau of Mines in China, he wired his proposal of marriage to Miss Lou Henry in Monterey, California.

Herbert Hoover and Lou Henry were married in California on February 11, 1899, and sailed for China the following day. In China, while her husband took trips into the interior, Mrs. Hoover studied Chinese and developed an interest in ancient Chinese porcelains, eventually becoming a collector in the precious Ming and K'ang Hsi periods. The Hoovers weathered the Boxer Rebellion in Tientsin, and lived later in England, Australia, New Zealand, Burma, and Russia. At one time Herbert Hoover maintained offices in a half-dozen countries simultaneously.

The scholarly Hoovers collected fifteenth and sixteenth century books on early science, engineering, metallurgy, mathematics, and alchemy. In 1905 they picked up in a bookshop a copy of Georgius Agricola's *De Re Metallica*, published in Latin in 1556 and used as a textbook and guide to miners and metallurgists for 180 years. The Hoovers spent five years in translating the work into English.

As United States Food Administrator and head of the Allied Food Council during and following World War I, Herbert Hoover established himself as a tireless and unselfish worker for the public good. His election to the Presidency was considered the climax to a life of devoted public service.

Wealthy and hospitable, the Hoovers set new records in White House entertaining, and Mrs. Hoover found it necessary to employ three secretaries to take care of her guest lists. For the afternoon receptions, invitations were sent to all who had left cards at the White House. The result was that days were spent in addressing the three or four thousand engraved invitations which were sent for one affair. Mary Randolph described in her reminiscences how they were sorted and stacked high on large tables, then wrapped and loaded on the trucks which delivered them in the environs of Washington.

To instill some variety into the evening functions, Mrs. Hoover liked to receive the guests in a different room each time, and in warm weather she often received while standing on the South Portico. The Hoovers stressed the democratic aspect of their social functions by having Cabinet members move about among the guests instead of staying in the vicinity of the receiving line.

"The Hoovers entertained incessantly," wrote Mary Randolph. Guests came to luncheon, to tea and to dinner, every day in the week. The kitchen staff got used to the possibility of feeding a dozen or so extra guests invited at the last moment. Even so the food sometimes ran short. At one big party when five hundred visitors showed up instead of the expected two hundred, the staff showed how truly resourceful it had become. Servants cleaned out the food shops in the neighborhood and when

231

Mr. and Mrs. Charles Lindbergh spend an afternoon with the Hoovers.

Piney, the Schnauzer pup, sits on the President's medicine ball; and below, Snowboy bestows a dubious greeting through the White House fence.

Mrs. Hoover smiles on an Easter crowd and a Maypole dance is the main event at an Easter egg-rolling.

even this provided inadequate refreshments, picnic baskets, packed earlier for the Hoovers' trip to their camp in Virginia, were hurriedly unpacked and the contents served to the crowd.

The commodious Hoover fishing camp, an hour's ride from Washington at the headwaters of the Rapidan River, served as a second home for the President and his wife. It was at Rapidan Camp that Hoover indulged his favorite sport of trout fishing and Mrs. Hoover entertained leaders of the Girl Scout movement, a prime interest. The First Lady, who was adamant in her resolve to avoid publicity, did not seem to mind when her name was mentioned in the press in connection with the Scouts.

On Christmas Eve it was routine to welcome a large group of Girl Scouts into the White House to sing carols. Bess Furman, noted newswoman and author, then a young reporter, determined to find out at first hand just what it was like at the White House on Christmas Eve. With the aid of Gertrude Bowman, custodian of the Girl Scouts' Little House on New York Avenue, Miss Furman disguised herself as a Scout and joined forty or so green-uniformed children on their way to the White House. Once inside the singers were lined up in the front foyer while the Marine Band stood by ready to accompany them. As the girls burst forth in "The First Noël," the Hoovers, in evening clothes, appeared spotlighted in the doorway of the Blue Room with their two tiny grand-

children. Mrs. Hoover requested additional carols—"Silent Night," "Good King Wenceslas," and "Joy to the World." Later the Scouts were taken to the East Room, where from a ceiling-high tree a silver candle and a red candle were plucked for each girl.

President Hoover's remarkable administrative talents, well demonstrated in his long public career, were put to good use in his early months in the White House. His plans were quickly undermined, however, for on Black Thursday, the twenty-fourth of October, 1929, the stock-market crash heralded the great depression which would outlast the Hoover administration. As President Hoover later expressed it, he had been "overtaken by the economic hurricane."

The Rapidan Camp became more than ever a retreat from the harrowing worries of the Presidency as Hoover strove valiantly to put into effect his solutions for the nation's economic problems. Private relief activities were organized, and the Reconstruction Finance Corporation was created to lend funds to big business.

In the summer of 1932, Hoover and Vice President Charles Curtis were renominated, but an arduous campaign led only to defeat by the Democratic candidates. Election returns that fall showed that Franklin D. Roosevelt of New York and his running mate, John N. Garner of Texas, had carried 42 states and 472 electoral votes.

During the Hoover occupancy, an invited public flocked to White House receptions.

"If it is a revolution it is a peaceful one," said F.D.R. in answer to attacks on the New Deal. Here the President exchanges banter with reporters near the Little White House in Warm Springs, Georgia.

A four-term lease

THE ROOSEVELTS—Franklin Delano and Eleanor—presented a refreshing contrast to the long line of Presidential couples who, from time to time, had suffered under the enormous demands of White House life. Taking to their new position with zest, the President and Mrs. Roosevelt soon had the White House fairly bursting with family and social activities and the diversified business of the New Deal.

The White House had long been familiar territory to both the Roosevelts. While a student at Harvard early in the century, Franklin D. Roosevelt had often visited the mansion, then occupied by a distant cousin, "Uncle Ted" Roosevelt. He had slept in its high-ceilinged, history-rich rooms and joined in the scintillating talk at TR's dinner table.

Eleanor Roosevelt, Theodore Roosevelt's favorite niece, had also had many chances to observe at close range the workings of the President's world, and it had been Uncle Ted who had given the bride away when Eleanor and Franklin Roosevelt were married in New York on St. Patrick's Day, 1905. When, twenty-eight years later, the Roosevelts moved into the White House, it was very much as though they were returning to a former home.

From his White House office President Roosevelt immediately directed the setting up of New Deal agencies to bring the country out of the depression. A rapid succession of relief measures, many of them formulated during Roosevelt's governorship of New York, were set up by Congress at a rate which surprised even Roosevelt. The Civilian Conservation Corps put a quarter of a million young men to work building dams, planting trees, and draining marshlands; in a year's time the Public Works Administration had removed a million men from relief rolls.

An amorphous group called the Brain Trusters, with Sam Rosenman, Raymond Moley, Rexford G. Tugwell, Adolf Berle, and Bernard Baruch prominent among its members, actively influenced the President's program.

President Roosevelt had original ideas on the handling of the press.

Every gadget and trinket on Roosevelt's cluttered desk in his study had its own meaning and, in addition, an anecdote. The bust is of his mother.

235

On his first Sunday morning in the White House the President
leaves for church with members of his family, including his
wife, Eleanor Roosevelt, and his mother, Sara Delano Roosevelt.

At his first press conference four days after entering the White House,
the President announced to a gathering of 125 newspaper and radio corre-
spondents that the practice of submitting written questions in advance
would no longer be observed. He would speak freely on all public issues
if it was politic to do so, and when he talked "off the record" the newsmen would be trusted to keep the information to themselves. The White
House at once became a leading source of interesting news.

Roosevelt reached out to the public more directly in his "fireside
chats"—simply phrased, lucid radio talks, delivered in a conversational
manner. As many as ten people worked over those "chats," but in the end
the President always rewrote or edited every speech himself. They were
always followed by an enormous increase in the White House mail.

In the early days of the New Deal, which Eleanor Roosevelt said were "exhilarating" to her husband, the President was never long away from his work. His day began early in the morning. After breakfast in bed, which was occasionally disrupted by grandchildren, he glanced through the newspapers, in the big bedroom facing south, submitted to a brief examination by his doctor, Ross McIntire, and planned his day with Marvin McIntyre and Steve Early, the appointments and press secretaries. The list of visitors expected during the day was already posted in the Press Room when the President arrived at his office in the executive wing.

The work day usually continued through the evening hours. Before that, however, there were cocktails served before dinner in the Oval Study, a room very much Roosevelt's own, with his collection of nautical prints and paintings hung against the white walls. The President mixed the cocktails himself, dispensing Martinis and old-fashioneds along with banter and stories.

A favorite sitting room, the upstairs Oval Room was also a second workshop, with its own huge desk loaded with trinkets and little figures. In this comfortable room Roosevelt often spent his evenings talking with off-the-record visitors, or waded through a pile of correspondence with Missy LeHand or Grace Tully, sometimes working far into the night.

The Roosevelts handled official social functions with urbanity and warmth, plus superhuman stamina. Thousands were entertained at dinners and receptions during their White House years. Mrs. Roosevelt might shake hands with 1500 visitors at a reception in the afternoon, and that night, along with the President, shake hands with another 1500. At times the First Lady's calendar listed as many as five functions in one day.

To the formal affairs the Roosevelts gradually added an imposing list of large, gay parties: annual entertainments for the press, with a hot buffet supper served to some 1500 members of the profession, garden parties for war veterans, and a yearly dinner for the President's Cuff-Links Club, an organization of cronies of long standing. While the President attended the Gridiron Club dinner, given every year for male members of the press, the Gridiron Widows had their own party at the White House.

As more than a million members of the general public also took a look at the White House each year, the wear and tear on the aging house became a serious problem. Henrietta Nesbitt, housekeeper under the Roosevelts, wrote in her *White House Diary* of the lengths to which the custodial staff was forced to go in order to keep the mansion in a presentable state. Sixty rooms and twenty baths had to be shined daily; the main floor polished every morning and touched up several times during the day; the entire house dusted two or three times a day. In the interest of hygiene and greater efficiency in this connection, Mrs. Nesbitt confiscated the maids' feather dusters and burned them wholesale. There was a ceaseless parade of painters, carpenters, and electricians through the house. Mrs. Nesbitt admitted she was kept on tenterhooks trying to find an interval when the Roosevelts were out of the house at the same time so she could conduct a thorough housecleaning, instead of, as she put it, "working around the Roosevelts."

Sistie and Buzzie, the darlings of the nation, have a session with the White House swing.

*"The greatest man the world has ever seen," was the opinion of
Roosevelt held by his long-time friend and adviser, Louis Howe.
Howe died during Roosevelt's first term.*

*Harry Hopkins in
the days when he
headed the W.P.A.*

It was mainly as visitors and sporadic residents that the White House
saw the Roosevelt children, now grown and pursuing their own lives.
The three older ones, Anna, James, and Elliott, were already married.
Franklin, Jr., and John Roosevelt were still at school. At the beginning of
Roosevelt's first term, Anna Roosevelt Dall, soon to be divorced from
Curtis Dall, brought her two small children, Anna Eleanor and Curtis,
to live in the White House; the childen, delights of the President's heart,
soon were "Sistie" and "Buzzie" to the entire country. Sara Delano Roosevelt, the President's mother, also came to the White House for long stays
and entertained her own friends at luncheon or tea.

Soon, in addition to carrying out her duties as First Lady, Eleanor
Roosevelt was traveling about the country, by plane, train, or car, acting
as a reporter for the President. Her talent for observing, for acting as "eyes
and ears" for her husband, had developed greatly during his 1921 attack
of poliomyelitis. Because he was bound to a wheel chair by a paralysis of
the lower limbs, President Roosevelt relied on his wife to keep him in
touch with the people of the nation. On her return from her travels he

238

F.D.R. thrived on press conferences. Although he might explode in anger afterward, during the meetings he usually was in command of the reporters and himself.

would question her closely on what she had seen and heard. During her first year in the White House, Mrs. Roosevelt covered nearly forty thousand miles—a figure she would top several times while she was First Lady.

F.D.R. begins a "fireside chat" from his study in the Oval Room.

The dynamic woman who had amazed the White House ushers when she ran the elevator herself, or poked up the fire without asking for help, gradually developed a career in her own right. Talks on the radio and lengthy lecture tours preceded the creation of her newspaper column, "My Day." The column became so popular that publishers entirely hostile to the Roosevelt administration found they were compelled to run it in their newspapers.

The Monroe Room became the setting for Mrs. Roosevelt's weekly press conferences at which she furthered the understanding of many of the New Deal measures for public welfare. Before she began this unusual activity, President Roosevelt's old friend and adviser, Louis McHenry Howe, coached Mrs. Roosevelt carefully in the handling of loaded questions sometimes skillfully slipped in by members of the press.

In the summer of 1934, the White House offices were given a badly

239

*The President and party
greet Queen Elizabeth
at Union Station
in June, 1939.
At right is
Secretary of State
Cordell Hull.*

needed enlargement by the rebuilding of the West Wing. An ingenious redesigning added space underground, leaving the outward appearance generally the same as in Theodore Roosevelt's renovation. Glass-walled offices and a new Cabinet Room were up-to-date features of the construction. The President's remarkable secretarial staff—Louis Howe, Stephen Early, Marvin McIntyre, Marguerite LeHand, and Grace Tully—received adequate working space. A swimming pool had already been installed through a public subscription started by a New York newspaper.

From his desk in his new oval office in the West Wing, Franklin D. Roosevelt carried out his program based on the responsibility of the government for the public welfare. He was seldom alone. To his desk there came a stream of men and women to hear Roosevelt talk and to air their own views. Even during luncheon, served from the refrigerated lunch wagon wheeled into the office from the kitchen, the President usually conferred with some close associate. Grace Tully revealed that the President's loquacity often disrupted his carefully planned schedule.

The President enjoyed the succession of visitors from other countries—national leaders who came to the White House to talk over the political and economic affairs of the world. Ramsey McDonald, Prime Minister of Great Britain, came with his daughter Ishbel. Edouard Herriot of France visited the President, and while he was there twenty-five French journalists were entertained at tea. Italian, German, Chinese, and South American envoys sat face to face with President Roosevelt in his study and discussed the problems of the world.

In the summer of 1939, three months before Great Britain went to war against Germany, the White House had a two-day visit from King George and Queen Elizabeth of England. For their short, highly publicized stay in the capital, no detail of protocol or entertainment was overlooked. President Roosevelt himself took part in making plans for their visit and came up with the idea of seating the Queen, instead of the King, at his right at the dinner table, an idea which proved very pleasing to them.

The White House domestic staff was "briefed like a small army" before the arrival of the royal couple. "We received orders from the ushers as to the duties of our floor men and women," wrote Mrs. Nesbitt in her *Diary.* "The women were . . . to contact the maids of Her Royal Majesty, and her ladies' maids' maids, and find out what they could do for them."

The amiable King and Queen were pleased with it all—with their newly renovated suites upstairs, with the affability of the Roosevelts, and especially with the all-American entertainment given by folk and opera singers, fifty-nine in all, following the State dinner.

The royal retinue was less happy in the White House, in spite of the attention given their comfort. When King George's valet complained about the quality of the food and drink he was being served and Queen Elizabeth's maid had the White House upstairs maids warm up her lunch for the third time, word got around among the White House staff that the royal attendants were putting on airs. But the staff was bemused by the English requests for blankets and hot-water bottles during a heat wave.

240

President and Mrs. Roosevelt in a springtime mood.

Roosevelt leaves for his 1941 inaugural, leaving a disappointed Fala behind.

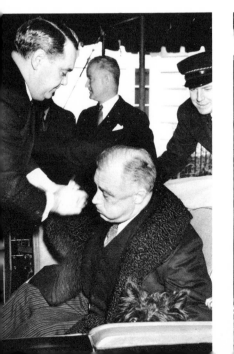

Margaret Suckley, the President's cousin, who gave Fala to the President, took this picture of them together.

The Japanese attack on Pearl Harbor was announced at the White House during lunch. President Roosevelt was eating in his study with Harry Hopkins, Mrs. Roosevelt was entertaining thirty guests. Before Christmas, Winston Churchill, with full entourage, including two Scotland Yard men and a valet, arrived at the White House for a stay of several weeks. There were days and nights of conferences between Churchill and the President as they made decisions on strategy. The Prime Minister napped during the afternoon while the President caught up on his regular work. Then, after dinner, the two men, often joined by American and English aides, worked late into the night. Mrs. Roosevelt remembers that it took the President several days to catch up on his sleep after Mr. Churchill left for England.

Under wartime security, the doors of the White House were closed to the public. Troops guarded the entrances and manned the machine guns on the roof. Blackout curtains were hung throughout the house and an order issued that no more planes could fly overhead. Employees in the White House had to show passes bearing their fingerprints before being admitted to the grounds each morning. A gas mask was attached to the President's wheel chair at all times.

The Trophy Room on the ground floor was turned into a map room, and it was there that President Roosevelt, as Commander in Chief, supervised the planning of the procedures of war. In code, over carefully guarded telephone lines, information concerning the latest moves on all fronts came to the White House from the War and Navy Departments. Winston Churchill, coming back to the White House for long visits, asked for his own map room and got it—in the Monroe Room on the second floor.

The White House had a necessary wartime remodeling, with addi-

The White House ablaze
with light on the night
of the "day that will
live in infamy,"
December 7, 1941.

tional office space provided in the rebuilt East Wing. The Social Bureau and the Secret Service, with its elaborate system of communications, were set up in new quarters there. In a subterranean basement the first White House bomb shelter was installed—a grim new note—with a small vault for highly important state papers built into its center.

Harry Hopkins, who had originally come to Washington at Roosevelt's invitation to carry out the New Deal relief measures, had become increasingly important to the President in his role of wartime adviser and personal emissary. When Hopkins told the President in June, 1942, that he was going to be married to Louise Macy, Roosevelt immediately asked that they move into the White House so that Hopkins would be nearby at all times. After their wedding they came to live in the President's House, bringing along Diana, Hopkins' small daughter by a former marriage.

In 1942 a fascinating string of guests came to dine and sleep at the White House. Alexander Woollcott, famous wit and raconteur, swapped stories with the President and made himself characteristically at home in his bedroom, inviting guests for meals and asking for coffee to be sent up at frequent intervals during the day and night.

President Roosevelt
and Prime Minister
Churchill hold a
council of war.

Mrs. Roosevelt and Madame Chiang Kai-shek on the lawn early in 1943.

Foreign Minister Molotov came from Russia, and the White House valet assigned to him found a picnic of black bread and sausages side by side with a pistol when he unpacked Molotov's bag. George II, King of Greece; Peter II of Yugoslavia; Queen Wilhelmina of Holland; all came to the White House to gain such succor as was obtainable. Madame Chiang Kai-shek arrived for a short stay, bringing, as only part of her usual entourage of forty persons: two nurses, two nieces, and a nephew. The Chinese settled in as though in a hotel; Madame Chiang demanded fresh silk sheets each day, and the party's peremptory method of summoning servants by clapping hands brought a variety of comment from White House residents. Mrs. Roosevelt said that Madame Chiang "could talk very convincingly about democracy . . . but hasn't any idea how to live it." A White House usher said more bluntly, "They think they're in China calling the coolies."

There were other visitors to the White House in those anxious days in which American troops were deployed all over the world. Probably the most important of all to Eleanor Roosevelt were the wounded service men who were able to leave briefly their rooms in Washington hospitals and come, often on crutches or in wheel chairs, to the White House for tea. Mrs. Roosevelt entertained the young men with little anecdotes about Fala, the President's dog, and a ghost story or two centering on the White House bedrooms. With four sons in dangerous spots on several different war fronts, Mrs. Roosevelt wanted to be of service to the men who were bearing the brunt of the war.

With Senator Harry S. Truman as running mate, President Roosevelt was elected to a fourth term of office in November, 1944. At his inauguration in January—a brief ceremony on the South Portico of the White House —many persons present were struck by the President's look of exhaustion. Roosevelt had paid dearly for the strain of his years as Commander in Chief of the armed forces.

It was after his return from the Big Three meeting in Yalta in early February that Grace Tully, the President's secretary, noticed the signs of a weariness that would not be erased and his heroic efforts to call up energy for each day's demands. When, on March 1, President Roosevelt went up to Capitol Hill to address a joint session of Congress, he spoke from a sitting position, explaining that he could thus dispense with the ten-pound locked leg braces which he always wore for public appearances.

In spite of his rapidly waning strength, the President found great satisfaction in the pattern of the war in the spring of 1945. The feel of victory was in the air; in Europe, the defeat of the enemy was accepted as imminent. Plans were being made for setting up an organization for peace, the United Nations. Delegates to the coming San Francisco conference were invited to the White House to be briefed for the important session. The President was in a hopeful mood when he left Washington on March 29 for a short rest in Warm Springs. He planned to address the opening session of the United Nations conference in San Francisco.

April 12, in the Little White House in Georgia, started out as a routine

244

Roosevelt and a solemn
Vice President-elect
Harry S. Truman, after
the election of 1944;
and below, Roosevelt
speaks in the quietest
of all inaugurals
from the back porch of
the White House in
January, 1945.

President and Mrs. Roosevelt were photographed with their thirteen grandchildren on the day of his fourth inauguration.

Chief Justice Stone swears Harry S. Truman in to the Presidency in the Executive Offices of the White House, on April 12, 1945.

vacation day for the President. He sat in his study signing papers and looking over important mail. Later in the day he planned to go to a barbecue, and in the evening the polio patients at the Foundation were to stage a minstrel show in his honor.

Around lunchtime, while the artist, Elizabeth Shoumatoff, sketched his features in preparation for doing an oil painting, the President slumped sideways in his chair, murmured, "I have a terrific headache," and fainted. At 3:35 that afternoon, President Franklin D. Roosevelt died of a massive cerebral hemorrhage.

Eleanor Roosevelt was attending a benefit tea in Washington that day when she was called back to the White House by phone. Harry S. Truman, called to the White House by Stephen Early, arrived at 5:25 P.M. and was taken to Mrs. Roosevelt in her study on the second floor. When the shocked Vice President wondered aloud what he could do to help, Mrs. Roosevelt's answer was, "What can we do for you?"

The White House rooms filled up with stricken-faced men and women. The dead President's Cabinet met in the Cabinet room in the Executive Offices for the short swearing-in of President Harry S. Truman.

Up the long track from Georgia came the funeral train, past towns and villages and through great cities, with bands playing "Hail to the Chief" when it paused for a moment; and weeping crowds pressing near the train.

Once again a President lay in state in the flower-banked East Room. At brief funeral services beside the flag-draped, closed coffin, Mrs. Roosevelt stood with her daughter, Anna, and one son, Elliott. Three sons had been unable to get back to the White House in time. Men in uniform were a reminder that there was still a war to be brought to an end.

The casket is carried into the White House on April 14, 1945; and below, friends of the President arrive for the funeral. Margaret Suckley leads Fala.

Mrs. Harry S. Truman and Margaret Truman photographed at Blair House,
where, with the President, they were to spend nearly half of their
White House years. At right, President Truman in a jovial mood.

Old house, new home

Harry S. Truman was "shocked" to learn that he was President. He has said it was "overwhelming to step right in and take charge." In the first three-month period of his Presidency, during which Mr. and Mrs. Truman and their college-age daughter, Margaret, moved into the White House, the war in Europe was ended, the Atomic Age began, the war with Japan was won, and the United Nations Charter was drafted.

The Trumans had moved from their modest Connecticut Avenue apartment on the day following the inauguration. Instead of going directly to the White House, however, they had moved into Blair House across Pennsylvania Avenue in order to give Mrs. Eleanor Roosevelt time to gather up the Roosevelt possessions, the accumulation of twelve years in the mansion.

When Mrs. Truman and Margaret looked over the big, vacant house, the high-ceilinged, barn-like family quarters seemed especially dismal. Margaret thought it would be impossible to give the rooms the cozy, friendly feeling the Truman family would like, but she was determined at least "to have something cheerful" when the house was redecorated.

Painters slapped on color in the bedrooms and private sitting rooms—pastels in blue and rose for Margaret, lavender and gray for Mrs. Truman, and cream and off-white for the President. Margaret had her grand piano installed in her chintz-hung sitting room and President Truman also had a piano in his study. Margaret then piled her bed with stuffed animals and dolls much as she would have done in the big house in Independence, Missouri, and she warmly welcomed the gift of a red Irish setter puppy.

By the war's end, social gatherings in the capital had become larger and larger, with those in the White House the largest of all. Guests at receptions stood four abreast as they waited to shake hands with President and Mrs. Truman in the Blue Room. Invitation lists for State dinners, luncheons, and teas were the longest in history.

In the midst of this excitement the Trumans managed to maintain

Crowds waiting in Lafayette Park for news of the Japanese surrender.

249

*The brisk Truman
walk was caught by
a photographer.*

a serene level of private life. Mrs. Truman's chief interest lay in the White House family which included her mother, Mrs. D. W. Wallace. Mrs. Truman appeared at as many of the teas, dinners, ship-christenings, and press luncheons as possible, but she never abandoned her early decision to give no personal interviews or press conferences.

On the occasions when they were not separately occupied, President and Mrs. Truman would spend an evening together in the family lounge at the end of the upstairs hall, enjoying a period of intimate talk and family gossip. Thinking that some of her school friends might be awed by the grandeur of her new home, Margaret encouraged them to call her and left orders at the switchboard that she was always "in" to them. The family icebox on the third floor was kept stocked with snacks for the younger set.

Margaret was thrilled when she discovered that she could ask for a showing of any Hollywood film, old or new, any time she pleased, and she sat through her old favorite, *The Scarlet Pimpernel*, sixteen times. She also liked the Secret Service-chauffeured rides to classes at George Washington University. These pleasures compensated hugely for the White House cooking, which she termed "institutional," and also for the annoyance of the role of belle which she found forced upon her.

Margaret Truman had heard the legend that Abraham Lincoln's ghost sometimes paced the floor of his old study, and after the Trumans had moved the huge Lincoln bed into the room where Lincoln signed the Emancipation Proclamation, the urge to sleep there was too strong for her to resist. Not quite daring to risk the adventure alone, she invited two girl friends to share the bed with her for the night.

No ghost appeared—the President had thought of hiring one for the occasion but was hesitant about giving the girls a bad fright—but it was a sleepless night for all of them nevertheless. What kept the girls awake, finally reducing them to sleeping on the floor, was the bed itself—the miserably uncomfortable bed which Mary Lincoln had left behind when she fled the White House to Illinois in the spring of 1865.

President Truman inherited an incredible number of problems from his predecessor, Franklin Roosevelt. "Don't look back," he has said. "You've got to keep going. . . . You've got to look ahead of you." To help him make decisions Mr. Truman set up a Central Intelligence Agency, which contributed secret information. Cabinet members and the department heads of the Army, Navy, and Air Force added their own ideas, but, in the end, Truman has said, "The President has to make the decisions. . . . A man to be President of the United States has to understand the whole picture. . . . He must be fundamentally honest. . . . He must have a policy. . . . He must be honest intellectually and otherwise. . . ."

It was at once evident that the White House did not have as its chief tenant the colorless personality which the quickly applied term "average man" suggested. President Harry S. Truman was as satisfactory a source of copy as any of his predecessors. He arose at 5:30 A.M. and each morning went for a vigorous walk. He pleased his public with his simple humility

Truman's plan for extended offices.

and his down-to-earth style of expression. His love of music, especially Mozart, Bach, and Chopin, was well known, and pictures of Truman at the keyboard appeared in the press constantly. In making decisions, however, the salty President went his own way, unmoved either by flattery or criticism. "I never give much weight or attention to the brickbats that are thrown my way," he confided to a journalist.

The first atomic bomb was produced at Los Alamos, New Mexico, and exploded at Alamogordo, New Mexico, July 16, 1945. The second bomb was dropped from a B-29 on Hiroshima, Japan, August 6; the third bomb on Nagasaki August 9. The decision to use the atomic bomb was President Truman's—a decision made inside the White House. Mr. Truman has said that the atomic bomb was dropped "on the theory that our troops were expecting to invade Japan in a short time." The official estimate was that 1.5 million men would have been used for the invasion; that there would have been five hundred thousand casualties and two hundred and fifty thousand dead. The atomic bomb was "a weapon of war. . . . In war you use every weapon you have. . . . You have to use it. . . ." President Truman has said that "I had no trouble sleeping. . . . I read myself to sleep every night in the White House, reading biography or the troubles of some President in the past."

HST's balcony.

The White House had already outgrown the changes made under Franklin Roosevelt, and early in 1946 President Truman had plans drawn up for an extension to the executive offices in the west wing. Congress, on learning that the cost of the project was to be $1,650,000, refused to grant an appropriation. Money was forthcoming, however, for straightening the pillars of the North Portico.

A furor arose the following year when President Truman spent $10,000 for a balcony behind the pillars of the South Portico. The President was proud of his balcony and the greater the outcry, the more he defended it. The balcony was defensible, he said, on the best grounds of architectural tradition. Scoffing at the idea that the balcony had been put on to provide an outdoor sitting area or, indeed, that he had time for rocking on a porch, he gave two reasons for adding it: first, to break what Truman considered the outlandish, disproportionate height of the portico columns, designed in Jefferson's day; and second to aid in shading the windows of the Blue Room. Dirt-collecting awnings could be done away with and neat wooden shades rolled up under the balcony, to be let down when needed.

At about the time the balcony was being built, President Truman had an opportunity to put to practical use the knowledge of architecture he

A White House custodian points out a crack in the upstairs hall.

A split beam, with steel brace, directly under Margaret Truman's upstairs sitting room.

had gained while he was a judge in Jackson County, Missouri, when he had overseen the construction of both the Independence and Kansas City courthouses. Toward the fall of 1947, the President's practiced eye detected some peculiarities in the structure of the house he and his family were occupying. The floor of the living quarters sagged badly, and in the upstairs Oval Room which he used as a study, the floor creaked and swayed under his feet. In his big bathroom, the tub appeared to be slowly sinking into the floor. The plaster on the parlor ceilings, too, was continuously cracking and one day a leg of Margaret's piano went through the ceiling of the family dining room directly below.

In February, 1948, President Truman called in a committee of architects and engineers, including Lorenzo S. Winslow, the official White House architect, and W. Englebert Reynolds, Commissioner of Public Buildings, and asked them to make a quick examination of the house. Their early discoveries of structural weakness and serious fire hazards made it clear that a more thorough examination of the building would be needed. In April, President Truman got $50,000 from Congress for such a study.

The Committee's findings were appalling. The White House was found to be resting on soft clay with footings only eight feet deep. Interior walls had settled and cracked, and beams were giving way. The foundation of the grand stairway was on the verge of collapse, and the heavy roof and third floor added in 1927 leaned on crumbling walls. No one could understand why the old mansion had not come tumbling down long before.

Through the long years since 1817, the building's beams and studs had been perforated to accommodate wires and pipes. Doors had been cut here and there according to the whim of a tenant, closed off and cut somewhere else. Commissioner Reynolds suggested that the family floor was staying put "purely from habit." A wag said that it was all holding together solely from pride. Only the outer walls were pronounced sound and worthy of preservation.

While the survey of the White House continued through the summer of 1948, the Trumans vacationed in their home town, Independence, Missouri. In the early fall, when the political polls had showed conclusively that Truman would be defeated by the Republican candidate, Thomas E.

Dewey, the President, accompanied by his wife and daughter, began his whistle-stop campaign journey. The stunning upset of Election Day surprised nearly everyone but Harry S. Truman.

The condition of the White House had been found so hazardous that it had to be evacuated immediately. The Trumans, on their return to Washington, moved into government-owned Blair House.

By February, 1949, the estimates for restoring the White House to a safely livable condition had risen from $1,400,000 to $5,400,000. At President Truman's request, Congress set up the Commission on Renovation of the Executive Mansion, consisting of two Senators, two Representatives, the President of the American Society of Civil Engineers, Mr. Richard E. Dougherty, and the President of the American Institute of Architects, Mr. Douglas W. Orr. The Commission was given authority to carry out all measures necessary to the complete restoration of the White House. Experts on engineering and architecture acted as advisers. Major General Glen E. Edgerton served as Executive Director and Mr. Lorenzo S. Winslow was Secretary of the Commission. A contract was made with the builder John McSwain.

The major question of whether to raze the original outer walls of the White House, or to use them as a shell for a new interior had already been debated in Congress. The Commission decreed that for historical and sentimental reasons, the walls should be preserved. The exterior walls would be under-pinned with concrete piers set from twenty-four to twenty-seven feet below ground level, the interior removed, and a steel frame erected inside the old walls. All interior loads would rest on this framework.

One of the most lengthy and intricate phases of the restoration of the White House involved the removal and storage of the irreplaceable chandeliers, mantelpieces, and woodwork. Ornamental plasterwork was carefully diagrammed before it was removed. Every inch of valuable architectural material was marked and filed away for the future.

While the giant reconstruction of the White House proceeded, the Trumans carried out their social duties on a scale appropriate to the smaller setting of Blair House. For very large affairs they took over an auditorium in a Washington hotel.

Truman removed this sign
after only one weekend.

The load on the marble
columns is measured
and concrete poured
in the new underpinning.

A well from the days of Jefferson; the gold-leafed corridor ceiling from 1817; stones from the original White House, fire-blackened in the burning of 1814; these were all uncovered at the start of the vast rebuilding of 1952.

Bulldozers excavated for a two-story baseme

a steel framework rose inside the shell of the outer walls.

The finish is removed from oak paneling
in the Dining Room before painting it green.

Ornamental plasterers prepare
decorations for White House moldings.

The Blue Room's wall covering nears completion.

A carpet of turf is laid across the south lawn.

A crystal chandelier, subtly remodeled and simplified, goes up again in the East Room.

Movers start bringing back the White House furniture from Blair House and from storage.

The new East Room suggested a simple elegance, with its crystal chandeliers and gold drapes against white walls.

There was a gold-and-white Louis XV mantel in the oval Blue Room, which carried a classic motif of gold on its deep-blue walls.

The soft green of the State Dining Room paneling was a notable change from the dark oak walls and trophy heads put there by Theodore Roosevelt.

In the first-floor China Room there were examples of china from almost every family who had lived in the White House. The Christy portrait of Mrs. Coolidge hangs there.

A Carrara marble mantel-piece bought in 1816 was placed in the Red Room.

The President's private study in the Oval Room.

The only Victorian room in the house was the Lincoln Room on the second floor.

The Great Seal was
woven into the carpet
in the Green Room.

Real candles burned
in the chandelier in the
Family Dining Room.

The Rose Room, where
queens and other ranking
visitors would sleep.

The Trumans return to the restored White House, and soon thereafter the President describes the new interior for television. Here, he descends the main stair for the benefit of the camera and chats with an announcer in the Red Room.

President Truman continuously faced new problems arising from Communist aggression in Europe and the Far East. The Korean war, which began in the summer of 1950, dragged on and on. Korea was "the most difficult decision in my eight years in the White House. . . . I wanted to establish the United Nations as a going concern. . . ." About Korea—in fact, about all his important decisions made in the White House—Harry Truman says he has "no regrets. Not the slightest." In his inaugural speech of 1949, President Truman had spoken of the urgency of helping the people of the world to help themselves. Only if the undeveloped areas of the world were made productive and their people self-reliant, he believed, could there ever be world peace. Truman's Point Four program, which he thought was his greatest move toward peace, was initiated to meet what he called "a growing crisis in a world torn between aggression and peace."

Margaret Truman chose this period for launching a singing career which kept her on the move giving concerts and making radio or television appearances. Between engagements, she managed a lively social schedule. President Truman was proud of his daughter's talent and of her courage in striking out for herself; when she received good notices, he believed she deserved them. When the music critic of the Washington *Post*, Paul Hume, wrote an unflattering review of one of her concerts, the President thought he was mistaken and answered him to that effect, using blunt, colloquial language to make sure he was understood.

President Harry S. Truman had been an avid letter writer all his life

262

I shall not be a candidate for re-election. I have served my country long and I think efficiently and honestly. I shall not accept a renomination. I do not feel that it is my duty to spend another four years in the White House.

Truman settles a question in the spring of 1952.

and only a small proportion of his letters had been anything but warm and friendly. His letter to Hume was the one the nation heard the most about, however, and opinions for and against his unconventional action were heard for weeks. The President wrote down his own defense in his diary: "A frustrated critic on the Washington *Post* wrote a lousy review. The only thing, General Marshall said, he didn't criticize was the varnish on the piano. He put my baby as low as he could and he made the young accompanist look like a dub.

"It upset me and I wrote him what I thought of him. I told him he was lower than Mr. X and that was intended to be an insult worse than a reflection on his ancestry. I would never reflect on a man's mother because mothers are not to be attacked, although mine was.

"Well, I've had a grand time this day. I'm accused of putting my baby who is the apple of my eye in a bad position. I don't think that is so. She doesn't either—thank the Almighty."

263

President and Mrs. Dwight D. Eisenhower.

14 | Dwight D. Eisenhower   1953–1961

The executive mansion

With the entry of Dwight D. Eisenhower into the Presidency in 1953, the White House became the home, for the first time in more than seventy years, of a former general and the general's wife. The extraordinary popularity that brought Eisenhower to the White House had already embraced Mrs. Eisenhower, whom the public had first got to know during the 1952 election campaign.

Although Washington hostesses longed to entertain the glamorous couple living in the White House, they were soon sighing over their inability to entice the Eisenhowers out of their new home. The President and First Lady were positive about the manner in which they meant to spend their leisure hours. By the time they had been in the White House for a year they were fairly well categorized as homebodies, rarely accepting invitations to large affairs but choosing to spend their evenings quietly, in front of a television set or watching a movie in the theatre on the ground floor. Sometimes friends were invited in for bridge or canasta. "At last I've got a job where I can stay home nights, and, by golly, I'm going to stay home," the President told a friend.

Since they had been on the go year after year, the attitude of the Eisenhowers was understandable. Since the summer day in 1916 when the young first lieutenant, Dwight D. Eisenhower, and Mamie Doud, aged nineteen, were married in her home in Denver, Colorado, the couple had been continuously on the move. As many as thirty times they had been abruptly uprooted from a new spot just as it began to feel like home, and transferred to another town or army post. They had lived in the Canal Zone, in the Philippines, on army posts everywhere, and finally in Europe. Their last home abroad had been the Villa St. Pierre, at Marnes-la-Coquette, a suburb of Paris.

It was a spectacular household that Mrs. Eisenhower became head of, early in 1953. The backstage areas of the White House had been completely remodeled and were efficiently run by a large household staff. Nevertheless Mrs. Eisenhower was said to devote more hours to domestic duties

The moving in. Deliverymen handle an Eisenhower painting with care.

265

The appointed moment for a state dinner approaches. The tablecloth has had its final touching up with an iron, the floral arrangements have been checked, and waiters hover in the soft light from the silver chandelier. Below, Winston Churchill, master of the magnificent entrance, pays a visit to the Eisenhowers at the White House.

than any other recent First Lady. Her day began with conferences with the head usher, who takes care of the social program; the maître-d'hôtel, who is in charge of the butlers; and the housekeeper, who oversees the cleaning of the big house. She then spent hours answering mail and meeting callers.

Early in her White House occupancy Mrs. Eisenhower expressed concern to a journalist friend that the public's impression was that the mansion had the proportions of a castle, and that the Eisenhowers were attended like royalty. Actually, she pointed out, a majority of the seventy-one White House servants mentioned in the press were engaged in maintenance of the recently restored house. As for the "hundred and two rooms," every bathroom and storeroom, small or large, was included in the figure.

President Eisenhower wisely permitted himself time to indulge in some hobbies. He was an ardent fisherman and golfer, an enthusiastic outdoor cook, and a good bridge player. Like his old friend Winston Churchill, Eisenhower had taken up oil painting solely as a means of relaxation. One day the President startled a friend by cleaning off the still-wet paint and starting the canvas over, explaining that "it was no fun once it was done."

So that the President could practice his golfing shots in private, a putting green was installed on the edge of the White House lawn in 1954. The following year the squirrels on the grounds came into prominence when it was reported that the President had ordered them banished because they were ruining his golf green. Senator Richard Neuberger, of Oregon, with tongue in cheek, began a "Save the White House Squirrels Fund" to pay for a fence to "prevent any . . . depredations by marauding squirrels."

A new interest had come into the lives of the Eisenhowers in 1949, with the purchase of a 189-acre farm in Gettysburg, Pennsylvania. The house, parts of which were more than two hundred years old, was slowly remodeled into a "modernized version of a Pennsylvania burgher's house," with occupancy planned for the spring of 1955. The farm became more and more a second home for the Eisenhowers.

President Eisenhower added two innovations to the Presidential press conferences which have taken place in the White House since the Wilson era, and which became major weekly events during the Roosevelt and Truman administrations. He allowed reporters to quote him verbatim, and he also admitted television cameras. Veteran actor and television producer Robert Montgomery was given an office in the White House so that he could act as adviser and coach to President Eisenhower on his broadcasts.

At 6:15 on the evening of November 25, 1957, reporters were summoned to the office of the associate White House Press Secretary, Mrs. Anne Wheaton, acting in the absence of James Hagerty. Mrs. Wheaton revealed to a packed room and an anxious nation that the President had "suffered a chill." Subsequent reports, however, stated that the President had had a mild stroke. His recovery was rapid, and a week later he was back at work in his office.

Whether or not the strain of the ever-growing burden of the Presidency was to blame, the cerebral hemorrhage, following a heart attack and an

267

Aftermath of an Easter egg-rolling.

Barbara Ann and Dwight David Eisenhower, the President's grandchildren, who often came to visit.

President Eisenhower limbers up on his own golf green.

East Room ceremonies in 1957 began second terms for both Eisenhower and Nixon.

In late 1957, President Eisenhower showed a television audience a missile nose cone which he said had been "hundreds of miles to outer space and back."

operation to relieve ileitis, was the third serious illness which had struck President Eisenhower since the fall of 1955. Each time the attention of the nation and the world had focused on the White House. The lingering death of Garfield and Wilson's paralytic stroke were recalled, and the near-disaster which attended them as governmental affairs came to a halt.

In contrast, under Eisenhower, the processes of the Executive branch were carried on by members of Eisenhower's official family. Vice President Nixon, Assistant to the President Sherman Adams, Press Secretary James C. Hagerty, and others kept the wheels of government turning until the President's recovery. *The New York Times* referred to this period as one of "government-by-committee."

Inevitably, as his illnesses were highlighted, the President's opponents dwelt on his absences from the White House, his long periods of convalescence, and the time spent in keeping well. A special Presidential assistant, Robert K. Gray, was quoted as saying that it made his blood boil to hear Eisenhower called "a part-time President." His opinion was that Eisenhower was the "world's hardest-working man."

Mrs. Eisenhower had always been flexible in regard to White House entertaining. When the President's coronary attack in 1955 made state dinners too exhausting, a luncheon was substituted for a visiting head of state and his wife. The traditional winter social schedule at the White House included six state dinners and five large receptions, but by the winter of 1957–1958 formal functions had been greatly curtailed. Receptions were omitted altogether that year, but the dinners were followed by musicales, to which additional guests were invited.

The space age opened with the orbiting Russian and American earth satellites. Indicative of the nation's heightened interest in science was a Science-Military dinner given at the White House in February, 1958. Dr. James R. Killian, Jr., Special Assistant to the President for Science, and various missile experts shared honors with the Joint Chiefs of Staff and the Secretaries of the Army, Navy, and Air Force.

268

A new way for a President to travel. Eisenhower approaches his helicopter.

The President, his wife, and his son, Major John S. Eisenhower, with his family, walk through the Christmas-decked hall of the White House.

*Britain's Queen
Elizabeth II
gets a warm welcome
from Mrs. Eisenhower.*

In the early months of President Eisenhower's second term, plans were made public for providing more space for the executive offices, which, it was disclosed, employed over 1,500 people. Times had changed since Theodore Roosevelt had found the White House office staff jammed into three rooms on the second floor. Roosevelt solved his space problem with the addition of the West Wing and had turned the entire upstairs into family quarters. Under Eisenhower, that same West Wing housed the hundred or so employees most closely linked to the office of the President. But the remainder worked in the old State-War-Navy Building, now called the Executive Office Building, or in office quarters scattered over the city.

The projected plans called for the razing of the block northwest of the White House and across Pennsylvania Avenue, leaving standing only Blair House, Lee House, and Decatur House. This space would be filled by a seven-story office building. A three- or four-story building on the site of the razed State Building, with a tunnel connecting it with the White House, would take care of the President and his staff.

Although it was too late for his administration to benefit from any changes, President Eisenhower was eager to settle the question of housing for the executive offices. In a press conference the President spoke freely of the meaning of the White House to the public: "We must never minimize what the White House, just as a building, means to America. I have seen strong men come into that building . . . with tears on their cheeks. . . . I think the White House should never be overshadowed by anything or ill-treated."

270

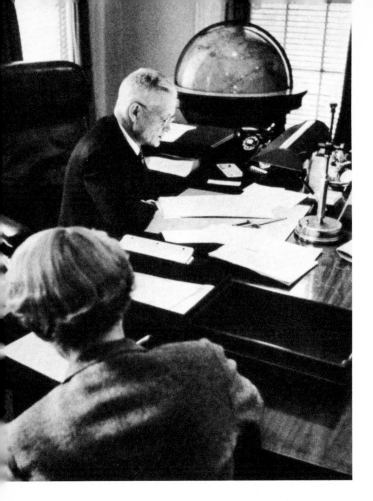

In the West Wing, home of the Executive Offices, are seen some of the men closest to the President. At left, Assistant to the President Sherman Adams dictates; at right, Press Secretary James C. Hagerty hands out a news release. Below, Secretary of Labor Mitchell waits in the office of Appointments Secretary Robert Gray for an interview with the President.

Seated between the American flag and the blue-and-white President's flag, President Dwight D. Eisenhower begins another long day in his office as an aide appears with documents. In addition to making crucial decisions, the President must daily meet with a wide range of visitors from America and abroad. King Saud of Saudi Arabia elucidates, below.

The President confers with Secretary of State John Foster Dulles and
James J. Wadsworth of the State Department on a question of international
policy. Below, a group of winners in a 4-H Club competition exchanges
gifts and pleasantries with Eisenhower. The President received a
bellows for his farm, the girls and boys pens and key rings.

Above, a dozen of the hundreds of behind-the-scenes workers who keep the wheels of government turning. Below, Jim Hagerty consults a teleprinter, switchboard girls carry on, and a clerk consults a distant file.

Here, President Eisenhower leaves his office to walk to an important meeting in a conference room just down the hall. Below, reporters wait in the White House Press Room, a center for the world's hottest news.

Dwight D. Eisenhower, thirty-fourth President
of the United States of America, stands for a
moment on the terrace outside his office. He
gazes across the south grounds, as have all the
men who have inherited the traditions and the
responsibilities of the Presidency and the loan
of the White House for a few years. Nothing has
really changed here. The mansion has been added
to and subtracted from, burned, rebuilt, and
demolished, and yet has emerged essentially the
same. The changes were all of the flesh and not
the spirit. The enduring qualities of the White
House have lived on within its thick sandstone
walls: the vision of Washington, who never lived
to see his dream; the spacious and ordered
concepts of Jefferson; the spirit of Jackson; the
patience of Lincoln; and the reason and daring
of other great Presidents—Grover Cleveland,
Theodore Roosevelt, Woodrow Wilson, Franklin
Delano Roosevelt. From the beginning, the White
House has been the social and ceremonial center
of the nation. It has been home to some
remarkable and gracious women: Dolley Madison,
Mary Todd Lincoln, Lucy Hayes, Frances Folsom
Cleveland, Grace Coolidge, Eleanor Roosevelt
among them. Great men and women have lived in
the White House and will continue to live there,
for as Abigail Adams wrote in 1800, "This house is
built for ages to come."

A new frontier

THE WHITE HOUSE, tranquil and unchanging, had stood for 160 years. The rowdy uses of its early years, its families' sorrows, the somber whisper of scandal, had all been in the nature of onslaughts against its cool and classic composure.

More fittingly, the White House had seen the heights of personal and official triumph. No other walls in America had looked on so much pomp and social brilliance, as well as simple domestic felicity. But events beyond the wildest imaginings of its builders had given it only a certain patina of age.

The White House newcomers of early 1961, President John F. Kennedy and his family, were to bring to the house their own new and highly individual style.

The impact of the Kennedys on the White House, and on the nation, was nothing less than stupendous. Seldom had such an amalgam of energy, youth, wealth, and ability been observed in persons occupying high positions. In the West Wing, in the family quarters, in the public parlors, something constructive was constantly afoot.

Mrs. Kennedy set to work on a project to restore the interior of the mansion to its classic style, with the ultimate objective of making it a showcase of history and art of the American Republic. A Fine Arts Committee, with various subcommittees under it, was appointed to seek out authentic American antiques and paintings of the eighteenth and nineteenth centuries. State functions took on a liveliness scarcely recalled by Washington's oldest citizens.

In the West Wing offices the challenges facing the New Frontier were attacked with vigor and optimism. A Cabinet member said that the Kennedy deadline for action would be "the day before yesterday." The coverage by all news media of these activities was overwhelmingly thorough.

There were many "firsts" attendant on the Kennedys' entry into the White House. John F. Kennedy was the first President to be elected to

As part of their program to encourage the arts, the Kennedys brought Shakespeare to the White House. Here, actors of the American Shakespeare Festival take a bow after a performance in the East Room.

President John F. Kennedy and his family pause for a moment at the entrance to the White House.

Caroline makes herself at home in her father's office and John F. Kennedy, Jr.,
enjoys the out-of-doors, while Charlie, the Welsh terrier, stands guard.

Caroline and her friends peer into the playground pool.

Macaroni, the pony, joins the Kennedys and visitors for an interlude on the White House grounds.

the office at the early age of forty-three. He was also the first Roman Catholic President. He held, for the first time, "live" television news conferences. Mrs. Kennedy was the first very youthful First Lady since the days of Mrs. Grover Cleveland. Dr. Janet G. Travell was the first woman ever to be named White House physician. It was the first time in many decades that the White House had had as its tenants parents of small children.

It was the Kennedys as a family that most intrigued the American public. The handsome and cultivated couple, their three-year-old daughter Caroline, and infant son John, Jr., seemed to meet all the requirements for White House families. They occupied family quarters consisting of fifteen rooms on the second floor, with the addition of a top-floor playroom for the children.

The new White House occupants dazzled their guests and the watching public with the sumptuousness of their state dinners and receptions. Like Thomas Jefferson, the Kennedys employed a French chef and realized the value of music at social affairs. The punch bowls were filled to the brim, and there was dancing in the East Room, led off by the President and First Lady.

At official functions, the tedious, traditional receiving line was often abandoned, permitting guests to go up to the main floor at once, and

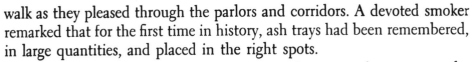

Preceding his concert in the White House, the Spanish 'cellist, Pablo Casals, rehearses in the Diplomatic Reception Room. He is flanked by Mieczyslaw Horszowski, pianist, and Alexander Schneider, violinist.

walk as they pleased through the parlors and corridors. A devoted smoker remarked that for the first time in history, ash trays had been remembered, in large quantities, and placed in the right spots.

Mrs. Kennedy soon shortened the state dinners to four courses, for her belief was that five courses provided too much food for White House guests. A little time was saved by shortening the meal, and it was usually devoted to after-dinner entertainment in the East Room.

A program of scenes from Shakespearean plays was given there following a state dinner in honor of President Ibrahim Abboud of the Sudan. On a specially constructed stage, backed by removable, dark-red screens, actors of the American Festival of Stratford, Connecticut, performed excerpts from *Macbeth*, *Henry V*, *As You Like It*, *Troilus and Cressida*, and *The Tempest*.

"I'd be willing to bet," said Dr. James G. McManaway of the Folger Shakespeare Library, "that this is the first time Shakespeare has been performed inside the White House."

There was great interest in the appearance of the renowned Spanish violoncellist, Pablo Casals, then in his eighty-fifth year, at the White House in November, 1961. The occasion was a state dinner for Gov. Luis Muñoz Marin of Puerto Rico. Breaking his vow never to play in any country recognizing the Franco regime, Casals, with the assistance of Alexander Schneider, violin, and Mieczyslaw Horszowski, piano, performed works by Mendelssohn, Schumann, and Couperin. In the distin-

Mrs. Kennedy points out an especially interesting spot on the White House grounds to Empress Farah of Iran. The Empress and Shah visited the United States in April, 1962.

Even formal affairs were
lively. Following a dinner
in honor of Nobel Prize
winners, poet Robert
Frost rises to greet
novelist Pearl Buck, while
the President and Mrs.
Kennedy look on.

guished audience was Alice Roosevelt Longworth, daughter of Theodore Roosevelt, who recalled that Casals had played in the White House in 1904, when her father was President.

The social and the serious in the Kennedy administration overlapped when the aristocracy of scientific America—forty-nine Nobel Prize winners of the western hemisphere—were honored guests at a White House dinner on April 29, 1962. Small tables for dining were set up in the State Dining Room and in the Blue Room, to seat 173 noted guests in all. Among them were Lieutenant Colonel John H. Glenn, the first American to orbit the earth, and writers Robert Frost, Katherine Anne Porter, Pearl Buck, and Van Wyck Brooks.

After dinner there was dancing—unscheduled—to the Strolling Strings of the U.S. Air Force, and readings—scheduled—by actor Fredric March, from the works of three deceased Nobel Prize winners: Ernest Hemingway, General George C. Marshall, and Sinclair Lewis.

Such appearances by fine artists were merely aspects of the Kennedys' wish to promote the best in the culture of America. As Mrs. Kennedy's project to embellish the White House with the art and furnishings of the nation's past began to take shape, the accent was almost solely on things American.

The White House had undergone four complete "restorations" since the fire of 1814. President James Monroe had brought in his own belongings and ordered new pieces from Paris to furnish the rebuilt White

283

The President and Mrs. Kennedy with French Minister of
Culture André Malraux before a state dinner
in his honor.

Mrs. Kennedy and her sister Princess Lee Radziwill (left) ride in a silver and gold howdah atop an elephant during their visit to India in the spring of 1962. Other exotic pictures from her India trip showed Mrs. Kennedy visiting the Taj Mahal, riding a gift horse named Princess, feeding an elephant, and recoiling from the startling behavior of a cobra.

House. Chester A. Arthur in 1881 had smothered the house under befringed and gilded trappings to the point of camouflage. Theodore Roosevelt in 1902 had restored the house to a cool simplicity, and the 1948 restoration had left the White House more than ever chaste and museum-like.

Under Mrs. Kennedy's sponsorship, the aim of the new restoration was to restyle the public rooms in such a way that they would reflect the history of the Presidents and their families, not to make the White House conform to the style of any particular period. One important step was to look for furniture originally used in the mansion.

The idea of furnishing the White House with authentic and appropriate pieces was not an entirely new one. Other First Ladies had taken steps in this direction but with less success. Mrs. Calvin Coolidge's appeal for donations of fine furniture to the house had netted only a few pieces. Mrs. Herbert Hoover had been interested in the Monroe period and had had several examples of furnishings from his era copied for the White House. Mrs. Eisenhower, through the National Society of Interior Designers, had inaugurated a refurbishing program in 1959.

The refurbished Green Room was in the style of a Federal parlor of about 1800. Over the fireplace was hung the great portrait of Benjamin Franklin, painted in London in 1767 by the Scottish artist, David Martin.

285

No more appropriate addition to the White House could have been made
than the superb paintings acquired during the Kennedy years. They evoked
memories of the nation's past and of former White House occupants, but of
even more importance, they presented a fine panorama of the art of painting
in America. Above, The Reception of General Grant, by Francis B. Carpenter.

Thomas Jefferson, an 1800
portrait by Rembrandt Peale.

John James Audubon, painted in
Scotland in 1826, by John Syme.

Under the Kennedys, however, the tempo was accelerated in this as in all things. In no time at all agreeable changes were noticeable in the looks of the White House. One visitor facetiously remarked that although it was most attractive, it was also very confusing. Furniture and pictures were switched around so much from day to day in an effort to find just the correct spots for them that a tourist going through on two consecutive days might think he was seeing different rooms.

To act as curator of antiques in the White House, Mrs. Lorraine Pearce was borrowed from the Smithsonian Institution, and every piece that came to the mansion was examined, catalogued, and placed in proper relationship to other pieces. Donors sent paintings, furniture, and the funds with which to purchase desirable additions.

Oddly enough, the first "find"—a heavily carved, oaken desk made from the timbers of a British ship—was discovered in the broadcasting room. A present from Queen Victoria to President Rutherford B. Hayes in 1878, the desk appealed so much to the Kennedys that it was placed in the President's office.

Isolated gifts of interest and value came only gradually to the White House. But eventually the Red Room was furnished in Empire style, with a sofa once belonging to Dolley Madison in an important spot; the Green Room was furnished with exquisite pieces of the mansion's earliest period. A chair ordered from Paris in 1817 by President Monroe; another chair which had stood in Lincoln's bedroom; a mirror used by George Washington; these and other prized gifts warmed up the high-ceilinged rooms.

Mrs. Kennedy deplored the poor quality of much of the art she found in the White House. With a few exceptions—especially the Stuart portraits of George Washington, and others by George P. A. Healy—the portraits of Presidents had been hit-or-miss products, sometimes copies of works of better painters. One ambition of the special committee appointed to build up the White House collection was to replace some of these mediocrities with paintings done from life.

Many worthwhile examples of nineteenth-century American art were given to or purchased by the White House. Some particularly interesting ones were: *Niagara Falls*, by John F. Kensett, painter of the Hudson River School; a still life by James Peale, and one by Rubens Peale; a landscape by Jasper Cropsie; two early paintings on tin of the Capitol.

One of the most beautiful additions to the White House was the 127-year-old French wallpaper hung in the Diplomatic Reception Room. It was this lovely but minor acquisition which brought forth the most publicized remark of the entire redecoration. "Somebody got stuck," was the opinion of Milton Glaser, president of the American Institute of Interior Designers, when it was learned that $12,500 had been paid for the wallpaper, removed from the walls of an old house in Maryland. "Why on earth did they go to all the trouble . . . when new paper is available from the same blocks?"

Above, Vice President Lyndon Johnson visits the President's office. The Kennedy rocking chair, probably the best-known rocker of modern times, served a good purpose. It was prescribed by Dr. Travell as part of her treatment for the President's back injury.

287

President and Mrs. Kennedy, with color-bearer and naval aide, start off the reception for the diplomatic corps in May, 1962.

The White House, through Miss Pamela Turnure, Mrs. Kennedy's press secretary, deplored the "undignified situation" thus arising. It was pointed out that the old wallpaper possessed subtleties of coloring not obtainable in the new, and many visitors to the White House were inclined to agree.

The restoration of the White House interior was climaxed on February 14, 1962, by the appearance on television networks of Mrs. Kennedy in the role of guide on a tour of the public rooms. Beginning with some lines from history, Mrs. Kennedy showed television viewers through rooms both completed and in the process of being restored. "Her effortless familiarity with dates and names attested to homework done for the occasion," commented *The New York Times* in a glowing review. Forty-six million viewers were said to have seen the film.

The response of the public to the changes in the White House was immediate. Tourists poured through the rooms en masse during the short daily visiting hours. In the first year of the Kennedy occupancy 1,332,279 visitors came to gaze on the old walls and the new styling in the public parlors.

Aside from her sponsorship of the White House redecoration, Jacqueline Bouvier Kennedy in her own right contributed much to the prestige of the United States during her trips to other lands. In the spring of 1961 she accompanied the President to Europe, in the autumn of the same year to South America. All the world noted her serenity and grace during her travels through India and Pakistan in the spring of 1962.

Mrs. Kennedy was a favorite subject for the magazine and woman's-page writers. During the first eighteen months in the White House, more than 300 "Jackie stories" appeared in the newspapers of one city alone. Inevitably many of the articles dwelt on her chic. Her influence on the world of fashion was tremendous. In view of the lift she had given the fashion industry, American designers could not object greatly when she suddenly abandoned her announced intention of wearing only American clothes, and from time to time appeared in French-made frocks.

For the nearly three years of the Kennedy administration the attention of the nation was focused upon the White House. Its occupants were subjects of wide and constant interest, and the press endlessly scrutinized their "style," their multifarious activities, their outlook on culture, social procedure, athletics and aesthetics. The age-old complaint of First Ladies was heard again: "There is so little privacy," said Jacqueline Kennedy in an interview.

In the new brisk order of getting things done, the comparative youth of the men closest to President Kennedy seemed a great asset. In the 51 top jobs in the administration, the average age was forty-eight. In choosing his top advisers, Kennedy accented scholarship as well as youth. There were sixteen members of Phi Beta Kappa, the national scholastic honor society; four men who had studied under Rhodes scholarships; one Nobel Prize winner.

The Kennedy administration was one of high hopes and lofty aspira-

President Kennedy is the center of the crush in the East Room. The informal affair for diplomats provided champagne, cocktails, and dancing for 300 guests.

Ambassador Frederic Guirma and his wife, from Upper Volta, brighten the scene with their colorful dress.

Caroline and a friend depart after taking a peek at the diplomatic goings-on.

There were educators and engineers, lawyers, economists, and politicians
filling top posts in the Kennedy administration. Whatever the background
these were the men who daily helped the President deal with crisis after c
Above, Theodore Sorensen, Special Counsel, speech writer, and adviser, co.

Pierre Salinger, press secretary.

Robert S. McNamara, Secretary of Defense.

Dean Rusk, Secretary of State.

Adlai Stevenson, Ambassador to the United Nations.

th President Kennedy, while Messrs.
ll, Staats, and Bundy wait their turn.
low, and to the right, are some of the
her men the President most relied on.

bert Kennedy, Attorney General.

Arthur J. Goldberg, Secretary of Labor.

tions. Courageous steps were taken in the field of civil rights. There was a striving for the furtherance and stabilization of the country's prosperity, and for the spread of peace throughout the world—an effort to "seek out the way of peace," as President Kennedy had expressed it in his inaugural speech.

Among achievements of President Kennedy's years was his handling of the perilous Cuban crisis in the fall of 1962. On October 22, the nation heard from the President of the build-up of Russian missiles on Cuba. After prolonged and painful deliberation, Kennedy set up a naval blockade, forcing the Soviet Union to dismantle and remove its missiles from the island.

Viewing it as a constructive step toward a world free of fear and hostilities, Kennedy took great pride in the signing of the nuclear test ban treaty, concluded by the United States, the Soviet Union and Britain on July 25, 1963. The treaty prohibited nuclear testing in the atmosphere, in space and under water. Kennedy termed it "a shaft of light cut into the darkness of cold war discords and tensions."

In his inaugural address President Kennedy had realistically said: "All this will not be finished in the first one thousand days, nor in the life of this administration, nor even perhaps in our lifetime on this planet. But let us begin." But the man who wanted to be returned to the White House in 1964 with a mandate—a mandate which would better enable him to work toward the desired goals—was not to be allowed to finish his first term.

On November 22, 1963, President John Fitzgerald Kennedy was assassinated as he sat in a motorcade in Dallas, Texas. Horror at the senseless shooting mingled with grief as people all over the world mourned a President of reason and humanity and grieved for a White House family of youth and grace and charm.

In the tumultuous hours after the shooting, events had crowded upon each others' heels: the death of the President in a Dallas hospital; the swearing-in of the new President, Lyndon Baines Johnson, aboard the presidential jet, *Air Force One*, while it stood on the runway at Love Field in Dallas; the swift flight back to Washington, with the anguished Mrs. Kennedy beside the dead President's casket; the arrival at dusk at Andrews Air Force Base and President Johnson's first words to the public.

On Saturday, November 23, there began three days of tribute to John F. Kennedy, of pageantry unforgettable in its sweep and style, of outpourings of grief movingly expressed. In the dismal pre-dawn hours of Saturday, John Kennedy was brought back to the White House for the last time—to a house with its flag at halfmast, its entrance black-draped. Mrs. Kennedy arrived too, for the first time since the tragedy in Dallas, still in the blood-spattered pink suit she had worn the day before.

Mindful of the sad similarities between her husband's death and President Lincoln's, Mrs. Kennedy had asked that certain details duplicate those of nearly a hundred years before. The East Room catafalque, on which the casket rested, was a replica of Lincoln's; as in 1865, black swathed the windows, the fireplaces, and chandeliers. In the pale light of candles,

292

The lonely figure of the President is silhouetted against a window of his office, and work hours in the White House grow longer and longe

Surrounded by Congressional leaders, President Kennedy signs
the test ban treaty in the newly restored Treaty Room in July, 1963.
Vice President Lyndon B. Johnson is at the right.

an honor guard made up of representatives of the various armed services came and went, was replaced again and again.

As hundreds huddled in the rain outside the White House gates, President and Mrs. Lyndon B. Johnson led the procession of personages of the Capital who came to pay their respects. Former President Eisenhower and former President Truman came to the hushed East Room and were followed by Judges of the Supreme Court, Congressmen and diplomats.

The people took pride, in the first dark hours, in the valor shown by Jacqueline Kennedy and the dignity with which she bore her grief. Behind the scenes her contributions to the ceremonies which lay ahead were many. She asked for bagpipers from the Special Services to appear, inspected the grave site at Arlington National Cemetery, and arranged for cards in memoriam to the late President to be placed on each seat in St. Matthew's Cathedral. She carried out duties which would further the transfer of the presidency and took an interest in clearing out the Kennedy effects from the West Wing offices—the Naval paintings, the ship models, the books, and the famous rocking chair.

The caisson leaves the White House for the trip to the Capitol.

The day began on Sunday with the muffled cadence of drums. There appeared under the North Portico the black caisson, drawn by seven matched gray horses, ready to carry the casket up the hill to the Capitol. On the lawn were gathered the White House employees—the cooks and laundresses, valets, secretaries and guides—assembled for a last goodbye.

All day and long into the night the crowds flowed slowly to the Capitol to pass by the casket which lay under the dome of the rotunda. At one point a line of mourners two miles long stood eight abreast in the chill air.

For those who wept for the dead President, who went to the Capitol, or stood among the crowds at Arlington on Monday, or who merely watched television, there were sights and sounds to be remembered forever. Perhaps it was the sight of the procession of world leaders led by Mrs. Kennedy, which went on foot behind the caisson from the White House to the Cathedral. Or it may have been some part of the religious or military ritual at Arlington. Perhaps it was the sight of Jacqueline Kennedy lighting the eternal flame at the head of the grave. It was the "something living" she had wanted.

Mrs. Kennedy performed one more duty in the White House that day. She received President de Gaulle of France, President Eamon de Valera of Ireland and Emperor Haile Selassie of Ethiopia in the family quarters. She then stood for the last time in the Red Room to greet other heads of state.

One tribute remained to be paid to the late President. It came to the White House in the form of a painting, *Matinée sur la Seine, beau temps*, by the French Impressionist Claude Monet. On a small plaque the following appeared:

In loving memory of John Fitzgerald Kennedy
35th President of the United States
from his family.

294

Matinée sur la Seine, beau temps by *Claude Monet.*

Consensus and hospitality

THIS IS A SAD TIME for all people. We have suffered a loss that cannot be weighed. For me it is a deep personal tragedy. I know the world shares the sorrow that Mrs. Kennedy and her family bear. I will do my best. That is all I can do. I ask for your help—and God's."

These moving words, spoken at Andrews Air Force Base, on the return from Dallas on November 22, 1963, were Lyndon Baines Johnson's first public utterance as President. He had already, within hours after the assassination of John F. Kennedy, demonstrated the skill and resolve which would reassure the world, and lead the nation through a period of grief and bewilderment.

It was immediately noted that the White House was different—different in style, in pace, in operation, and general accessibility. How the changes reflected the personalities of its new occupants—President and Mrs. Johnson and their two young daughters—was gradually revealed.

Since their coming to the White House had been abrupt, the Johnsons were less well known throughout the country than would normally have been true. Comparisons with predecessors quickly followed in an effort to know them better.

President Johnson, in his democratic approach to the people, was compared with Andrew Jackson; Mrs. Johnson's knowledge of politics and her talent for public speaking brought to mind the activities of Eleanor Roosevelt. The lively presence of Lynda Bird, nineteen, and Luci Baines, sixteen, stirred memories of the early Franklin Roosevelt White House which had been filled with young people.

Such simplicities naturally were inadequate, for the Johnsons were completely and most remarkably themselves—hardworking, energetic and outgoing, and with an enormous capacity for enjoyment.

The flavor of their native Texas was in their easy hospitality; they exercised the personal touch in public life to a degree unmatched in this

The President and Mrs. Johnson at Andrews Air Force Base on the evening of November 22, 1963.

297

The Johnsons share a moment of privacy in the White House garden.

The President greets some of his public at the White House fence.

century. The President could relate a folksy, homely anecdote to thousands with as much ease as to a group of friends. He never hesitated to use the colloquial when emphasizing a point. ". . . we can have, as they say in my country, the coonskins on the wall," he said when predicting success for his Medicare program, "instead of just a lot of conversation about them."

The President plainly enjoyed all the prerogatives of his office. He was "larger than life," wrote a journalist friend—in ego, talents, ambition, temper. He admired speed—in cars, air-travel, and in getting things done, and the pace of activities in the West Wing offices was swift.

In days filled to the limit, President Johnson made the air crackle with his energy. He worked: in the office, in his bedroom upstairs, in conference on the grounds, at the LBJ ranch in Texas, in his car, in his plane. He made speeches, held press conferences, often unscheduled to the annoyance of reporters, shook hands with tourists through the fence around the White House grounds, entertained businessmen at luncheon and Congressmen at dinner.

The President delighted innumerable guests by showing them through the private upstairs quarters. More persons penetrated the upper floor of the White House than since the 19th century—the days of the crowded, inadequate upstairs offices. More flattered female guests were danced around the East Room at parties than ever before.

Although at first Mrs. Johnson had said that she felt as though she were in an unrehearsed role, her qualifications were unusual. A graduate of the University of Texas, with degrees in both liberal arts and journalism, she had matched her husband's career with her own—as hostess, world traveler, political speaker, and business woman.

Claudia Taylor Johnson—called Lady Bird since early childhood—emerged as a lady without pretensions but with charm and poise. As it had been said of Mrs. Cleveland in the 1880's, Mrs. Johnson was capable of making every White House guest feel that her smile was just for him. Her interest in the old house was genuine, her interest in people constant. "A woman who listens," was how her press secretary, Elizabeth Carpenter described the new First Lady.

Mrs. Johnson had been listening and learning throughout the nearly thirty years of her husband's career as Representative, Senator, and Vice President. She had played an ever more active part in his rise and as First Lady was considered a political force. In her first year in the White House she made trips to 35 states, always with the aim of promoting the President's plans and policies.

Lynda and Luci went off to school in the mornings accompanied by Secret Service agents, Lynda to George Washington University, Luci to the National Cathedral School. While the presence of an agent was unobjectionable in the classroom, on a date it was a different matter. "It doesn't exactly breed romance," observed Lynda.

298

*President and Mrs. Johnson
and their daughters,
Luci Baines and Lynda Bird.*

Luci, who played the piano and danced several variations of the frug, was outspoken about her role in White House life. "I don't really realize I am a President's daughter and that I represent American youth," she told reporters. "If I did, I would go out of my mind trying to represent the best of American youth." She concluded that it was best "to be yourself" even if mistakes were made at times.

The President aroused the ire of both his attractive daughters when he oversimplified them thus: "I will never have to worry about either girl. Lynda Bird is so smart that she will always be able to make a living for herself. And Luci Baines is so appealing and feminine that there will always be some man around wanting to make a living for her."

Sudden and abrupt as his taking office had been, President Johnson was widely considered the best prepared President of all time. His political career in Congress had extended through the terms of three Presidents; his nearly three years in the Vice Presidency had seen his involvement in governmental affairs at the highest level.

Unusual because of its setting, a state dinner in the rose garden
honored Chancellor Ludwig Erhard of West Germany in June, 1964.

American Indians meet the President in the East Room.
Visiting groups to the White House were frequent and
diverse, causing Mrs. Johnson to observe that daily
life was much like one "big educational seminar."

There were important accomplishments immediately. All of President Johnson's influence was used to bring off the passage of the civil rights and tax-cut bills. His anti-poverty program to lift the depression from a ten-state area of the Appalachians got off to a promising start.

When Johnson cut the Federal budget, his economies extended to demanding that unused White House lights be turned off when not in use. This small, symbolical economy met with mixed reactions. While much of the public applauded, one facetious story ran that the girls were now, like the youthful Abraham Lincoln, doing their homework by firelight. The First Lady's reaction was one of quiet amusement: "Lyndon," she said, "has that light complex to an advanced degree."

Knowing the Johnsons' devotion to their LBJ ranch in Texas—"our heart's home" Lady Bird had called it—the ever-present detractors of White House occupants half-seriously predicted that its open-handed ways would be transplanted to the White House, with barbecues and camp-fires on the White House grounds.

But no such large-scale social gestures were imposed on White House life. Diplomats, ambassadors, government officials, and a cross-section of American citizenry, were however, entertained with the Johnson warmth and style. A new informality pervaded affairs honoring world leaders. Since the old-fashioned "state" visit had been shortened and its ceremony simplified, the President was more than likely to greet his important guests on the South lawn when they arrived by helicopter.

The entertainment following state dinners was as varied as the guests were diverse. Shakespearean drama, ballet, opera and hootenanny to the thwack of guitars all had their moment in the East Room.

The Johnson flexibility was demonstrated in other ways too. In July, 1964, a state dinner was given in honor of Costa Rican President Francisco Orlich. Since the night was warm there was dancing on the roof-top adjoining the East Wing. Passers-by on Pennsylvania Avenue stood agape as the President whirled Luci around in what was described as a presidential version of the current "bird." A rather typical Johnson guest-list included names of a famous entertainer, an author, cabinet members, and twenty-five of Luci's teenage friends.

"I want to be a People's President," Johnson said, "and in order to do so you have to see the people and talk to them and know something about them and not be too secluded." Both the President and Mrs. Johnson seemed happiest when surrounded by crowds. "I wish I could look into every face and shake every hand," said the President during a trip through the impoverished Southern mountains.

This wish became increasingly hard to fulfill as campaign time came on in the fall of 1964, calling for thousands of miles of travel, countless hands to shake, multitudes to address. A novel feature of the campaign was the first whistle-stop tour ever carried out by a First Lady, in which Lady Bird Johnson stumped the South from Alexandria to New Orleans. Before she began the tour, Mrs. Johnson talked by phone to the governors and senators of eight Southern states.

301

Luci Baines takes a look in the Red Room mirror before a party.

Lynda Bird Johnson.

Luci took an enthusiastic part in the campaign of 1964.

The ten-car Lady Bird Special, red, white and blue inside and out, blaring stirring music as it approached each town, traveled 1700 miles through the South in four days. At each of the 180 stops Mrs. Johnson made a short speech from the observation platform. At intervals Lynda and Luci joined the tour and contributed to the speech-making.

At the finish, President Johnson had traveled 50,000 miles by plane, conducting an old-fashioned, long-talking campaign in villages, towns, and cities. The able, ebullient Hubert Horatio Humphrey, candidate for Vice President, traveled as far on his own aboard his plane dubbed the "Happy Warrior."

On November 3, 1964, President Johnson, with the greatest popular vote in history, won in a landslide over the Republican candidate Barry Goldwater. By way of celebration everyone within earshot was invited to the LBJ ranch on the next day. It would be a great barbecue in honor of a great victory.

On January 4, at nine o'clock in the evening, President Johnson went up to the Capitol to deliver his annual State of the Union speech to Congress. Near the start of his first full term of office, the President outlined a wide-ranging plan for the bettering of life in America. It was in broad outline, the program for his Great Society goals. Based largely on improvements in education, the Great Society would aspire to wipe out poverty,

President Johnson appeared to enjoy every minute of the campaign.

improve the national health, conserve and restore the beauty of the nation's towns and countryside.

As the celebrations preceding the inauguration began, the White House bulged at the seams with relatives and old friends of the Johnsons. The President's uncle, Huffman Baines, and his aunt Josepha Saunders, who had been the first White House guests fourteen months before, came up from Texas. There were as well brothers and sisters, cousins, nieces and nephews of both the President and First Lady. Luci gave up her bed to friends and slept on a cot in the dressing-room. Governor Connally of Texas drew Lincoln's ornate bed when sleeping arrangements were made for guests.

In the thin sunlight of January 20, 1965, Lyndon Baines Johnson was inaugurated 36th President of the United States. His hand rested on a Bible held by Mrs. Johnson as he took the oath of office. The tone of the inaugural address was prayerful and aspiring and the President reminded the nation of its proud beginnings—"conceived in justice, written in liberty, bound in union."

Following the solemn words there came the spectacle, the optimistic, noisy, extravagant celebration. It was part hoopla, part patriotism, made up of marching troops, dancing Indians, mountain men, flags, high-stepping horses, and hours of cheers, songs, and band music.

Lynda made use of her inherited gift for public speaking in 1964.

The Johnsons leave the pre-inaugural gala to return to the White House.

President Johnson with
Vice President
Hubert Horatio Humphrey.

The President with two
important staff members,
Jack Valenti and Bill Moyers.

By sundown the parade was over. Five inaugural balls scattered throughout the city finished off the great day and the President and First Lady danced at all of them.

The hours of handshaking through receptions preceding the inauguration, the inaugural-eve gala, the parade and balls had called for an excessive expenditure of energy from the President. At 2:55 on the morning of January 23, he was admitted to Bethesda Naval Hospital with a severe cold. The nation, which had just nervously lived through a period of 14 months without a Vice President, waited out the few days of the illness with great concern. After recovering, one of Johnson's first requests of Congress was for a Constitutional amendment which would provide for a transfer of power in case a President should become incapacitated.

As was often the case in the Johnson White House, business and pleasure intermingled as the new social season began. A series of receptions for Congress began in February—ten in all to accommodate all members of the House and Senate. While Mrs. Johnson entertained the wives of Senators and Representatives downstairs in the movie theatre with a film on White House history—or, at times, a color film on the paintings hanging in the White House, the President and Cabinet officers carried on detailed discussions with members of Congress concerning affairs both foreign and domestic. This was the first time in history that the rank and file of Congress, as opposed to a favored few, had been so carefully briefed on White House plans.

As President Johnson began the first year of the term he had won in his own right, the problems of the presidency appeared as prodigious as ever. Abroad, the ten-year-old involvement in the war in Vietnam seemed ever more serious.

At home, the principles of the Great Society were repeated by the President: "... not how much, but how good; not only how to create wealth but how to use it; not only how fast we are going but where we are headed. It proposes as the first test for a nation, the quality of its people. People are the purpose and object of this endeavor."

Acting on the mandate he had received from the people, President Johnson proposed—and Congress passed—a long list of bills concerning the rights of the common man—his right to decent medical care and housing and a good education. A new Cabinet division, the Department of Housing and Urban Development, was created and conservation measures taken. The Negro, striving to break out of the restrictions of the past, found his greatest champion in the President.

Under the broad umbrella of the administration's programs, Mrs. Johnson's role as First Lady took on a more positive character. So that she might use her energies in a meaningful way, she decided to try limiting her work efforts to facets of education and conservation, areas in which she felt most at home. *Headstart* and *Beautification*, projects always to be associated with her name, came into being. The first concerned itself with preparing underprivileged children of kindergarten age for regular school, the second with improving the general environment in America.

*At the end of the upstairs corridor, President Johnson
confers with Secretary of State Dean Rusk and
Secretary of Defense Robert S. McNamara.*

Her Beautification program began in Washington with litter removal and the transformation of desolate public areas into pleasant parks. Thousands of trees and flowering shrubs were planted in the Capital's open spaces and at the entrances to the city.

The endeavor took on new dimensions as all over the country persons in positions of authority began to ponder what could be done to improve their own areas. It was no longer merely something to be discussed, as Mrs. Johnson put it, "by garden club ladies over a cup of tea." The subject also embraced the problems of air and water pollution, and it was becoming an important part of industrial and public planning.

Few White House families had been as hospitable as the Johnsons, and the house had rarely teemed with such constant activity. Nor had many residents there ever used the mansion so flexibly as a kind of theatre for the presentation of their proposals and programs.

The President held many of his news conferences in the big East Room surrounded by the gadgetry of the television broadcast. "Mother" was the name given by the press corps to his large, custom-built lectern, which boasted hidden microphones and teleprompters and which could be seen as enfolding the President in its electronic arms. He brought the Blue Room into his work day with special meetings for members of Con-

Mrs. Johnson's travels found her in a wide variety of settings. In New England, after dedicating a historic site, she donned a 1910 bonnet and rode in a parade in an antique car.

gress. He held meetings out of doors in the Rose Garden, just off the Executive Offices.

Mrs. Johnson, whose "office" was a desk in a corner of her bedroom, also moved her business meetings freely around the house. She particularly liked the dark green Treaty Room on the second floor for talks with committees. There she discussed with experts the next move on Headstart or Beautification or the new painting in the process of being acquired. When ladies came to tea she took them into one of the formal parlors or into the family sitting room at the end of the west hall.

The sitting room was also a haven to which the President sometimes brought associates at the end of the day, and it was the spot in which Mrs. Johnson often awaited him while the dinner hour grew later and later.

The sitting room was a point too from which Mrs. Johnson could sometimes see, past the offices, certain portentous signs on Executive Avenue—the television van, the spotlighted news announcer—which might mean the start of another crisis, either domestic or international.

In the summer of 1966 the Johnson family gained a new member when on the sixth of August nineteen-year-old Luci married Patrick John Nugent. As usual when a festive occasion was in the making, relatives

A trip to spur interest in the rural schools of the
Appalachians took Mrs. Johnson into the wooded dells of
eastern Kentucky—to the delight of both teachers and pupils.

and friends from Texas and Alabama were invited, and before the wedding day they filled up the bedrooms on the top floors.

Luci, a recent convert to Roman Catholicism, had chosen to be married in the National Shrine of the Immaculate Conception in Washington, instead of in the White House.

In the church, hidden television cameras transmitted the glamour of the wedding to the public. When the wedding party and guests flocked to the White House for the reception, television again flashed scenes across the nation from the grounds and state rooms.

Late in October the President, with Mrs. Johnson, left for a seventeen-day diplomatic errand in Asia. The purpose of the trip was to boost the rapidly slipping support for the Vietnam war at home, and to encourage in the Asians a "spirit of regional unity." The Johnsons put in long days of ceremony and conference as they visited Australia and New Zealand, the Philippines and Thailand, Malaysia and Korea. When he stopped briefly in South Vietnam, Johnson became the first President ever to visit an active foreign battlefield.

By 1967, President Johnson was forced to run two wars; the rapidly escalating and bewilderingly drawn-out war in Asia, and the war on the home front against inflation, dissension, and anti-war protest.

Again the President sought to dramatize his efforts to attain harmony in the world by a meeting with Premier Aleksei Nikolayevich Kosygin of the Soviet Union. In the little town of Glassboro, New Jersey, the two heads of state from the two greatest powers on earth talked about world trouble spots—about South Vietnam, the Arab-Israeli conflict in the Middle East, about control of nuclear power.

Little more than a year after Luci's marriage in church the White House itself became the scene of a wedding—its first in fifty-three years. On December 9, 1967, Lynda Johnson and Marine Captain Charles S. Robb were married in the East Room. Nearly 500 guests packed the big chamber and the long cross-hall and craned their necks for the best possible view of the splendid proceedings: the bride's entry on the arm of the President, the brief ceremony in front of evergreens a-twinkle with tiny electric candles, the newly married couple walking under raised swords as they left the East Room.

One departure from the strictly conventional was the color of the bridesmaids' long velvet gowns—a deep ruby red.

The President experienced a minor defeat after the ceremony when he tried to bring his little white mongrel dog, Yuki, into a photographic session. Yuki wore a red coat with "congratulations" written on it, red stockings, and an L.B.J. pin. But Mrs. Johnson said "no" to the suggestion and Yuki was photographed alone.

By late 1967 there was another new member of the devoted family —Luci's baby son, Patrick Lyndon Nugent, called Lyn for short. When the Nugents went on a vacation trip, the infant stayed with his grandparents, and the public was treated to pictures of the President showing Lyn around the White House, and showing the White House to Lyn;

When Lynda Johnson and Marine Captain Charles Robb were married in
the East Room in 1967, guests thought the entire proceeding
enchanting—from the entry of the President with his
daughter until the moment at the reception for cutting the wedding cake.

The Johnson family spent Christmas in the White House only once—in 1967. "...the most glorious Christmas ever," said Mrs. Johnson of the holiday.

Lyn on the lawn with Yuki; Lyn cradled in the arms of the President or Mrs. Johnson.

Christmas of 1967—the only one the family spent in the White House—was an especially emotional one for the Johnsons. The President returned home on Christmas morning from a whirlwind trip around the world and Luci's baby got his first look at a Christmas tree and the toy-filled velvet stockings that hung near the fireplace. The President and Mrs. Johnson, as they looked at their sons-in-law, tried to stifle the realization that before the next Christmas came around these young men would probably have departed for the battlefield in Southeast Asia.

It was the war and its accompanying woes that hung most heavily over the administration at the start of its final year. As the end of the war seemed ever farther away, the drop in the President's popularity was so radical that polls showed only 26 percent of the public favoring the way he was handling it with 36 percent approving of his conduct of office in general.

The President could not appear in public without the chance of provoking rude or even violent demonstrations. The campaign year loomed ahead, with its monstrous demands on a candidate's time and energy.

On March 31, 1968, on national television, at the end of a speech announcing a halt in bombing in Vietnam, Mr. Johnson spoke these words: "I shall not seek and I will not accept the nomination of my party as your President." The President spoke of "division in the American house," and of national unity, which he called "the ultimate strength of our country."

"I do not believe," he continued, "that I should devote an hour or a day of my time ... to any duties other than the awesome duties of this office, the Presidency of your country." Political contenders were left speechless; the nation was astounded.

Many columnists did an about-face and wrote warmly of the man they had been denouncing, suggesting that perhaps after all, some of the attacks on him had been unfair; that the President was not solely responsible for the crime, violence, and discord which wracked America and the world. Even Hanoi warmed up slightly and agreed to start preliminary talks on ways to bring the war to a close.

When peace talks began in Paris in May, 1968, there was a surge of hope that the war would be over before Johnson left office.

In the autumn the President and First Lady became grandparents for a second time when Lynda gave birth to a daughter she named Lucinda.

Mrs. Johnson revealed in an interview late in 1968 that she had known long before the announcement of March 31 that the President was thinking of retiring from public life. At the same time she offered some insights into living in the White House, amid the constant reminders of its awesome place in history and of its former tenants. She mentioned her enjoyment of the glorious vistas, the fresh flowers in the rooms, and the excitement of the comings and goings of the powerful of the world.

Other knowledge of the meaning of living in the mansion had been

The President, First Lady, and the Robbs look at part of the photographic record of the past five years.

more painfully acquired. Mrs. Johnson spoke of the White House as a place for the most painful decisions, a house in which the President—any President—after listening to every side of a question, still had the lonely burden of making up his own mind.

Asked what part of White House living she would be happiest to leave behind, Mrs. Johnson was quick to answer: the eighteen-hour day, and the 4 A.M. phone calls to the President from the situation room.

She was positive in her defense of the domestic gains of the administration, saying that she was sure they would be permanent.

It had been written of the President that he had taken it into his own hands to escalate a remote and futile war, that much of the rancorous tone which prevailed across America stemmed from distrust of him. It was widely believed that he lacked the ability to persuade the people of the rightness of his programs.

But it was also said that he labored with all his strength for what he believed to be right; that he had imparted to the federal government an awareness of new goals and the authority to pursue them for the welfare of the people.

It was appropriate that he end his farewell speech to Congress on January 15 with these words: "I hope it may be said a hundred years from now that by working together we helped to make our country more just— more just for all of its people, as well as to insure and guarantee the blessings of liberty for all of our posterity. That's what I hope. But I believe that at least it will be said that we tried."

311

The winds of change

For millions of Americans the winning of the Presidency by Richard Milhous Nixon represented the classic triumph of determination and patience over all obstacles.

The road to the White House had been a long and often arduous one. After serving for eight years as Vice President under Dwight Eisenhower, Richard Nixon had lost the presidential election of 1960 to John F. Kennedy. In 1962 he had again been defeated in the contest for the governorship of California. Widely looked upon by that time as a permanent "loser," he had nevertheless gone on to be elected President of the United States in 1968.

Sharing the irregular fortunes of political life had been Patricia Ryan Nixon, like her husband the possessor of boundless strength and patience. Mrs. Nixon had taught school in the days when Richard Nixon was a struggling lawyer. She had been homemaker, mother to two daughters, campaign worker when her husband ran for the House of Representatives and later for the Senate from California, hostess and world traveler when Nixon was Vice President.

The Nixons moved into the White House in January, 1969, with only one of their daughters—twenty-two-year-old Tricia. Julie, two years younger, had recently been married to David Eisenhower, grandson of the former President. The young Eisenhowers were still in college, David at Amherst, Julie at Smith.

The public soon got a view of the private side of the Nixon household —most incomplete as was later revealed—in a manner seemingly reserved for White House occupants.

It was learned that the President was fond of sports and that he followed the subject of baseball assiduously, that he liked to golf and bowl, and that he often talked sports with his new son-in-law.

The Nixons were said to look upon a quiet dinner together or with a few friends with particular pleasure, with perhaps a movie afterward in the elegant little White House theatre. Mrs. Nixon said that she thought the public rooms were perfectly beautiful and that she saw no reason whatsoever for making changes in them.

The President's chair in the Cabinet Room receives an alteration on January 20, 1969.

313

President Richard Nixon.

Mrs. Nixon.

If Tricia Nixon were to have her way, her life would be private indeed. "When you don't read about me in the newspapers, you'll know I'm having a good time," she told an interviewer. But by her second year in the White House she would have overcome any shyness sufficiently to appear on television—in a tour of the living quarters—and also to act as hostess at a lawn concert for 2,000 children.

Tricia's recently won degree from Finch College was in French political history. On the subject of American politics her tendency was to be conservative. Once her father had made her a gift of a loving cup inscribed to "The World's Greatest Republican."

At eight o'clock on the morning of January 22 the new President went to the East Room for the swearing-in of his Cabinet by Chief Justice Earl Warren. The ceremony was performed in the presence of the new members' wives, each one in turn holding the Bible for her husband.

Mr. Nixon took the occasion to make some informal remarks on "cabinets" of the past. "Kitchen Cabinet" had been the label placed on Andrew Jackson's assemblage of political cronies, "Tennis Cabinet" on Theodore Roosevelt's pool of partners for tennis, hiking, climbing, fencing, and medicine ball. Since the present group was an actual Cabinet, and in view of the unusually early hour, the President suggested that it should be called the "Working Cabinet."

Prompt changes in the West Wing offices pointed up superficial differences between the Nixon and Johnson administrations. Banished were clamorous teletypes and the three-screen television console that President Johnson had kept an eye on. The positive colorations of avant-garde paintings came off the office walls and were replaced by pictures in more traditional styles.

Mr. Nixon was partial to order and privacy and did much of his work in private or with a very few members of his staff or Cabinet. He chose two spots for talk and quiet reflection in addition to his Oval Office: an office in the Executive Office Building across the street from the West Wing, and a small study next door to the Lincoln Bedroom—a cozy room with a fireplace and with a record player close at hand.

Early in the Nixon tenancy it was announced that the White House would revive its old formality of dress and seating at state dinners. Guests would sit at large U-shaped or E-shaped tables instead of the round ones seating ten guests which had been in recent use. White tie and diplomatic medals and ribbons would be in order.

"After all, it is the White House. It should be special," said one guest in praise of the reversion to the Eisenhower era.

Since the early days of the White House the East Room had been the setting for balls, promenades, weddings, press conferences, and concerts. It was now to be put to still another use.

The first Sunday of the Nixon occupancy saw minister Billy Graham —an old friend of the President—conducting a religious service in the big chamber, building his short sermon around a quote from the Nixon Inaugural Address. "To a crisis of the spirit we need an answer of the spirit,"

*The entire family, including Julie's husband, David Eisenhower,
early in the Nixons' first White House year.*

Mr. Nixon had said, and Mr. Graham elaborated upon that theme, speaking from a lectern set up in front of the gold draperies.

Other ministers, a Catholic bishop, and a rabbi followed. Visiting choirs contributed music. Since it was the first time that sacred services had been held regularly in the White House, they drew a variety of comment. "The administration that prays together, stays together," said one quipster of the affairs, while others looked upon them as evidence of the President's emphasis on the spiritual.

But the Protestant theologian Reinhold Niebuhr wrote in serious vein that in his opinion the practice tended to undermine the principle of separation of church and state. "It is wonderful," he commented, "what a simple White House invitation will do to dull the critical faculties, thereby confirming the fears of the Founding Fathers."

The President's first months in office were a time of crowded days and of many departures and arrivals. Little more than a month after the inauguration he made an eight-day trip to the capitals of Western Europe. He warned that spectacular news must not be expected from the journey, but rather "a new spirit of consultation, which will lead to a new spirit of confidence among our European friends and ourselves."

Sorrow entered Mr. Nixon's life when former President Eisenhower died in late March of 1969. In his honor, heads of state came to Washington from all over the world. Later Mr. Nixon's virtuosity as both host

In the China Room, Julie points out an especially interesting White House heirloom to a touring group.

In the corridor Tricia poses for another of the often-requested photographs.

and diplomat was brought into play, as there came to his office at pre-arranged intervals men who were representatives of the chaotically troubled spots of the world. The Vice President of South Vietnam, Nguyen Cao Ky, had his session with the President, as did Mohammed Reza Pahlavi, the Shah of Iran, and President Zalman Shazar of Israel.

In the spring of 1969 complaints were being voiced in Washington that the quietude of the Nixon White House had spilled over into the social life of the city, cutting the seasonal parties to a fraction of the usual number.

But the Nixons were hosts at some lively entertainments and in fact in their first year received an unprecedented number of invited guests.

Duke Ellington, a great name in American jazz, was guest of honor at a dinner party on his seventieth birthday. In a long, swinging evening in the East Room, Ellington's own sophisticated music, played and sung by a variety of singers and instrumentalists (including both Mr. Nixon and Vice President Spiro Agnew at the piano), was the main attraction. In May Tricia gave a masked ball for many of Washington's most attractive twenty-to-thirty-year-olds. The evening belonging entirely to Tricia, Mrs. Nixon had said she would stay away and merely "peep down at the fun from the top of the stairs."

As always there was interest in the kind of role the new First Lady would play. "I really want to work, I don't want just to lend my name," Mrs. Nixon had said. And in June she went on a working trip—the initial one on her own as First Lady.

The journey was planned to draw attention to the volunteer projects of the nation. A four-day stay in California and Oregon was devoted to visits to just such projects: a day nursery for children of migrant workers; social welfare and teaching centers for the underprivileged; gardens which provided vegetables for welfare recipients.

Amid the warm welcomes for Mrs. Nixon and her party, there was a rude reminder of unfinished business in Southeast Asia. In Portland, Oregon, anti-war demonstrators interrupted a quiet meeting and showered confetti on the visitors. A close look showed that the scraps of paper were printed: "If this was napalm, you would be dead."

In mid-July of 1969, the world thrilled to the landing of two American astronauts on the moon. A large proportion of the peoples of the world were able, through television, to watch the undertaking.

The President, exuberant over the success of the effort, watched the splashdown of the astronauts in mid-Pacific from the aircraft carrier *Hornet*. It was a propelling start to his tour of six nations of Asia—a trip on which he was accompanied by Mrs. Nixon.

Mr. Nixon had entered office with his first aim the disengagement of the United States from the war in Southeast Asia. To the anxious leaders of the Philippines, of Indonesia, Thailand, India, Pakistan, and South Vietnam, he brought reassurance that America would continue to play a significant role in Asia. The war over, the United States would look to the Asians to take on their own development and the burden of their defense.

316

Later, by his brief stay in Bucharest, Rumania, Nixon became the first American President to visit any Communist capital.

As in the case of every new administration, the "honeymoon"—that period of grace and good will on all sides—was soon over. Mr. Nixon was soon being charged with postponing decisive action on crucial domestic problems, particularly the desegregation of schools. But in another area steps had been taken which were highly praised.

In his first week in office, President Nixon had signed an order creating the new Council of Urban Affairs to deal with housing, welfare, crime, mass transit, and racial problems. Headed by Daniel Patrick Moynihan, the council also had Vice President Agnew and cabinet officers as members.

The greatest step was taken in the direction of welfare reform. The plans called for the complete overhaul of the existing hodgepodge of welfare setups and the provision of a basic federal subsidy for its recipients. A second proposal, made at the same time, dealt with the subject of revenue-sharing with the states. The President's proposals were called innovative, even revolutionary, by some observers.

The Nixons spent much of their first summer out of Washington, but for some of that period the White House had as tenants Julie and David Eisenhower, out of school for the summer and occupying the same quarters as had David's parents in earlier days.

Restoration had been in progress for many weeks on the Nixons' newly purchased home in Southern California, overlooking the Pacific Ocean. In August they were to be found in San Clemente in their Western White House—never, according to Mr. Nixon, to be called the "summer" White House, since that might suggest an idleness he did not anticipate.

A forty-five-year-old Spanish-style white stucco with red tile roof, the house was built around a square courtyard and offered ideal privacy for work or rest. A few minutes away by golf cart, on the grounds of a coast guard station, a complex of three buildings, prefabricated and removable, was erected to provide office space for the President, his aides, and the Secret Service.

Security measures for the Nixon family were tight and omnipresent in the idyllic hideaway on a Pacific bluff. The swimming pool had a bulletproof glass wall on the side next to the ocean. On the grounds, glassed-in posts for the Secret Service agents were matched architecturally to the gazebos. The entire complex was linked by wire and jet plane to the White House and to the Nixon home in Key Biscayne, Florida.

In the fall the Nixons returned to Washington and the daily round of meetings, planning, parties, interviews, and travel. The President returned to slave over the gigantic problems which made up his job—problems which had in fact accompanied him to the Pacific coast and back again. The most crucial was still the war in Vietnam.

In spite of troop withdrawals begun in June, 1969, in spite of the reasonableness of peace proposals offered the enemy, the war continued.

Music heard at the White House ranged from sophisticated jazz...

...to chamber music, a very special branch of the classical.

317

Amid a storm of criticism from Congress and the press over his procedures in Vietnam, and discordant cries from a nation beset by inflation, high taxes, anti-war demonstrations, and riots, Mr. Nixon appealed to the public for national unity. He asked for time, and for the moral support he felt he must have in order to bring about an honorable peace.

The peace movement, well-established on the campuses of America and touching every aspect of American life, reached a new level with huge rallies in November, 1969. In Washington, protesters against the war carried out a forty-hour *March Against Death*, taking it past the White House and along the reaches of Pennsylvania Avenue. The war had become, perhaps unjustly, but painfully and regrettably, Mr. Nixon's war.

Well within White House tradition in periods of war, the Nixons continued a glittering chain of social affairs—luncheons, receptions, teas, dinners formal and informal with entertainment amusing or edifying. Bob Hope came to dinner, bringing along the entire troupe of his Christmas show then in readiness for servicemen in Europe and Asia. The paintings of Andrew Wyeth were exhibited in the East Room—against gold velvet panels—and following a dinner in his honor, guests listened to Rudolph Serkin play works of Beethoven and Chopin. The Duke and Duchess of Windsor were treated to a white tie dinner for 100 guests.

Of unusual originality were the Nixon "Evenings at the White House," receptions at which a variety of entertainers appeared. At the initial one in January, 1970, Red Skelton performed in pantomime and skit. The "last of the great clowns" had the pleasure of arriving at the White House to a tune he had composed, played by the Marine Corps Orchestra. For George Washington's Birthday on February 22, the Broadway musical "1776" was performed on the East Room stage.

On Sundays after religious services in the East Room, guests
were invited into the State Dining Room for coffee.

President Georges Pompidou of France and Madame Pompidou
pause with President and Mrs. Nixon before a
state dinner in the Pompidous' honor.

In the spring the British actor Nicol Williamson appeared alone in an evening of dramatic excerpts and songs, and a little later the popular singer of gospel and country songs, Johnny Cash, brought his talents to the White House. The "Evenings" were correctly spoken of as light-hearted and happy occasions.

In the President's office, however, the frustrations, the woes, the need to find answers to agonizing questions pressed ever nearer.

For many months withdrawals of troops from Vietnam had continued at the rate of nearly 12,000 each month. In April, the President appeared on television and announced a long-range plan for recalling 150,000 men during the coming year.

On April 30 in a seeming reversal of his Vietnam policies, Mr. Nixon aired his decision to send American combat troops into Cambodia to destroy enemy bases. The response—shock, bewilderment, and anger—swelled to a nationwide eruption of fury and despair after four students at Ohio's Kent State University were shot and killed by National Guardsmen during an anti-war rally. War protest increased radically; students went on strike; hundreds of colleges were affected.

The President, astonished at the violence of the reaction to his moves, had entered his most difficult period in office. Faced with revolt within his own administration, beleaguered from right and left, he was treated to further accusations of widening the war, isolation from all the aspirations of the young, and even of taking over the prerogatives of Congress. The Senate voted against unlimited authority for the President to send military forces into any country without the consent of Congress.

May 9 was the day of a huge peace rally in the Capital. Early in the morning crowds had already begun to gather in the parks south of the White House. Mr. Nixon dropped a note of surprise into the beginning of a portentous day when before dawn he was driven to the Lincoln Memorial, where he talked to a small band of drowsy students. He asked that they "try to understand what we are doing. . . . I know you want to get the war over . . . that's all right," he continued. "Just keep it peaceful."

If from the start the President had known that his success in domestic affairs depended on the ending of the war, he had also been aware of the need for flexibility within his office. His immediate reaction to the national turbulence was to move quickly to restore lines of communication with the young. Meetings with college students, conferences with university presidents followed. A nine-man commission was appointed to

Anti-war protesters crowd the grounds south of the White House in May, 1970, following the entry into Cambodia and its tragic aftermath at Kent State University. Hundreds of such rallies and demonstrations had taken place in the cities and on the campuses of America in the preceding year.

Mr. Nixon faces the press during a televised news conference.

look closely at campus turmoil. Washington conferences for youth of different age groups were scheduled for the coming year.

New steps were taken to expedite the running of the United States government. An Office of Management and Budget under Labor Secretary George Shultz got its start. New talent was brought to the White House. At the head of the new Domestic Affairs Council the President placed an aide, John Ehrlichman.

It was in an effort to find ways to deal with the complex relationships between the United States and other nations, and in an attempt to find solutions to the overwhelming problems at home, that the President labored each long day. It was for these reasons he was in the White House.

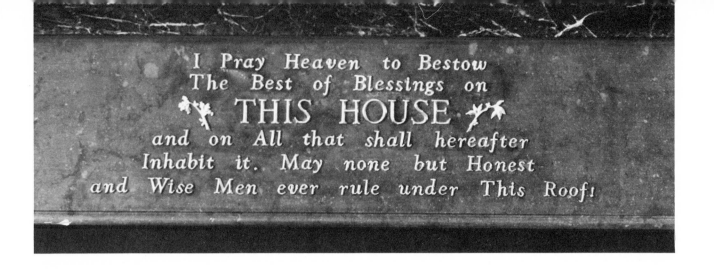

I Pray Heaven to Bestow
The Best of Blessings on
THIS HOUSE
and on All that shall hereafter
Inhabit it. May none but Honest
and Wise Men ever rule under This Roof!

BIBLIOGRAPHY

Adams, Abigail, *New Letters of Abigail Adams, 1788–1801,* edited by Stewart Mitchell. Boston: Houghton Mifflin Company, 1947

Adams, Charles Francis, ed., *Memoirs of John Quincy Adams.* Philadelphia: J. B. Lippincott Company, 1874–1877

Alexander, Holmes, *The American Talleyrand.* New York: Harper & Brothers, 1935

Allen, Frederick Lewis, *Since Yesterday: The Nineteen-Thirties in America.* New York: Harper & Brothers, 1940

Architecture and Building Magazine, Vol. 13, December 6, 1890

Baker, Ray Stannard, *Woodrow Wilson, Life and Letters.* Garden City, N. Y.: Doubleday, Page & Company, 1927

Belden, Thomas Graham and Marva Robins Belden, *So Fell the Angels.* Boston: Little, Brown & Company, 1956

Beloff, Max, *Thomas Jefferson and American Democracy.* New York: The Macmillan Company, 1949

Bemis, Samuel Flagg, *John Quincy Adams and the Union.* New York: Alfred A. Knopf, Inc., 1956

Bishop, Joseph Bucklin, *Theodore Roosevelt and His Time.* Authorized. New York: Charles Scribner's Sons, 1920

Blum, John M., *Joe Tumulty and the Wilson Era.* Boston: Houghton Mifflin Company, 1951

Bobbé, Dorothie, *Mr. and Mrs. John Quincy Adams.* New York: Minton, Balch & Company, 1930

Bowers, Claude J., *The Tragic Era.* Cambridge: Houghton Mifflin Company, 1929

Brant, Irving, *James Madison the President, 1809–1812.* Indianapolis: The Bobbs-Merrill Company, Inc., 1956

Brown, Glenn, *1860–1930, Memories: A Winning Crusade to Revive George Washington's Vision of a Capital City.* Washington: W. F. Roberts Company, 1931

Bryan, Wilhelmus Bogart, *A History of the National Capital from Its Foundation Through the Period of the Adoption of the Organic Act.* 2 vol. New York: The Macmillan Company, 1914–1916

Burns, James MacGregor, *Roosevelt: The Lion and the Fox.* New York: Harcourt, Brace and Company, Inc., 1956

Butt, Archibald W., *Taft and Roosevelt: The Intimate Letters of Archie Butt.* Garden City, N. Y.: Doubleday, Doran & Company, Inc., 1930

Chitwood, Oliver Perry, *John Tyler: Champion of the Old South.* New York: D. Appleton-Century Company, Inc., 1939

Cleaves, Freeman, *Old Tippecanoe: William Henry Harrison and His Time.* New York: Charles Scribner's Sons, 1939

Colman, Edna M., *Seventy-five Years of White House Gossip: From Washington to Lincoln.* Garden City, N. Y.: Doubleday, Page & Company, 1926

Coolidge, Calvin, *The Autobiography of Calvin Coolidge.* New York: Cosmopolitan Book Corp., 1929

Coolidge, Grace A., "Home Again!" *American Magazine,* vol. 109, January 1930

——— "How I Spent My Days at the White House," *American Magazine,* vol. 108, October 1929

——— "Making Ourselves at Home in the White House," *American Magazine,* vol. 108, November 1929

——— "Our Family Pets," *American Magazine,* vol. 108, December 1929

Corning, A. Elwood, *William McKinley: A Biographical Study.* New York: Broadway Publishing Company, 1907

Cresson, William Penn, *James Monroe.* Chapel Hill: The University of North Carolina Press, 1946

Crook, William H., *Memories of the White House,* edited by Henry Rood. Boston: Little, Brown & Company, 1911

Cutts, Lucia B., ed., *Memoirs and Letters of Dolly Madison.* Boston: Houghton Mifflin Company, 1886

Daugherty, Harry M. and Thomas Dixon, *The Inside Story of the Harding Tragedy.* New York: The Churchill Company, 1932

Dos Passos, John, *The Head and Heart of Thomas Jefferson.* Garden City, N. Y.: Doubleday & Company, Inc., 1954

Eaton, Margaret O'Neale Timberlake, *The Autobiography of Peggy Eaton.* New York: Charles Scribner's Sons, 1932

Eckenrode, H. J., *Rutherford B. Hayes.* New York: Dodd, Mead & Company, 1930

Fuess, Claude M., *Calvin Coolidge: The Man from Vermont.* Boston: Little, Brown & Company, 1940

Furman, Bess, *Washington By-Line.* New York: Alfred A. Knopf, Inc., 1949

——— *White House Profile.* Indianapolis: The Bobbs-Merrill Company, Inc., 1951

Garraty, John A., *Woodrow Wilson: A Great Life in Brief.* New York: Alfred A. Knopf, Inc., 1956

Grant, Jesse R., *In the Days of My Father, General Grant.* New York: Harper & Brothers, 1925

Hamlin, Talbot, *Benjamin Henry Latrobe.* New York: Oxford University Press, 1955

Helm, Katherine, *The True Story of Mary, Wife of Lincoln.* New York: Harper & Brothers, 1928

Hillman, William, *Mr. President.* New York: Farrar, Straus & Young, Inc., 1952

Hoover, Herbert, *The Memoirs of Herbert Hoover.* 3 vol. New York: The Macmillan Company, 1951–1952

Hoover, Irwin H., *Forty-two Years in the White House.* Boston: Houghton Mifflin Company, 1934

Howe, George Frederick, *Chester A. Arthur: A Quarter-Century of Machine Politics.* New York: Dodd, Mead & Company, 1934

Jaffray, Elizabeth, *Secrets of the White House.* New York: Cosmopolitan Book Corp., 1927

James, Marquis, *The Life of Andrew Jackson.* Indianapolis: The Bobbs-Merrill Company, 1938

Keckley, Elizabeth Hobbs, *Behind the Scenes.* New York: G. W. Carleton & Company, 1868

Kohlsaat, Herman H., *From McKinley to Harding.* New York: Charles Scribner's Sons, 1923

Langford, Laura Holloway, *The Ladies of the White House.* Philadelphia: Bradley & Company, 1881

Leech, Margaret, *Reveille in Washington.* New York: Harper & Brothers, 1941

Lewis, Ethel, *The White House.* New York: Dodd, Mead & Company, 1937

Lewis, Lloyd, *Myths After Lincoln.* New York: Harcourt, Brace and Company, Inc., 1929

Longworth, Alice Roosevelt, *Crowded Hours.* New York: Charles Scribner's Sons, 1933

Lynch, Denis Tilden, *An Epoch and a Man: Martin Van Buren and His Times.* New York: H. Liveright, 1929

Lyons, Eugene, *Our Unknown President.* Garden City, N. Y.: Doubleday & Company, Inc., 1948

McAdoo, Eleanor Randolph, and Margaret Y. Gaffey, *The Woodrow Wilsons.* New York: The Macmillan Company, 1937

McLean, Evalyn Walsh, with Boyden Sparks, *Father Struck It Rich.* Boston: Little, Brown & Company, 1936

Milhollen, Hirst D. and Milton Kaplan, *Presidents on Parade.* New York: The Macmillan Company, 1948

Monoghan, Jay, *Diplomat in Carpet Slippers.* Indianapolis: The Bobbs-Merrill Company, 1945

Morgan, George, *The Life of James Monroe.* Boston: Small, Maynard & Company, 1921

Nesbitt, Victoria Henrietta, *White House Diary.* Garden City, N. Y.: Doubleday & Company, Inc., 1948

Nevins, Allan, *Grover Cleveland: A Study in Courage.* New York: Dodd, Mead & Company, 1933

——— *Hamilton Fish: The Inner History of the Grant Administration.* New York: Dodd, Mead & Company, 1936

———, ed., *Polk: The Diary of a President, 1845–1849.* New York: Longmans, Green & Company, Inc., 1929

Nicolay, Helen, *Andrew Jackson: The Fighting President.* New York: The Century Company, 1929

Olcott, Charles S., *The Life of William McKinley.* Boston: Houghton Mifflin Company, 1916

Padover, Saul K., *A Jefferson Profile as Revealed in His Letters.* New York: The John Day Company, Inc., 1956

Pendel, Thomas F., *Thirty-six Years in the White House: Lincoln–Roosevelt.* Washington: The Neale Publishing Company, 1902

Perkins, Frances, *The Roosevelt I Knew.* New York: The Viking Press, Inc., 1946

Poore, Ben: Perley, *Perley's Reminiscences of Sixty Years in the National Metropolis.* Tecumseh, Mich.: A. W. Mills, 1886

Pringle, Henry F., *The Life and Times of William Howard Taft.* New York: Farrar & Rinehart, Inc., 1939

Randall, J. G., *Midstream: Lincoln the President.* New York: Dodd, Mead & Company, 1952

Randall, Ruth Painter, *Lincoln's Sons.* Boston: Little, Brown & Company, 1955

———*Mary Lincoln: Biography of a Marriage.* Boston: Little, Brown & Company, 1953

Randolph, Mary, *Presidents and First Ladies.* New York: D. Appleton-Century Company, Inc., 1936

Randolph, Sarah N., *The Domestic Life of Thomas Jefferson.* Cambridge, Mass.: Harvard University Press, 1939

Reid, Edith Gittings, *Woodrow Wilson: The Caricature, the Myth, and the Man.* New York: Oxford University Press, 1934

Reilly, Michael, *Reilly of the White House.* New York: Simon and Schuster, Inc., 1947

Roberts, Kenneth L., *Concentrated New England.* Indianapolis: The Bobbs-Merrill Company, 1924

Roosevelt, Eleanor, *This I Remember.* New York: Harper & Brothers, 1949

Russell, Phillips, *Jefferson, Champion of the Free Mind.* New York: Dodd, Mead & Company, 1956

Sandburg, Carl, *Abraham Lincoln: The War Years.* New York: Harcourt, Brace and Company, Inc., 1939

Schachner, Nathan, *Thomas Jefferson: A Biography.* New York: Appleton-Century-Crofts, Inc., 1951

Seaton, Josephine, *William Winston Seaton.* Boston: J. R. Osgood & Company, 1871

Singleton, Esther, *The Story of the White House.* New York: The McClure Company, 1907

Smith, Margaret Bayard, *The First Forty Years of Washington Society,* edited by Gaillard Hunt. New York: Charles Scribner's Sons, 1906

Smith, Theodore C., *The Life and Letters of James Abram Garfield.* New Haven: Yale University Press, 1925

Snead, Austine, *The unpublished letters of "Miss Grundy,"* from the Rutherford B. Hayes Library

Starling, Edmund W., *Starling of the White House, As Told to Thomas Sugrue.* New York: Simon and Schuster, 1946

Stiles, Lela, *The Man Behind Roosevelt: The Story of Louis McHenry Howe.* Cleveland, New York: The World Publishing Company, 1954

Taft, Helen Herron, *Recollections of Full Years.* New York: Dodd, Mead & Company, 1914

Tebbel, John, *George Washington's America.* New York: E. P. Dutton & Company, Inc., 1954

Tugwell, Rexford G., *The Democratic Roosevelt: A Biography of Franklin D. Roosevelt.* Garden City, N. Y Doubleday & Company, Inc., 1957

Tully, Grace, *F.D.R., My Boss.* New York: Charles Scribner's Sons, 1949

Tumulty, Joseph P., *Woodrow Wilson as I Know Him.* Garden City, N. Y.: Doubleday, Page & Company, 1921

White, William Allen, *A Puritan in Babylon.* New York: The Macmillan Company, 1938

Whitney, Janet, *Abigail Adams.* Boston: Little, Brown & Company, 1947

Whitton, Mary Ormsbee, *First First Ladies, 1789–1865.* New York: Hastings House Publishers, Inc., 1948

Williams, T. Harry, *Lincoln and His Generals.* New York: Alfred A. Knopf, Inc., 1952

Wilson, Edith Bolling, *My Memoir.* Indianapolis: The Bobbs-Merrill Company, 1939

Winston, Robert W., *Andrew Johnson: Plebian and Patriot.* New York: Henry Holt and Company, 1928

Woodward, William E., *Meet General Grant.* New York: Liveright Publishing Corp., 1946

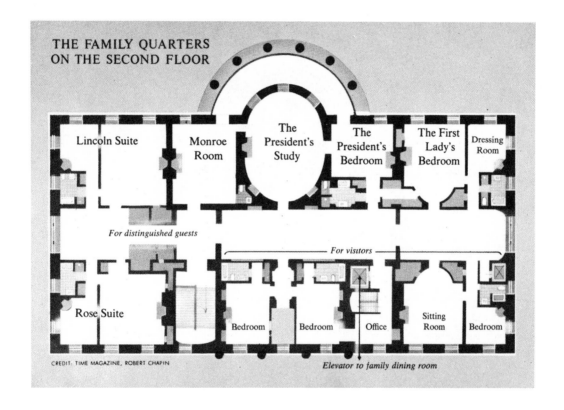

THE FAMILY QUARTERS ON THE SECOND FLOOR

Lincoln Suite

Monroe Room

The President's Study

The President's Bedroom

The First Lady's Bedroom

Dressing Room

For distinguished guests

For visitors

Rose Suite

Bedroom

Bedroom

Office

Sitting Room

Bedroom

CREDIT: TIME MAGAZINE, ROBERT CHAPIN

Elevator to family dining room